A Textbook of Data Structures and Algorithms 1

*One of the greatest lessons I have learnt in my life is
to pay as much attention to the means of work as to its end...
I have been always learning great lessons from that one principle,
and it appears to me that all the secret of success is there;
to pay as much attention to the means as to the end....
Let us perfect the means; the end will take care of itself.*

– Swami Vivekananda
(Lecture Delivered at Los Angeles, California, January 4, 1900)

# A Textbook of Data Structures and Algorithms 1

*Mastering Linear Data Structures*

G A Vijayalakshmi Pai

WILEY

First published 2022 in Great Britain and the United States by ISTE Ltd and John Wiley & Sons, Inc.

Previous edition published in 2008 as "Data Structures and Algorithms: Concepts, Techniques and Applications" by McGraw Hill Education (India) Pvt Ltd. © McGraw Hill Education (India) Pvt Ltd. 2008

ISTE Ltd
27-37 St George's Road
London SW19 4EU
UK

www.iste.co.uk

John Wiley & Sons, Inc.
111 River Street
Hoboken, NJ 07030
USA

www.wiley.com

Library of Congress Control Number: 2022945771

British Library Cataloguing-in-Publication Data
A CIP record for this book is available from the British Library
ISBN 978-1-78630-869-6

# Contents

Preface . . . . . . . . . . . . . . . . . . . . . . . . . . . . . . . . .   ix

Acknowledgments . . . . . . . . . . . . . . . . . . . . . . . . . . .   xv

Chapter 1. Introduction . . . . . . . . . . . . . . . . . . . . . . . .   1

  1.1. History of algorithms . . . . . . . . . . . . . . . . . . . . . . .   3
  1.2. Definition, structure and properties of algorithms . . . . . . . . . . .   4
    1.2.1. Definition . . . . . . . . . . . . . . . . . . . . . . . . . .   4
    1.2.2. Structure and properties . . . . . . . . . . . . . . . . . . .   4
  1.3. Development of an algorithm . . . . . . . . . . . . . . . . . . . .   5
  1.4. Data structures and algorithms . . . . . . . . . . . . . . . . . . .   6
  1.5. Data structures – definition and classification . . . . . . . . . . .   7
    1.5.1. Abstract data types . . . . . . . . . . . . . . . . . . . . . .   7
    1.5.2. Classification . . . . . . . . . . . . . . . . . . . . . . . .   9
  1.6. Algorithm design techniques . . . . . . . . . . . . . . . . . . . .   9
  1.7. Organization of the book . . . . . . . . . . . . . . . . . . . . . .   11

Chapter 2. Analysis of Algorithms . . . . . . . . . . . . . . . . . .   13

  2.1. Efficiency of algorithms . . . . . . . . . . . . . . . . . . . . . .   13
  2.2. Apriori analysis . . . . . . . . . . . . . . . . . . . . . . . . . .   15
  2.3. Asymptotic notations . . . . . . . . . . . . . . . . . . . . . . . .   17
  2.4. Time complexity of an algorithm using the $O$ notation . . . . . . . .   19
  2.5. Polynomial time versus exponential time algorithms . . . . . . . . . .   20
  2.6. Average, best and worst case complexities . . . . . . . . . . . . . .   21

2.7. Analyzing recursive programs. . . . . . . . . . . . . . . . . . . . . . . . .    23
    2.7.1. Recursive procedures  . . . . . . . . . . . . . . . . . . . . . . . .    23
    2.7.2. Apriori analysis of recursive functions . . . . . . . . . . . . . . .    27
2.8. Illustrative problems  . . . . . . . . . . . . . . . . . . . . . . . . . . . .    31

**Chapter 3. Arrays** . . . . . . . . . . . . . . . . . . . . . . . . . . . . . . . .    45

3.1. Introduction. . . . . . . . . . . . . . . . . . . . . . . . . . . . . . . . . .    45
3.2. Array operations. . . . . . . . . . . . . . . . . . . . . . . . . . . . . . . .    46
3.3. Number of elements in an array. . . . . . . . . . . . . . . . . . . . . . . .    46
    3.3.1. One-dimensional array. . . . . . . . . . . . . . . . . . . . . . . .    46
    3.3.2. Two-dimensional array  . . . . . . . . . . . . . . . . . . . . . . .    47
    3.3.3. Multidimensional array  . . . . . . . . . . . . . . . . . . . . . . .    47
3.4. Representation of arrays in memory . . . . . . . . . . . . . . . . . . . . .    48
    3.4.1. One-dimensional array. . . . . . . . . . . . . . . . . . . . . . . .    49
    3.4.2. Two-dimensional arrays. . . . . . . . . . . . . . . . . . . . . . . .    51
    3.4.3. Three-dimensional arrays . . . . . . . . . . . . . . . . . . . . . .    52
    3.4.4. N-dimensional array . . . . . . . . . . . . . . . . . . . . . . . . .    53
3.5. Applications  . . . . . . . . . . . . . . . . . . . . . . . . . . . . . . . . .    54
    3.5.1. Sparse matrix  . . . . . . . . . . . . . . . . . . . . . . . . . . . .    54
    3.5.2. Ordered lists. . . . . . . . . . . . . . . . . . . . . . . . . . . . .    55
    3.5.3. Strings  . . . . . . . . . . . . . . . . . . . . . . . . . . . . . . .    56
    3.5.4. Bit array . . . . . . . . . . . . . . . . . . . . . . . . . . . . . . .    58
3.6. Illustrative problems  . . . . . . . . . . . . . . . . . . . . . . . . . . . .    60

**Chapter 4. Stacks** . . . . . . . . . . . . . . . . . . . . . . . . . . . . . . . .    71

4.1. Introduction. . . . . . . . . . . . . . . . . . . . . . . . . . . . . . . . . .    71
4.2. Stack operations . . . . . . . . . . . . . . . . . . . . . . . . . . . . . . .    72
    4.2.1. Stack implementation . . . . . . . . . . . . . . . . . . . . . . . .    73
    4.2.2. Implementation of push and pop operations . . . . . . . . . . . . .    74
4.3. Applications  . . . . . . . . . . . . . . . . . . . . . . . . . . . . . . . . .    76
    4.3.1. Recursive programming. . . . . . . . . . . . . . . . . . . . . . . .    76
    4.3.2. Evaluation of expressions. . . . . . . . . . . . . . . . . . . . . .    79
4.4. Illustrative problems  . . . . . . . . . . . . . . . . . . . . . . . . . . . .    83

**Chapter 5. Queues** . . . . . . . . . . . . . . . . . . . . . . . . . . . . . . . .    101

5.1. Introduction. . . . . . . . . . . . . . . . . . . . . . . . . . . . . . . . . .    101
5.2. Operations on queues. . . . . . . . . . . . . . . . . . . . . . . . . . . . .    102
    5.2.1. Queue implementation. . . . . . . . . . . . . . . . . . . . . . . .    102
    5.2.2. Implementation of insert and delete operations on a queue . . . . .    103

5.2.3. Limitations of linear queues. . . . . . . . . . . . . . . . . . . . . .    105
5.3. Circular queues. . . . . . . . . . . . . . . . . . . . . . . . . . . . . . . .    106
    5.3.1. Operations on a circular queue . . . . . . . . . . . . . . . . . . . .    106
    5.3.2. Implementation of insertion and deletion operations in
circular queue . . . . . . . . . . . . . . . . . . . . . . . . . . . . . . . . . . .    109
5.4. Other types of queues. . . . . . . . . . . . . . . . . . . . . . . . . . . .    112
    5.4.1. Priority queues . . . . . . . . . . . . . . . . . . . . . . . . . . . . . .    112
    5.4.2. Deques . . . . . . . . . . . . . . . . . . . . . . . . . . . . . . . . . . .    117
5.5. Applications . . . . . . . . . . . . . . . . . . . . . . . . . . . . . . . . . .    119
    5.5.1. Application of a linear queue . . . . . . . . . . . . . . . . . . . . . .    119
    5.5.2. Application of priority queues . . . . . . . . . . . . . . . . . . . . .    120
5.6. Illustrative problems . . . . . . . . . . . . . . . . . . . . . . . . . . . .    125

**Chapter 6. Linked Lists** . . . . . . . . . . . . . . . . . . . . . . . . . . . .    143

6.1. Introduction. . . . . . . . . . . . . . . . . . . . . . . . . . . . . . . . . .    143
    6.1.1. Drawbacks of sequential data structures . . . . . . . . . . . . . .    143
    6.1.2. Merits of linked data structures. . . . . . . . . . . . . . . . . . . .    145
    6.1.3. Linked lists – structure and implementation . . . . . . . . . . . .    145
6.2. Singly linked lists . . . . . . . . . . . . . . . . . . . . . . . . . . . . . .    147
    6.2.1. Representation of a singly linked list . . . . . . . . . . . . . . . .    147
    6.2.2. Insertion and deletion in a singly linked list . . . . . . . . . . . .    149
6.3. Circularly linked lists . . . . . . . . . . . . . . . . . . . . . . . . . . . .    155
    6.3.1. Representation. . . . . . . . . . . . . . . . . . . . . . . . . . . . . . .    155
    6.3.2. Advantages of circularly linked lists over singly linked lists . . . .    155
    6.3.3. Disadvantages of circularly linked lists . . . . . . . . . . . . . . .    156
    6.3.4. Primitive operations on circularly linked lists . . . . . . . . . . .    158
    6.3.5. Other operations on circularly linked lists . . . . . . . . . . . . .    159
6.4. Doubly linked lists. . . . . . . . . . . . . . . . . . . . . . . . . . . . . .    160
    6.4.1. Representation of a doubly linked list. . . . . . . . . . . . . . . .    161
    6.4.2. Advantages and disadvantages of a doubly linked list . . . . . . .    162
    6.4.3. Operations on doubly linked lists . . . . . . . . . . . . . . . . . .    163
6.5. Multiply linked lists. . . . . . . . . . . . . . . . . . . . . . . . . . . . .    166
6.6. Unrolled linked lists. . . . . . . . . . . . . . . . . . . . . . . . . . . . .    171
    6.6.1. Retrieval of an element . . . . . . . . . . . . . . . . . . . . . . . .    172
    6.6.2. Insert an element . . . . . . . . . . . . . . . . . . . . . . . . . . . .    172
    6.6.3. Delete an element. . . . . . . . . . . . . . . . . . . . . . . . . . . .    173
6.7. Self-organizing lists . . . . . . . . . . . . . . . . . . . . . . . . . . . . .    175
6.8. Applications . . . . . . . . . . . . . . . . . . . . . . . . . . . . . . . . . .    175
    6.8.1. Addition of polynomials. . . . . . . . . . . . . . . . . . . . . . . .    176
    6.8.2. Sparse matrix representation . . . . . . . . . . . . . . . . . . . . .    178
6.9. Illustrative problems . . . . . . . . . . . . . . . . . . . . . . . . . . . .    182

**Chapter 7. Linked Stacks and Linked Queues** . . . . . . . . . . . . . . .   201

7.1. Introduction. . . . . . . . . . . . . . . . . . . . . . . . . . . . . .   201
   7.1.1. Linked stack . . . . . . . . . . . . . . . . . . . . . . . . . . .   202
   7.1.2. Linked queues . . . . . . . . . . . . . . . . . . . . . . . . . .   203
7.2. Operations on linked stacks and linked queues . . . . . . . . . . . . . .   203
   7.2.1. Linked stack operations . . . . . . . . . . . . . . . . . . . . . .   203
   7.2.2. Linked queue operations. . . . . . . . . . . . . . . . . . . . . . .   204
   7.2.3. Algorithms for Push/Pop operations on a linked stack . . . . . . .   205
   7.2.4. Algorithms for insert and delete operations in a linked queue. . . .   206
7.3. Dynamic memory management and linked stacks . . . . . . . . . . . .   209
7.4. Implementation of linked representations . . . . . . . . . . . . . . . . .   214
7.5. Applications . . . . . . . . . . . . . . . . . . . . . . . . . . . . . .   216
   7.5.1. Balancing symbols . . . . . . . . . . . . . . . . . . . . . . . . .   216
   7.5.2. Polynomial representation. . . . . . . . . . . . . . . . . . . . . .   218
7.6. Illustrative problems . . . . . . . . . . . . . . . . . . . . . . . . . .   222

**References** . . . . . . . . . . . . . . . . . . . . . . . . . . . . . . . . .   241

**Index** . . . . . . . . . . . . . . . . . . . . . . . . . . . . . . . . . . . .   243

**Summaries of other volumes** . . . . . . . . . . . . . . . . . . . . . . . .   245

# Preface

Efficient problem solving using computers, irrespective of the discipline or application, calls for the design of efficient algorithms. The inclusion of appropriate data structures is of critical importance to the design of efficient algorithms. In other words, *good algorithm design must go hand in hand with appropriate data structures for an efficient program design to solve a problem.*

***Data structures and algorithms*** is a fundamental course in computer science, which most undergraduate and graduate programs in computer science and other allied disciplines in science and engineering offer during the early stages of the respective programs, either as a core or as an elective course. The course enables students to have a much-needed foundation for efficient programming, leading to better problem solving in their respective disciplines.

Most of the well-known text books/monographs on this subject have discussed the concepts in relation to a programming language – beginning with Pascal and spanning a spectrum of them such as C, C++, C#, Java, Python and so on, essentially calling for ample knowledge of the language, before one proceeds to try and understand the data structure. There does remain a justification in this. The implementation of data structures in the specific programming language need to be demonstrated or the algorithms pertaining to the data structures concerned need a convenient medium of presentation and when this is the case, why not a programming language?

Again, while some authors have insisted on using their books for an advanced level course, there are some who insist on a working knowledge of the specific programming language as a prerequisite to using the book. However, in the case of a core course, as it is in most academic programs, it is not uncommon for a novice or a sophomore to be bewildered by the "miles of code" that demonstrate or explain a data structure, rendering the subject difficult to comprehend. In fact, the efforts that one needs to put in to comprehend the data structure and its applications are distracted by the necessity to garner sufficient programming knowledge to follow the code. It is indeed ironic that while a novice is taught data structures to appreciate programming, in reality it turns out that one learns programming to appreciate data structures!

In my decades-old experience of offering the course to graduate programs, which admits students from diverse undergraduate disciplines, with little to no strong knowledge of programming, I had several occasions to observe this malady. In fact, it is not uncommon in some academic programs, especially graduate programs which, due to their shorter duration, have a course in programming and data structures running in parallel in the same semester, much to the chagrin of the novice learner! That a novice is forced to learn data structures through their implementation (in a specific programming language), when in reality it ought to be learning augmented with the implementation of the data structures, has been the reason behind the fallout.

A solution to this problem would be to

i) Frame the course such that the theory deals with the concepts, techniques and applications of data structures and algorithms, not taking recourse to any specific programming language, but instead settling for a pseudo-language, which clearly expounds the data structure. Additionally, supplementing the course material with illustrative problems, review questions and exercises to reinforce the students' grasp of the concepts would help them gain useful insights while learning.

ii) Augment the theory with laboratory sessions to enable the student to implement the data structure in itself or as embedded in an application, in the language of his/her own choice or as insisted upon in the curriculum. This would enable the student who has acquired sufficient knowledge and insight into the data structures to appreciate the beauty and merits of employing the data structure by programming it themselves, rather than "look" for the data structure in a prewritten code.

This means that text books catering to the fundamental understanding of the data structure concepts for use as course material in the classroom are as much needed as the books that cater to the implementation of data structures in a programming language for use in the laboratory sessions. While most books in the market conform to the latter, bringing out a book to be classroom course material and used by instructors handling a course on data structures and algorithms, comprehensive enough for the novice students to benefit from, has been the main motivation in writing this book.

As such, the book details concepts, techniques and applications pertaining to data structures and algorithms, independent of any programming language, discusses several examples and illustrative problems, poses review questions to reinforce the understanding of the theory, and presents a suggestive list of programming assignments to aid implementation of the data structures and algorithms learned.

In fact, the book may either be independently used as a textbook since it is self-contained or serve as a companion for books discussing data structures and algorithms implemented in specific programming languages such as C, C++, Java, Python, and so on.

At this juncture, it needs to be pointed out that a plethora of programming resources and freely downloadable implementations of the majority of the data structures in almost all popular languages are available on the Internet, which can undoubtedly serve as good guides for the learner. However, it has to be emphasized that an earnest student of data structures and algorithms must invest a lot of time and self-effort in trying to implement the data structures and algorithms learned, in a language of one's choice, all by oneself, in order to attain a thorough grasp of the concepts.

## About this edition

This edition is a largely revised and enlarged version of its predecessor, published by McGraw Hill, USA. The earlier edition published in 2008 saw 15 reprints in its life span of 13 years (ending January 2022) and was recommended as a text book for the course in several universities and colleges. It comprised 17 chapters categorized into five parts and reinforced learning through 133 illustrative problems, 215 review questions and 74 programming assignments.

The features of this new edition are as follows:

– There are 22 chapters spread across three volumes that detail sequential linear data structures, linked linear data structures, nonlinear data structures, advanced data structures, searching and sorting algorithms, algorithm design techniques and NP-completeness.

– The data structures of $k$-d trees and treaps have been elaborated in a newly included chapter (Chapter 15) in Volume 3.

– The data structures of strings, bit rays, unrolled linked lists, self-organizing linked lists, segment trees and $k$-ary trees have been introduced in the appropriate sections of the existing chapters in Volumes 1 and 2.

– The concepts of counting binary search trees and Kruskal's algorithm have been detailed in the appropriate sections of the existing chapters in Volume 2.

– Skip list search, counting sort and bucket sort have been included in the chapters on searching and sorting algorithms in Volume 3.

– The algorithm design techniques of divide and conquer, the greedy method and dynamic programming have been elaborately discussed in Chapters 19–21 in Volume 3.

– The concept of NP-completeness has been detailed in a newly included chapter, Chapter 22 in Volume 3.

– Several illustrative problems, review questions and programming assignments have been added to enrich the content and aid in understanding the concepts. The new edition thus includes 181 illustrative problems, 276 review questions and 108 programming assignments.

## Organization of the book

The book comprises three volumes, namely, Volume 1: Chapters 1–7, Volume 2: Chapters 8–12 and Volume 3: Chapters 13–22.

**Volume 1** opens with an *introduction to data structures* and concepts pertaining to the *analysis of algorithms*, detailed in Chapters 1 and 2, which is essential to appreciate the theories and algorithms related to data structures and their applications.

Chapters 3–5 detail sequential linear data structures, namely, *arrays, strings, bit arrays, stacks, queues, priority queues* and *dequeues*, and their applications. Chapters 6 and 7 elucidate linked linear data structures, namely *linked lists, linked stacks* and *linked queues*, and their applications.

**Volume 2** details nonlinear data structures. Chapters 8 and 9 elaborate on the nonlinear data structures of *trees, binary trees* and *graphs*, and their applications. Chapters 10–12 highlight the advanced data structures of *binary search trees, AVL trees, B trees, tries, red-black trees* and *splay trees*, and their applications.

**Volume 3** details an assortment of data structures, algorithm design strategies and their applications.

Chapters 13–15 discuss *hash tables, files, k-d trees* and *treaps*. Chapter 16 discusses the search algorithms of *linear search, transpose sequential search, interpolation search, binary search, Fibonacci search, skip list search* and other search techniques.

Chapter 17 elaborates on the internal sorting algorithms of *bubble sort, insertion sort, selection sort, merge sort, shell sort, quick sort, heap sort, radix sort, counting sort* and *bucket sort*, and Chapter 18 discusses the external sorting techniques of *sorting with tapes, sorting with disks, polyphase merge sort* and *cascade merge sort*.

Chapters 19–21 detail the algorithm design strategies of *divide and conquer*, the *greedy method* and *dynamic programming* and their applications.

Chapter 22 introduces the theories and concepts of *NP-completeness*.

For a full list of the contents of Volumes 2 and 3, see the summary at the end of this book.

## Salient features of the book

The features of the book are as follows:

– all-around emphasis on theory, problems, applications and programming assignments;

– simple and lucid explanation of the theory;

– inclusion of several applications to illustrate the use of data structures and algorithms;

– several worked-out examples as illustrative problems in each chapter;

– list of programming assignments at the end of each chapter;

– review questions to strengthen understanding;

– self-contained text for use as a text book for either an introductory or advanced level course.

## Target audience

The book could be used both as an introductory or an advanced-level textbook for undergraduate, graduate and research programs, which offer data structures and algorithms as a core course or an elective course. While the book is primarily meant to serve as a course material for use in the classroom, it could be used as a companion guide during the laboratory sessions to nurture better understanding of the theoretical concepts.

An introductory level course for a duration of one semester or 60 lecture hours, targeting an undergraduate program or first-year graduate program or a diploma program or a certificate program, could include Chapters 1–7 of Volume 1, Chapter 8 of Volume 2, Chapters 13, 16 (sections 16.1, 16.2, 16.5) and 17 (sections 17.1–17.3, 17.5, 17.7) of Volume 3 in its curriculum.

A middle-level course for a duration of one semester or 60 lecture hours targeting senior graduate-level programs and research programs such as MS/PhD could include Chapters 1–7 of Volume 1, Chapters 8–11 of Volume 2, Chapter 13 and selective sections of Chapters 16–17 of Volume 3.

An advanced level course that focuses on advanced data structures and algorithm design could begin with a review of Chapter 8 and include Chapters 9–12 of Volume 2, Chapters 14 and 15 and selective sections of Chapters 16–18, and Chapters 19–22 of Volume 3 in its curriculum based on the level of prerequisite courses satisfied.

Chapters 8–10 and Chapter 11 (sections 11.1–11.3) of Volume 2 and Chapters 13, 14 and 18 of Volume 3 could be useful to include in a curriculum that serves as a prerequisite for a course on database management systems.

To re-emphasize, all theory sessions must be supplemented with laboratory sessions to encourage learners to implement the concepts learned in an appropriate language that adheres to the curricular requirements of the programs concerned.

# Acknowledgments

The author is grateful to ISTE Ltd., London, UK, for accepting to publish the book, in collaboration with John Wiley & Sons Inc., USA. She expresses her appreciation to the publishing team, for their professionalism and excellent production practices, while bringing out this book in three volumes.

The author expresses her sincere thanks to the Management and Principal, PSG College of Technology, Coimbatore, India for the support extended while writing the book.

The author would like to place on record her immense admiration and affection for her father, Late Professor G. A. Krishna Pai and her mother Rohini Krishna Pai for their unbounded encouragement and support to help her follow her life lessons and her sisters Dr. Rekha Pai and Udaya Pai, for their unstinted, anywhere-anytime-anything kind of help and support, all of which were instrumental and inspirational in helping this author create this work.

G. A. Vijayalakshmi Pai
August 2022

# Introduction

While looking around and marveling at the technological advancements of this world – both within and without, one cannot help but perceive the intense and intrinsic association of the disciplines of science and engineering and their allied and hybrid counterparts, with the ubiquitous machines called *computers*. In fact, it is difficult to spot a discipline that has distanced itself from the discipline of computer science. To quote a few, be it a medical surgery or diagnosis performed by robots or doctors on patients halfway across the globe, or the launching of space crafts and satellites into outer space, or forecasting tornadoes and cyclones, or the more mundane needs of the online reservation of tickets or billing at supermarkets, or the control of washing machines, etc., one cannot help but deem computers to be *omnipresent*, *omnipotent*, why even *omniscient*! (Figure 1.1).

In short, any discipline that calls for *problem solving using computers* looks up to the discipline of computer science for efficient and effective methods of solving the problems in their respective fields. From the view point of problem solving, the discipline of computer science could be naively categorized into the following four sub areas, notwithstanding the overlaps, extensions and gray areas within themselves:

– *Machines*: What machines are appropriate or available for the solution of the problem? What is the machine configuration – its processing power, memory capacity, etc. – that would be required for the efficient execution of the problem solution?

– *Languages*: What is the language or software with which the problem solution needs to be coded? What are the software constraints that would hamper the efficient implementation of the solution to the problem?

– *Foundations*: What is the problem model and its solution? What methods need to be employed for the efficient design and implementation of the solution? What is its performance measure?

– *Technologies*: What are the technologies that need to be incorporated to solve the problem? For example, does the solution call for a web-based implementation, need activation from mobile devices, call for hand shaking broadcasting devices or merely need to interact with high-end or low-end peripheral devices?

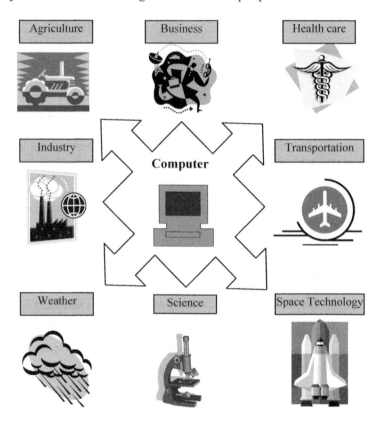

**Figure 1.1.** *Omnipresence of computers. For a color version of this figure, see www.iste.co.uk/pai/algorithms1.zip*

Figure 1.2 illustrates the categorization of the discipline of computer science from the perspective of problem solving.

One of the core fields that belongs to the foundations of computer science addresses the design, analysis and implementation of *algorithms* for the efficient solution of the problems concerned. An algorithm may be loosely defined as a *process, procedure, method* or *recipe*. It is a specific set of rules to obtain a definite output from specific inputs provided to the problem.

The subject of ***data structures*** is intrinsically connected with the design and implementation of efficient algorithms. ***Data structures deal with the study of methods, techniques and tools to organize or structure data.***

The history, definition, classification, structure and properties of algorithms are discussed in the following.

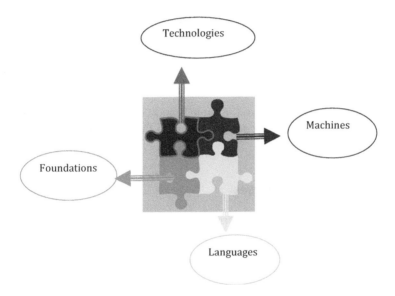

**Figure 1.2.** *Discipline of computer science from the perspective of problem solving. For a color version of this figure, see www.iste.co.uk/pai/algorithms1.zip*

## 1.1. History of algorithms

The word ***algorithm*** originates from the Arabic word *algorism*, which is linked to the name of the Arabic mathematician Abu Jafar Mohammed Ibn Musa Al Khwarizmi (825 CE). Al Khwarizmi is accredited as the first algorithm designer for adding numbers represented in the Hindu numeral system. The algorithm designed by him and followed until today calls for summing the digits occurring at a specific position and the previous carry digit repetitively, moving from the least significant digit to the most significant digit until the digits have been exhausted.

EXAMPLE 1.1.–

Demonstration of Al Khwarizmi's algorithm for the addition of 987 and 76:

| 987 + | 987 + | 987 + |
|---|---|---|
| 76 | 76 + | 76 + |
| | Carry 1 | Carry 1 |
| **(Carry 1)   3** | **(Carry 1)   63** | **1,063** |

## 1.2. Definition, structure and properties of algorithms

### 1.2.1. *Definition*

DEFINITION.–

An algorithm may be defined as a finite sequence of instructions, each of which has a clear meaning and can be performed with a finite amount of effort in a finite length of time.

### 1.2.2. *Structure and properties*

An algorithm has the following structure:

i) input step;

ii) assignment step;

iii) decision step;

iv) repetitive step;

v) output step.

EXAMPLE 1.2.–

Consider the demonstration of Al Khwarizmi's algorithm shown on the addition of the numbers 987 and 76 in example 1.1. In this, the input step considers the two operands 987 and 76 for addition. The assignment step sets the pair of digits from the two numbers and the previous carry digit if it exists, for addition. The decision step decides at each step whether the added digits yield a value that is greater than 10 and, if so, whether an appropriate carry digit should be generated. The repetitive step repeats the process for every pair of digits beginning from the least significant digit onward. The output step releases the output, which is 1063.

An algorithm is endowed with the following properties:

– *Finiteness*: an algorithm must terminate after a finite number of steps.

– *Definiteness*: the steps of the algorithm must be precisely defined or unambiguously specified.

– *Generality*: an algorithm must be generic enough to solve all problems of a particular class.

– *Effectiveness*: the operations of the algorithm must be basic enough to be put down on pencil and paper. They should not be too complex to warrant writing another algorithm for the operation!

– *Input–output*: the algorithm must have certain initial and precise inputs, and outputs that may be generated both at its intermediate or final steps.

An algorithm does not enforce a language or mode for its expression; it only demands adherence to its properties. Thus, one could even write an algorithm in one's own expressive way to make a cup of hot coffee! However, there is this observation that a cooking recipe that calls for instructions such as "add a pinch of salt and pepper", "fry until it turns golden brown" and so on, are "anti-algorithmic" because terms such as "a pinch" and "golden brown" are subject to ambiguity and hence violate the property of definiteness!

An algorithm may be represented using pictorial representations such as *flow charts*. An algorithm encoded in a programming language for implementation on a computer is called a *program*. However, there exists a school of thought that distinguishes a program from an algorithm. The claim put forward by them is that programs need not exhibit the property of finiteness, which algorithms insist upon and quote an *operating systems* program as a counter example. An operating system is supposed to be an "infinite" program that terminates only when the system crashes! At all other times other than its execution, it is said to be in "wait" mode!

## 1.3. Development of an algorithm

The steps involved in the development of an algorithm are as follows:

i) problem statement;

ii) model formulation;

iii) algorithm design;

iv) algorithm correctness;

v) implementation;

vi) algorithm analysis;

vii) program testing;

viii) documentation.

Once a clear statement of the problem is made, the model for the solution of the problem is formulated. The next step is to design the algorithm based on the solution model formulated. It is here that one sees the role of data structures. The right choice of the data structure needs to be made at the design stage itself since data structures influence the efficiency of the algorithm. Once the correctness of the algorithm is checked and the algorithm is implemented, the most important step of measuring the performance of the algorithm is performed. This is what is termed *algorithm analysis*. It can be seen how the use of appropriate data structures results in better performance of the algorithm. Finally, the program is tested, and the development ends with proper documentation.

## 1.4. Data structures and algorithms

As detailed in the previous section, the design of an *efficient* algorithm for the solution of the problem calls for the *inclusion of appropriate data structures*. A clear, unambiguous set of instructions following the properties of the algorithm alone does not contribute to the efficiency of the solution. It is essential that the data on which the problems need to work on are appropriately *structured* to suit the needs of the problem, thereby contributing to the efficiency of the solution.

For example, let us rewind to the past and consider the problem of searching for a telephone number of a person in the telephone directory book provided to the subscribers. It is well known that searching for a phone number in the directory is an easy task since the data are sorted according to the alphabetical order of the subscribers' names. All that the search calls for is to turn over the pages until one reaches the page that is approximately closest to the subscriber's name and undertake a sequential search moving one's finger down the relevant page. Now, what if the telephone directory were to have its data arranged according to the order in which the subscriptions for telephones were received? What a mess it would be! One may need to go through the entire directory – name after name, page after page in a sequential fashion until the name and the corresponding telephone number is retrieved!

This is a classic example to illustrate the significant role played by data structures in the efficiency of algorithms. The problem was the retrieval of a telephone number. The algorithm was the simple search for the name in the directory and the subsequent retrieval of the corresponding telephone number. In the first case, since the data were appropriately structured (sorted according to alphabetical order), the search algorithm undertaken turned out to be efficient. However, in the second case, when the data were unstructured, the search algorithm turned out to be crude and therefore inefficient.

Therefore, for the design of efficient programs for the solution of problems, it is essential that *algorithm design goes hand in hand with appropriate data structures* (Figure 1.3).

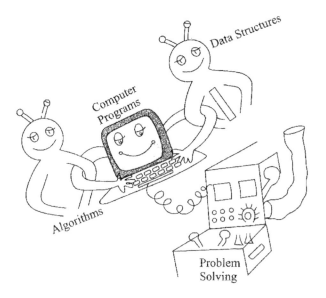

**Figure 1.3.** *Algorithms and data structures for efficient problem solving using computers*

## 1.5. Data structures – definition and classification

### 1.5.1. *Abstract data types*

A *data type* refers to the type of values that variables in a programming language hold. Thus, the integer, real, character and Boolean data types that are inherently provided in programming languages are referred to as *primitive data types*.

A list of elements is called a *data object*. For example, we could have a list of integers or a list of alphabetical strings as data objects.

The data objects that comprise the data structure and their fundamental operations are known as **abstract data types** (ADTs). In other words, an ADT is defined as a **set of data objects D** defined over a **domain L** and supporting a **list of operations O**.

## EXAMPLE 1.3.–

Consider an ADT for the data structure of positive integers called POSITIVE_INTEGER defined over a domain of integers $Z^+$, supporting the operations of addition (ADD) and subtraction (MINUS) and checking if positive (CHECK_POSITIVE). The ADT is defined as follows:

$$L = Z^+, \quad D = \{x | x \in L\}, \quad O = \{ADD, MINUS, CHECK\_POSITIVE\}.$$

A descriptive and clear presentation of the ADT is as follows:

**ADT positive integer**

**Data objects:**
Set of all positive integers D

$$D = \{x | x \in L\}, \quad L = Z^+$$

**Operations:**
Addition of positive integers INT1 and INT2 into RESULT

ADD (INT1, INT2, RESULT)

Subtraction of positive integers INT1 and INT2 into RESULT

SUBTRACT (INT1, INT2, RESULT)

Check if a number INT1 is a positive integer

CHECK_POSITIVE(INT1)    (Boolean function)

An ADT promotes **data abstraction** and focuses on *what* a data structure does rather than *how* it does what it does. It is easier to comprehend a data structure by means of its ADT since it helps a designer plan the implementation of the data objects and its supportive operations in any programming language belonging to any paradigm, such as **procedural**, **object oriented** or **functional**. Quite often, it may be essential that one data structure calls for other data structures for its implementation. For example, the implementation of stack and queue data structures calls for their implementation using either arrays or lists, which are themselves data structures.

While deciding on the ADT of a data structure, a designer may decide on the set of operations $O$ that are to be provided, based on the application and accessibility options provided to various users making use of the ADT implementation.

The ADTs for various data structures discussed in the book are presented in the respective chapters.

### 1.5.2. Classification

Figure 1.4 illustrates the classification of data structures. The data structures are broadly classified as *linear data structures* and *nonlinear data structures*. Linear data structures are unidimensional in structure and represent linear lists. These are further classified as *sequential* and *linked representations*. On the other hand, nonlinear data structures are two-dimensional representations of data lists. The individual data structures listed under each class are shown in the figure.

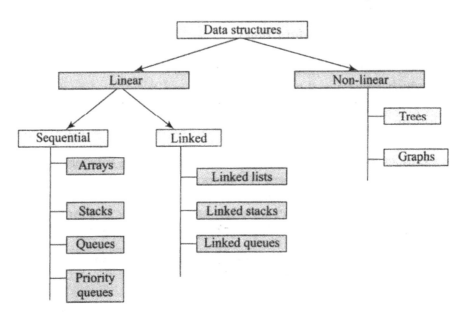

**Figure 1.4.** *Classification of data structures*

## 1.6. Algorithm design techniques

*Algorithm design* concerns strategic methods that strive to find effective solutions or efficient solutions to large classes of problems. Given a problem, it is possible to solve the problem by working over all possible combinations of input sequences, one or more of which may lead to the solution of the problem. Such a method of problem solving is referred to as the ***brute force*** or ***exhaustive search*** method. Brute force methods, therefore, do not explore ways and means to strategically solve the problem by exploiting the problem characteristics or the data structure that describes the problem. For example, a brute force method to find an element in a list would involve merely sequentially searching for the element, one by one, until the element is found or not found. A strategic method, on the other hand, would try to explore ways and means by which finding the element can be done efficiently without searching the entire list or minimizing the number of comparisons during the search and so on.

Several algorithm design techniques have been identified to solve various classes of problems. The following are some of them:

– divide and conquer;

– greedy method;

– backtracking;

– dynamic programming;

– branch and bound;

– local search;

– randomized algorithms.

This book discusses the three strategies of divide and conquer, greedy method and dynamic programming, which are popular methods and have been employed by problems and applications discussed in the rest of the book.

However, there are also problem classes that do not yield effective solutions, no matter which algorithm design technique is employed to tackle it. These have been categorized into two classes, namely, ***NP-complete*** and ***NP-hard***, where NP denotes ***non-deterministic polynomial***. A non-deterministic polynomial simply means that efficient algorithms are not available to solve them. However, studies are still under way to look for efficient ways to solve these problem classes. Considering the fact that several of these problems are of great practical importance, a class of algorithms known as ***approximation algorithms*** have emerged, which aim to solve specific problem instances through ***heuristics*** that strive to deliver solutions to the problem instances within a reasonable amount of time. Heuristics involve methods that are intuitive and help to attain near-optimal or acceptable solutions.

The book concludes with a discussion on NP-complete and NP-hard problems.

## 1.7. Organization of the book

The book is divided into three volumes (1–3) comprising 22 chapters covering concepts, techniques and applications of fundamental, linear, nonlinear and advanced data structures, including elaborating on searching and sorting algorithms and selective algorithm design strategies and concluding with a concise discussion on NP-completeness.

**Volume 1** includes Chapters 1–7 as briefed below:

– Chapter 1 addresses an *introduction* to the subject of algorithms and data structures. Chapter 2 introduces the *analysis of algorithms*.

– Chapters 3–5 discuss linear data structures that are *sequential*. Thus, the three chapters detail the data structures of *arrays*, *stacks* and *queues*, respectively.

– Chapters 6 and 7 discuss linear data structures that are *linked*. Thus, Chapter 6 elaborates on *linked lists* and Chapter 7 details *linked stacks* and *linked queues.*

**Volume 2** includes Chapters 8–12 as briefed below:

– Chapters 8 and 9 discuss the *nonlinear data structures* of *trees* and *graphs*, respectively.

– Some of the *advanced data structures* such as *binary search trees* and *AVL trees* (Chapter 10), *B trees* and *tries* (Chapter 11) and *red–black trees* and *splay trees* (Chapter 12), are elaborately covered in their respective chapters.

**Volume 3** covers Chapters 13–22 as briefed below:

– Chapter 13 discusses *hash tables*. Chapter 14 describes the methods of *file organization* and Chapter 15 provides details on *k-d trees* and *treaps*.

– The *sorting and searching techniques* are elaborated next. Chapter 16 discusses *searching* techniques, Chapter 17 details *internal sorting methods* and Chapter 18 describes *external sorting methods*.

– The *algorithm design strategies* are examined next. Thus, the popular algorithm design strategies of *divide and conquer*, *greedy method* and *dynamic programming* are elaborately discussed over application problems in Chapters 19–21, respectively.

– Finally, the concept of *NP-completeness* is covered. Chapter 22 elaborates on the *P-class* and *NP-class* of problems.

# Summary

– Any discipline in science and engineering that calls for problem solving using computers looks up to the discipline of computer science for its efficient solution.

– From the point of view of problem solving, computer science can be naively categorized into the four areas of machines, languages, foundations and technologies.

– The subjects of algorithms and data structures fall under the category of foundations. The design formulation of algorithms for the solution of the problems and the inclusion of appropriate data structures for their efficient implementation must progress hand in hand.

– An abstract data type (ADT) describes the data objects that constitute the data structure and the fundamental operations supported on them.

– Data structures are classified as linear and nonlinear data structures. Linear data structures are further classified as sequential and linked data structures. While arrays, stacks and queues are examples of sequential data structures, linked lists, linked stacks and queues are examples of linked data structures.

– The nonlinear data structures include trees and graphs.

– The tree data structure includes variants such as binary search trees, AVL trees, B trees, tries, red–black trees and splay trees.

– Algorithm design concerns strategic methods to solve problems efficiently.

– Divide and conquer, greedy method and dynamic programming are popular algorithm design strategies.

# 2

# Analysis of Algorithms

In the previous chapter, we introduced the discipline of computer science from the perspective of problem solving. It was detailed how problem solving using computers calls not only for good algorithm design but also for the appropriate use of data structures to render them efficient. This chapter discusses methods and techniques to analyze the efficiency of algorithms.

## 2.1. Efficiency of algorithms

When there is a problem to be solved, it is probable that several algorithms crop up for its solution, and therefore, one is at a loss to know which one is the best. This raises the question of how one decides which among the algorithms is preferable or which among them is the best.

The performance of algorithms can be measured on the scales of *time* and *space.* The former would mean looking for the fastest algorithm for the problem or that which performs its task in the minimum possible time. In this case, the performance measure is termed *time complexity*. The time complexity of an algorithm or a program is a function of the *running time* of the algorithm or program. In the case of the latter, it would mean looking for an algorithm that consumes or needs limited memory space for its execution. The performance measure in such a case is termed *space complexity*. The space complexity of an algorithm or a program is a function of the space needed by the algorithm or program to run to completion. However, in this book, our discussions mostly emphasize the time complexities of the algorithms presented.

The time complexity of an algorithm can be computed either by an empirical or theoretical approach.

The *empirical* or *posteriori testing* approach calls for implementing the complete algorithms and executing them on a computer for various instances of the problem. The time taken by the execution of the programs for various instances of the problem are noted and compared. The algorithm whose implementation yields the least time is considered to be the best among the candidate solutions.

The *theoretical* or *apriori* approach calls for mathematically determining the resources such as time and space needed by the algorithm as a function of a parameter related to the instances of the problem considered. A parameter that is often used is the *size of the input instances*.

For example, for the problem of searching for a name in the telephone directory, an apriori approach could determine the efficiency of the algorithm used in terms of the size of the telephone directory, that is, the number of subscribers listed in the directory. In addition, algorithms exist for various classes of problems that make use of the number of *basic operations*, such as additions, multiplications or element comparisons, as a parameter to determine their efficiency. The apriori analysis of sorting algorithms, for example, is generally undertaken based on the basic operation of *element comparisons*.

An apriori analysis of an algorithm therefore yields a mathematical function of the parameters that describe either the problem inputs or the basic operations of the algorithm.

The disadvantage of posteriori testing is that it is dependent on various other factors, such as the machine on which the program is executed, the programming language with which it is implemented and why, even on the skill of the programmer who writes the program code! On the other hand, the advantage of apriori analysis is that it is entirely machine, language and program independent.

The efficiency of a newly discovered algorithm over that of its predecessors can be better assessed only when they are tested over large input instance sizes. For smaller to moderate input instance sizes, it is highly likely that their performances may break even. In the case of posteriori testing, practical considerations may permit testing the efficiency of the algorithm only on input instances of moderate sizes. On the other hand, apriori analysis permits the study of the efficiency of algorithms on any input instance of any size.

## 2.2. Apriori analysis

Let us consider a program statement, for example, x = x + 2, in a sequential programming environment. We do not consider any parallelism in the environment. An apriori estimation is interested in the following for the computation of efficiency:

i) the number of times the statement is executed in the program, known as the *frequency count* of the statement;

ii) the time taken for a single execution of the statement.

Considering the second factor would render the estimation machine dependent since the time taken for the execution of the statement is determined by the machine instruction set, the machine configuration and so on. Hence, apriori analysis considers only the first factor and computes the efficiency of the program as a function of the *total frequency count* of the statements comprising the program. The estimation of efficiency is restricted to the computation of the total frequency count of the program.

Let us estimate the frequency count of the statement x = x + 2 occurring in the following three program segments (A, B, C):

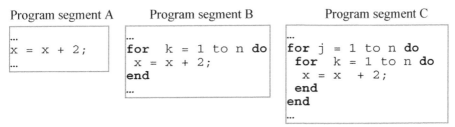

Program segment A          Program segment B                    Program segment C

```
...
x = x + 2;
...
```

```
...
for  k = 1 to n do
   x = x + 2;
end
...
```

```
...
for j = 1 to n do
   for  k = 1 to n do
      x = x  + 2;
   end
end
...
```

The frequency count of the statement in program segment A is 1. In program segment B, the frequency count of the statement is $n$, since the **for** loop in which the statement is embedded executes $n$ ($n \geq 1$) times. In program segment C, the statement is executed $n^2$ ($n \geq 1$) times since the statement is embedded in a nested **for** loop, executing $n$ times each.

In apriori analysis, the frequency count $f_i$ of each statement $i$ of the program is computed and summed to obtain the total frequency count $T = \sum_i f_i$.

The computation of the total frequency count of the program segments A–C is shown in Tables 2.1–2.3. It is well known that the opening statement of a **for** loop such as **for** i = low_index **to** up_index executes ((up_index – low_index +1) +1) times and the statements within the loop are executed ((up_index-low_index)+1) times. A top tested loop such as **for** necessitates testing the opening statement of the loop one more time before quitting the loop, hence the extra " +1" for the frequency count of the opening statement of the **for** loop.

| Program statements | Frequency count |
|---|---|
| ... | |
| x = x + 2; | 1 |
| ... | |
| **Total frequency count** | 1 |

**Table 2.1.** *Total frequency count of program segment A*

| Program statements | Frequency count |
|---|---|
| ... | |
| for k = 1 to n do | $(n+1)$ |
| x = x + 2; | $n$ |
| end | $n$ |
| ... | |
| **Total frequency count** | $3n+1$ |

**Table 2.2.** *Total frequency count of program segment B*

| Program statements | Frequency count |
|---|---|
| ... | |
| for j = 1 to n do | $(n+1)$ |
| for k = 1 to n do | $\sum_{j=1}^{n} (n+1) = (n+1)n$ |
| x = x + 2; | $n^2$ |
| end | $\sum_{j=1}^{n} n = n^2$ |
| end | $n$ |
| ... | |
| **Total frequency count** | $3n^2+3n+1$ |

**Table 2.3.** *Total frequency count of program segment C*

In the case of nested **for** loops, it is easier to compute the frequency counts of the embedded statements, making judicious use of the following fundamental mathematical formulae:

$$\sum_{i=1}^{n} 1 = n \qquad \sum_{i=1}^{n} i = \frac{n(n+1)}{2} \qquad \sum_{i=1}^{n} i^2 = \frac{n(n+1)(2n+1)}{6}$$

Observe how in Table 2.3, the frequency count of the statement **for** k = 1 **to** n **do** is computed as $\sum_{j=1}^{n}(n - 1 + 1) + 1 = \sum_{j=1}^{n}(n+1) = (n+1)n$.

The total frequency counts of the program segments A–C given by 1, $(3n+1)$ and $3n^2+3n+1$, respectively, are expressed as $O(1)$, $O(n)$ and $O(n^2)$, respectively. These notations mean that the orders of magnitude of the total frequency counts are proportional to 1, $n$ and $n^2$, respectively.

The notation $O$ has a mathematical definition, as discussed in section 2.3. These are referred to as the time complexities of the program segments since they are indicative of the running times of the program segments.

In a similar manner, one could also discuss the space complexities of a program, which is the amount of memory it requires for its execution and completion. The space complexities can also be expressed in terms of mathematical notations.

## 2.3. Asymptotic notations

Apriori analysis employs the following notations to express the time complexity of algorithms. These are termed *asymptotic notations* since they are meaningful approximations of functions that represent the time or space complexity of a program.

DEFINITION 2.1.–

$f(n) = O(g(n))$ (read as $f$ of $n$ is "big oh" of $g$ of $n$), iff there exists a positive integer $n_0$ and a positive number C such that $|f(n)| \leq C|g(n)|$, for all $n \geq n_0$.

## Example

| $f(n)$ | $g(n)$ | |
|---|---|---|
| $16n^3 + 78n^2 + 12n$ | $n^3$ | $f(n) = O(n^3)$ |
| $34n - 90$ | $n$ | $f(n) = O(n)$ |
| $56$ | $1$ | $f(n) = O(1)$ |

Here, $g(n)$ is the upper bound of the function $f(n)$.

### DEFINITION 2.2.–

$f(n) = \Omega(g(n))$ (read as $f$ of $n$ is the omega of $g$ of $n$), iff there exists a positive integer $n_0$ and a positive number $C$ such that $|f(n)| \geq C|g(n)|$, for all $n \geq n_0$.

## Example

| $f(n)$ | $g(n)$ | |
|---|---|---|
| $16n^3 + 8n^2 + 2$ | $n^3$ | $f(n) = \Omega(n^3)$ |
| $24n + 9$ | $n$ | $f(n) = \Omega(n)$ |

Here, $g(n)$ is the lower bound of the function $f(n)$.

### DEFINITION 2.3.–

$f(n) = \Theta(g(n))$ (read as $f$ of $n$ is theta of $g$ of $n$), iff there exist two positive constants $c_1$ and $c_2$ and a positive integer $n_0$ such that $c_1|g(n)| \leq |f(n)| \leq c_2|g(n)|$ for all $n \geq n_0$.

## Example

| $f(n)$ | $g(n)$ | |
|---|---|---|
| $28n + 9$ | $n$ | $f(n) = \Theta(n)$  since $f(n) > 28n$ and $f(n) \leq 37\,n$ for $n \geq 1$ |
| $16n^2 + 30n - 90$ | $n^2$ | $f(n) = \Theta(n^2)$ |
| $7.2^n + 30n$ | $2^n$ | $f(n) = \Theta(2^n)$ |

From the definition, it implies that the function $g(n)$ is both an upper bound and a lower bound for the function $f(n)$ for all values of $n$, $n \geq n_0$. This means that $f(n)$ is such that $f(n) = O(g(n))$ and $f(n) = \Omega(g(n))$.

## DEFINITION 2.4.–

$f(n) = o(g(n))$ (read as $f$ of $n$ is "little oh" of $g$ of $n$) iff $f(n) = O(g(n))$ and $f(n) \neq \Omega(g(n))$. In other words, the growth rate of $f(n)$ cannot be the same as that of $g(n)$.

In mathematical terms, this is expressed as

$$\underset{n \to \infty}{Lim} \frac{f(n)}{g(n)} = 0$$

which is easier to compute when powerful calculus techniques such as *L'Hôpital's Rule* are applied.

## *Example*

| $f(n)$ | $g(n)$ |
| --- | --- |
| $18n + 9$ | $n^2$ |

$f(n) = o(n^2)$ since $f(n) = O(n^2)$ and $f(n) \neq \Omega(n^2)$

Observe that $f(n) \neq o(n)$.

## 2.4. Time complexity of an algorithm using the *O* notation

*O* notation is widely used to compute the time complexity of algorithms. It can be gathered from its definition (Definition 2.1) that if $f(n) = O(g(n))$, then $g(n)$ acts as an upper bound for the function $f(n)$. $f(n)$ represents the computing time of the algorithm. When we say the time complexity of the algorithm is $O(g(n))$, we mean that its execution takes a time that is no more than constant times $g(n)$. Here, $n$ is a parameter that characterizes the input and/or output instances of the algorithm.

Algorithms reporting $O(1)$ time complexity indicate **constant running time**. The time complexities of $O(n)$, $O(n^2)$ and $O(n^3)$ are called **linear, quadratic** and **cubic** time complexities, respectively. The $O(logn)$ time complexity is referred to as *logarithmic*. In general, the time complexities of the type $O(n^k)$ are called ***polynomial time complexities***. In fact, it can be shown that a polynomial

$A(n) = a_m n^m + a_{m-1} n^{m-1} + \ldots + a_1 n + a_0 = O(n^m)$ (see illustrative problem 2.2). Time complexities such as $O(2^n)$ and $O(3^n)$, in general $O(k^n)$, are called *exponential time complexities*.

Algorithms that report $O(\log n)$ time complexity are faster for sufficiently large $n$ than if they have reported $O(n)$. Similarly, $O(n.\log n)$ is better than $O(n^2)$ but not as good as $O(n)$. Some of the commonly occurring time complexities in their ascending orders of magnitude are listed below:

$$O(1) \leq O(\log n) \leq O(n) \leq O(n.\log n) \leq O(n^2) \leq O(n^3) \leq O(2^n)$$

## 2.5. Polynomial time versus exponential time algorithms

If $n$ is the size of the input instance, the number of operations for polynomial time algorithms are of the form $P(n)$, where $P$ is a polynomial. In terms of $O$ notation, polynomial time algorithms have time complexities of the form $O(n^k)$, where $k$ is a constant.

In contrast, in exponential time algorithms, the number of operations are of the form $k^n$. In terms of $O$ notation, exponential time algorithms have time complexities of the form $O(k^n)$, where $k$ is a constant.

| Time complexity function \ Size | 10 | 20 | 50 |
|---|---|---|---|
| $n^2$ | $10^{-4}$ s | $4 \times 10^{-4}$ s | $25 \times 10^{-4}$ s |
| $n^3$ | $10^{-3}$ s | $8 \times 10^{-3}$ s | $125 \times 10^{-3}$ s |
| $2^n$ | $10^{-3}$ s | 1 s | 35 years |
| $3^n$ | $6 \times 10^{-2}$ s | 58 min | $2 \times 10^3$ centuries |

**Table 2.4.** *Comparison of polynomial time and exponential time algorithms*

It is clear from the above that polynomial time algorithms are much more efficient than exponential time algorithms. From Table 2.4, it can be seen how exponential time algorithms can quickly surpass the capacity of any sophisticated computer due to their rapid growth rate (refer to Figure 2.1). Here, it is assumed that the computer takes 1 microsecond per operation. While the time complexity functions of $n^2$ and $n^3$ can be executed in reasonable time, which are just fractions of a second, one can never hope to finish execution of exponential time algorithms even if the fastest computers were employed. Note how for an algorithm whose time complexity function is $2^n$, the running time for input size $n = 20$ is 1 s but when the input size $n$ is increased to 50, the running time is a whopping 35 years! Again, for an algorithm whose time complexity function is $3^n$, for input size $n = 20$, the running time is 58 min whereas for $n = 50$, it takes a giant leap touching 2000 centuries! Thus, if one were to find an algorithm for a problem that reduces from exponential time to polynomial time then that is indeed a great accomplishment!

## 2.6. Average, best and worst case complexities

The time complexity of an algorithm is dependent on parameters associated with the input/output instances of the problem. Very often, the running time of the algorithm is expressed as a function of the input size. In such a case, it is fair enough to presume that the larger the input size of the problem instance is, the larger its running time. However, such is not always the case. There are problems whose time complexity is dependent not only on the size of the input but also on the nature of the input. Example 2.1 illustrates this point.

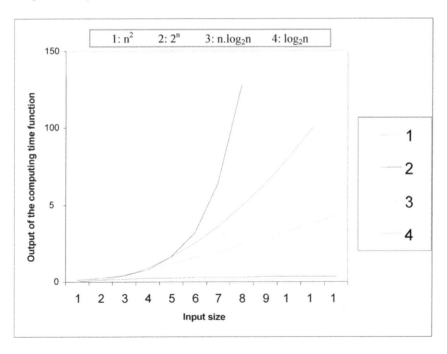

**Figure 2.1.** *Growth rate of some computing time functions. For a color version of this figure, see www.iste.co.uk/pai/algorithms1.zip*

## EXAMPLE 2.1.–

Algorithm: To sequentially search for the first occurring even number in the list of numbers given.

Input 1: –1, 3, 5, 7, –5, 7, 11, –13, 17, 71, 21, 9, 3, 1, 5, –23, –29, 33, 35, 37, 40.

Input 2: 6, 17, 71, 21, 9, 3, 1, 5, –23, 3, 64, 7, –5, 7, 11, 33, 35, 37, –3, –7, 11.

Input 3: 71, 21, 9, 3,  1,  5, –23, 3,  11, 33, 36, 37, –3, –7, 11, –5, 7, 11, –13, 17, 22.

Let us determine the efficiency of the algorithm for the input instances presented in terms of the number of comparisons performed before the first occurring even number is retrieved. All three input instances are of the same size of 21 numbers each.

In the case of Input 1, the first occurring even number occurs as the last element in the list. The algorithm would require 21 comparisons, equivalent to the size of the list, before it retrieves the element. On the other hand, in the case of Input 2, the first occurring even number appears as the very first element of the list, thereby calling for only one comparison before it is retrieved! If Input 2 is the *best* possible case that can happen for the quickest execution of the algorithm, then Input 1 is the *worst* possible case that can happen when the algorithm takes the longest possible time to complete. Generalizing, the time complexity of the algorithm in the best possible case would be expressed as $O(1)$, and in the worst possible case, it would be expressed as $O(n)$, where $n$ is the size of the input.

This justifies the statement that the running time of algorithms is dependent not only on the size of the input but also on its nature. That input instance (or instances) for which the algorithm takes the maximum possible time is called the **worst case,** and the time complexity in such a case is referred to as the **worst case time complexity**. That input instance for which the algorithm takes the minimum possible time is called the **best case,** and the time complexity in such a case is referred to as the **best case time complexity**. All other input instances that are neither of the two are categorized as **average cases**, and the time complexity of the algorithm in such cases is referred to as the **average case time complexity**. Input 3 is an example of an average case since it is neither the best case nor the worst case. By and large, analyzing the average case behavior of algorithms is harder and mathematically involved when compared to their worst case and best case counterparts. Additionally, such an analysis can be misleading if the input instances are not chosen at random or not chosen appropriately to cover all possible cases that may arise when the algorithm is deployed.

Worst case analysis is appropriate when the response time of the algorithm is critical. For example, in the case of a nuclear power plant controller, it is critical to know the maximum limit of the system response time regardless of the input instance that is to be handled by the system. The algorithms designed cannot have a running time that exceeds this response time limit.

On the other hand, in the case of applications where the input instances may be wide and varied and there is no knowledge beforehand of the kind of input instance that has to be worked upon, it is prudent to choose algorithms with good average case behavior.

## 2.7. Analyzing recursive programs

**Recursion** is an important concept in computer science. Many algorithms are best described in terms of recursion.

### 2.7.1. Recursive procedures

If $P$ is a procedure containing a call statement to itself (Figure 2.2(a)) or to another procedure that results in a call to itself (Figure 2.2(b)), then the procedure $P$ is said to be a **recursive procedure**. In the former case, it is termed **direct recursion,** and in the latter case, it is termed **indirect recursion**.

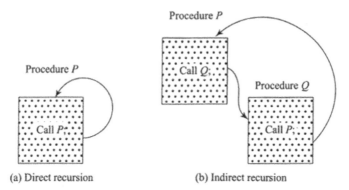

(a) Direct recursion          (b) Indirect recursion

**Figure 2.2.** *Skeletal recursive procedures*

Extending the concept to programming can yield program functions or programs themselves that are recursively defined. In such cases, they are referred to as **recursive functions** and **recursive programs**, respectively. Extending the concept to mathematics would yield what are called **recurrence relations**.

To ensure that the recursively defined function may not run into an infinite loop, it is essential that the following properties be satisfied by any recursive procedure.

i) There must be criteria, one or more, called the **base criteria** or simply **base case(s)**, where the procedure does not call itself either directly or indirectly.

ii) Each time the procedure calls itself directly or indirectly, it must be closer to the base criteria.

Example 2.2 illustrates a recursive procedure, and example 2.3 illustrates a recurrence relation.

EXAMPLE 2.2.–

A recursive procedure to compute the factorial of a number $n$ is shown as follows:

$$n! = 1, \quad \text{if } n = 1 \text{ (base criterion)}$$

$$n! = n. (n-1)!, \quad \text{if } n > 1$$

Note the recursion in the definition of factorial function(!). $n!$ calls $(n-1)!$ for its definition. The pseudo-code recursive function for the computation of $n!$ is shown as follows:

```
        function factorial(n)
1-2.    if   (n = 1) then factorial = 1
        else
3.         factorial = n* factorial(n-1);
        end factorial.
```

EXAMPLE 2.3.–

A recurrence relation $S(n)$ is defined as follows:

$S(n) = 0$, if $n = 1$ (base criterion)

$\quad = S(n/2) + 1$, if $n > 1$.

### EXAMPLE 2.4. *(The Tower of Hanoi Puzzle).–*

The Tower of Hanoi puzzle was invented by the French mathematician Edouard Lucas in 1883. However, there are numerous myths both ancient and mystical surrounding this puzzle and one such traces its origins to a custom prevalent in an ancient Hindu temple at Varanasi, India. Legend has it that there are 64 golden discs to be shuffled over 3 age old pegs, one move a day by the temple priests, at the end of which when the puzzle is solved, the world would come to an end! The puzzle therefore is also known as Tower of Brahma.

In the Tower of Hanoi puzzle, there are three pegs: source (S), intermediary (I) and destination (D). Peg S contains a set of disks stacked to resemble a tower, with the largest disk at the bottom and the smallest at the top. Figure 2.3 illustrates the initial configuration of the pegs for six disks. The objective is to transfer the entire tower of disks in Peg S to Peg D, maintaining the same order of the disks. Additionally, only one disk can be moved at a time, and never can a larger disk be placed on a smaller disk during the transfer. Peg I is for intermediate use during the transfer.

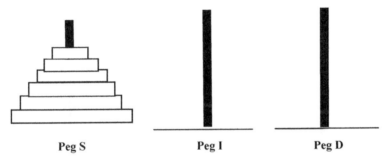

**Peg S**                    **Peg I**                    **Peg D**

**Figure 2.3.** *Tower of Hanoi puzzle (initial configuration)*

A simple solution to the problem, for $N = 3$ disks, is given by the following transfers of disks:

1) transfer disk from Peg S to D;

2) transfer disk from Peg S to I;

3) transfer disk from Peg D to I;

4) transfer disk from Peg S to D;

5) transfer disk from Peg I to S;

6) transfer disk from Peg I to D;

7) transfer disk from Peg S to D.

The solution to the puzzle calls for an application of recursive functions and recurrence relations. A skeletal recursive procedure for the solution of the problem for N number of disks is as follows:

1) move the top N-1 disks from Peg S to I (using D as an intermediary peg);

2) move the bottom disk from Peg S to D;

3) move N-1 disks from Peg I to D (using Peg S as an intermediary peg).

A pictorial representation of the skeletal recursive procedure for $N = 6$ disks is shown in Figure 2.4. Function TRANSFER illustrates the recursive function for the solution of the problem.

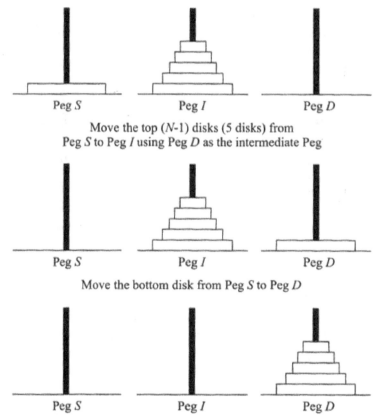

Peg S                    Peg I                    Peg D

Move the top ($N$-1) disks (5 disks) from
Peg S to Peg I using Peg D as the intermediate Peg

Peg S                    Peg I                    Peg D

Move the bottom disk from Peg S to Peg D

Peg S                    Peg I                    Peg D

Move ($N$-1) disks from Peg I to Peg D using Peg S as the intermediate Peg

**Figure 2.4.** *Pictorial representation of the skeletal recursive procedure for the Tower of Hanoi puzzle*

## 2.7.2. *Apriori analysis of recursive functions*

The apriori analysis of recursive functions is different from that of iterative functions. In the latter case, as was seen in section 2.2, the total frequency counts of the programs were computed before approximating them using mathematical functions such as $O$. In the case of recursive functions, we first formulate recurrence relations that define the behavior of the function. The solution of the recurrence relation and its approximation using the conventional $O$ or any other notation yields the resulting time complexity of the program.

```
function TRANSFER(N, S, I, D)
   /* N disks are to be transferred from Peg S to Peg D
      with Peg I as the intermediate peg*/
   if  N is 0 then exit();

   else
           {TRANSFER(N-1, S, D, I); /* transfer N-1 disks
                           from Peg S to Peg I with Peg D as the
                           intermediate peg*/


      Transfer disk from S to D; /* move the disk which
                           is the last and the largest disk,
                           from Peg S to Peg D*/


      TRANSFER(N-1, I, S, D); /* transfer N-1 disks from
                           Peg I to Peg D with Peg S as the
                           intermediate peg*/
           }
   end TRANSFER.
```

To frame the recurrence relation, we associate an unknown time function $T(n)$, where $n$ measures the size of the arguments to the procedure. We then obtain a recurrence relation for $T(n)$ in terms of $T(k)$ for various values of $k$.

Example 2.5 illustrates how the recurrence relation for the recursive factorial function FACTORIAL (n) shown in example 2.2 is obtained.

### EXAMPLE 2.5.–

Let $T(n)$ be the running time of the recursive function FACTORIAL (n). The running times of lines 1 and 2 are $O(1)$. The running time for line 3 is given by $O(1) + T(n-1)$. Here, $T(n-1)$ is the time complexity of the call to the recursive function FACTORIAL (n-1). Thus, for some constants $c$, $d$,

$$T(n) = c + T(n-1), \text{ if } n > 1$$
$$= d, \text{ if } n \leq 1$$

Example 2.6 derives the recurrence relation for the Tower of Hanoi puzzle.

## EXAMPLE 2.6.–

Let $T(N)$ be the minimum number of transfers needed to solve the puzzle with $N$ disks. From the function TRANSFER, it is evident that for $N = 0$, no disks are transferred. Again, for $N > 0$, two recursive calls each enabling the transfer of $(N - 1)$ disks and a single transfer of the last (largest) disk from Peg S to D are performed. Thus, the recurrence relation is given by

$$T(N) = 0, \text{ if } N = 0$$
$$= 2. \; T(N - 1) + 1, \text{ if } N > 0$$

Now what remains to be done is to solve the recurrence relation $T(n)$. Such a solution where $T(n)$ expresses itself in a form where no $T$ occurs on the right side is termed a ***closed form solution*** in conventional mathematics.

Despite the availability of different methods to solve recurrence relations, a general method of solution is to repeatedly replace terms $T(k)$ occurring on the right side of the recurrence relation by the relation itself with appropriate change of parameters. The substitutions continue until one reaches a formula in which $T$ does not appear on the right side. Quite often, at this stage, it may be essential to sum a series that could be either an arithmetic progression or geometric progression or some such mixed series. Even if we cannot obtain a sum exactly, we could work to obtain at least a close upper bound on the sum, which could act as an upper bound for $T(n)$.

Example 2.7 illustrates the solution of the recurrence relation for the function FACTORIAL (n), discussed in example 2.5, and example 2.8 illustrates the solution of the recurrence relation for the Tower of Hanoi puzzle, discussed in example 2.6.

## EXAMPLE 2.7.–

Solution of the recurrence relation

$$T(n) = c + T(n - 1), \text{ if } n > 1$$
$$= d, \text{ if } n \leq 1$$

yields the following steps.

$$T(n) = c + T(n-1)........(\text{step 1})$$

$$= c + (c + T(n-2))\sqrt{a^2 + b^2}$$
$$= 2c + T(n-2)........(\text{step 2})$$

$$= 2c + (c + T(n-3))$$
$$= 3c + T(n-3)........(\text{step 3})$$

In the $k$th step, the recurrence relation is transformed as

$$T(n) = k.c + T(n-k), \text{ if } n > k,......... (\text{step k})$$

Finally, when ($k = n - 1$), we obtain

$$T(n) = (n-1).c + T(1), \quad .........(\text{step n-1})$$
$$= (n-1)c + d$$
$$= O(n)$$

Observe how the recursive terms in the recurrence relation are replaced to move the relation closer to the base criterion, namely, $T(n) = 1$, $n \leq 1$. The approximation of the closed-form solution obtained, namely, $T(n) = (n - 1)c + d$, yields $O(n)$.

## EXAMPLE 2.8.–

Solution of the recurrence relation for the Tower of Hanoi puzzle,

$$T(N) = 0, \text{ if } N = 0$$
$$= 2. T(N - 1) + 1, \text{ if } N > 0$$

yields the following steps.

$$T(N) = 2.T(N-1) + 1.........(\text{step 1})$$

$$= 2.(2.T(N-2) + 1) + 1$$
$$= 2^2.T(N-2) + 2 + 1........(\text{step 2})$$

$$= 2^2(2.T(N-3)+1)+2+1$$
$$= 2^3.T(N-3)+2^2+2+1.........(\text{step } 3)$$

In the $k$th step, the recurrence relation is transformed as

$$T(N) = 2^k T(N-k)+2^{(k-1)}+2^{(k-2)}+........2^3+2^2+2+1, \quad ........(\text{step } k)$$

Finally, when ($k = N$), we obtain

$$T(N) = 2^N T(0)+2^{(N-1)}+2^{(N-2)}+.............2^3+2^2+2+1 \quad ........(\text{step } N)$$
$$= 2^N.0+(2^N-1)$$
$$= 2^N-1$$
$$= O(2^N)$$

## Summary

– When several algorithms can be designed for the solution of a problem, the need to determine which among them is the best arises. The efficiency of a program or an algorithm is measured by computing its time and/or space complexities. The time complexity of an algorithm is a function of the running time of the algorithm and the space complexity is a function of the space required by it to run to completion.

– The time complexity of an algorithm can be measured using apriori analysis or posteriori testing. While the former is a theoretical approach that is general and machine independent, the latter is completely machine dependent.

– The apriori analysis computes the time complexity as a function of the total frequency count of the algorithm. Frequency count is the number of times a statement is executed in a program.

– $O$, $\Omega$, $\Theta$ and $o$ are asymptotic notations that are used to express the time complexity of algorithms. While $O$ serves as an upper bound of the performance measure, $\Omega$ serves as the lower bound.

– The efficiency of algorithms is not just dependent on the input size but is also dependent on the nature of the input. This results in the categorization of worst, best and average case complexities. Worst case complexity is that input instance(s) for which the algorithm reports the maximum possible time and best case time complexity is that for which it reports the minimum possible time.

– Polynomial time algorithms are highly efficient when compared to exponential time algorithms. The latter can quickly get beyond the computational capacity of any sophisticated computer due to their rapid growth rate.

– Apriori analysis of recursive algorithms calls for the formulation of recurrence relations and obtaining their closed form solutions, before expressing them using appropriate asymptotic notations.

## 2.8. Illustrative problems

### PROBLEM 2.1.–

If $T_1(n)$ and $T_2(n)$ are the time complexities of two program fragments $P_1$ and $P_2$, where $T_1(n) = O(f(n))$ and $T_2(n) = O(g(n))$, find $T_1(n) + T_2(n)$ and $T_1(n).T_2(n)$.

### Solution:

Since $T_1(n) \leq c.f(n)$ for some positive number $c$ and positive integer $n_1$ such that $n \geq n_1$ and $T_2(n) \leq d.g(n)$ for some positive number $d$ and positive integer $n_2$ such that $n \geq n_2$, we obtain $T_1(n) + T_2(n)$ as follows:

$T_1(n) + T_2(n) \leq c. f(n) + d. g(n)$, for $n > n_0$ where $n_0 = \max(n_1, n_2)$

i.e., $T_1(n) + T_2(n) \leq (c + d) \max(f(n), g(n))$ for $n > n_0$

Hence, $T_1(n) + T_2(n) = O(\max(f(n), g(n)))$.

(This result is referred to as **Rule of Sums of $O$ notation**.)

To obtain $T_1(n).T_2(n)$, we proceed as follows:

$T_1(n).T_2(n) \leq c. f(n). d. g(n)$

$\leq k. f(n). g(n)$

Therefore, $T_1(n).T_2(n) = O(f(n).g(n))$.

(This result is referred to as **Rule of Products of $O$ notation**.)

## PROBLEM 2.2.–

If $A(n) = a_m n^m + a_{m-1} n^{m-1} + \ldots + a_1 n + a_0$, then $A(n) = O(n^m)$ *for* $n \geq 1$.

### Solution:

Let us consider $|A(n)|$. We have

$$
\begin{aligned}
|A(n)| &= |a_m n^m + a_{m-1} n^{m-1} + \ldots + a_1 n + a_0| \\
&\leq |a_m n^m| + |a_{m-1} n^{m-1}| + \ldots |a_1 n| + |a_0| \\
&\leq (|a_m| + |a_{m-1}| + \ldots |a_1| + |a_0|) . n^m \\
&\leq c.n^m \qquad \text{where } c = |a_m| + |a_{m-1}| + \ldots |a_1| + |a_0|
\end{aligned}
$$

Hence, $A(n) = O(n^m)$.

NOTE.– This result is useful when the time complexity of an algorithm in terms of $O$ notation is to be obtained, given the total frequency count of the algorithm, which when computed results in a polynomial in input variable $n$ of degree $m$.

## PROBLEM 2.3.–

Two algorithms $A$ and $B$ report time complexities expressed by the functions $n^2$ and $2^n$, respectively. They are to be executed on a machine $M$ that consumes $10^{-6}$ s to execute an instruction. What is the time taken by the algorithms to complete their execution on machine $A$ for an input size of 50? If another machine $N$ that is 10 times faster than machine $M$ is provided for the execution, what is the largest input size that can be handled by the two algorithms on machine $N$? What are your observations?

### Solution:

Algorithms $A$ and $B$ report time complexities of $n^2$ and $2^n$, respectively. In other words, each of the algorithms execute approximately $n^2$ and $2^n$ instructions, respectively. For an input size of $n = 50$ and with a speed of $10^{-6}$ s per instruction, the time taken by the algorithms on machine $M$ are as follows:

Algorithm $A$: $50^2 \times 10^{-6} = 0.0025$ s

Algorithm $B$: $2^{50} \times 10^{-6} \cong 35$ years

If another machine $N$ that is 10 times faster than machine $M$ is provided, then the number of instructions that algorithms $A$ and $B$ can execute on machine $N$ would also be 10 times more than that on $M$. Let $x^2$ and $2^y$ be the number of instructions that algorithms $A$ and $B$ execute on machine $N$. Then, the new input size that each of these algorithms can handle is given by

Algorithm $A$:

$$x^2 = 10 \times n^2$$

$$\therefore x = \sqrt{10} \times n \cong 3.n$$

That is, algorithm $A$ can handle three times the original input size that it could handle on machine $M$.

Algorithm $B$:

$$2^y = 10 \times 2^n$$
$$\therefore y = \log_2 10 + n \cong 3 + n$$

That is, algorithm $B$ can handle just three units more than the original input size than it could handle on machine $M$.

*Observations*: Since algorithm $A$ is a polynomial time algorithm, it displays a superior performance of executing the specified input on machine $M$ in 0.0025 s. Additionally, when provided with a faster machine $N$, it is able to handle three times the original input size that it could handle on machine $M$.

In contrast, algorithm $B$ is an exponential time algorithm. While it takes 35 years to process the specified input on machine $M$, despite the faster machine provided, it is able to process just three units more over the input data size than it could handle on machine $M$.

## PROBLEM 2.4.–

Analyze the behavior of the following program, which computes the $n$th Fibonacci number, for appropriate values of $n$. Obtain the frequency count of the statements (that are given line numbers) for various cases of $n$.

```
procedure Fibonacci(n)
1.       read(n);
2-4.     if (n<0) then print ("error"); exit();
5-7.     if (n=0) then print ("Fibonacci number is 0");
                   exit();
8-10.    if (n=1) then print ("Fibonacci number is 1");
                   exit();
11-12.   f1=0;
         f2=1;
13.      for i = 2 to n do
14-16.      f  = f1 + f2;
            f1 = f2;
            f2 = f;
17.      end
18.      print("Fibonacci number is", f);
end Fibonacci
```

## Solution:

The behavior of the program for the cases concerned can be analyzed as shown in Table P2.4.

| Line number | Frequency count of the statements | | | |
|---|---|---|---|---|
| | $n < 0$ | $n = 0$ | $n = 1$ | $n > 1$ |
| 1 | 1 | 1 | 1 | 1 |
| 2 | 1 | 1 | 1 | 1 |
| 3, 4 | 1, 1 | 0 | 0 | 0 |
| 5 | 0 | 1 | 1 | 1 |
| 6, 7 | 0 | 1, 1 | 0 | 0 |
| 8 | 0 | 0 | 1 | 1 |
| 9, 10 | 0 | 0 | 1, 1 | 0 |
| 11, 12 | 0 | 0 | 0 | 1, 1 |
| 13 | 0 | 0 | 0 | $(n - 2 + 1) + 1$ |
| 14, 15, 16 | 0 | 0 | 0 | $(n - 1), (n - 1), (n - 1)$ |
| 17 | 0 | 0 | 0 | $(n - 1)$ |
| 18 | 0 | 0 | 0 | 1 |
| Total frequency count | 4 | 5 | 6 | $5n + 3$ |

Table P2.4. Frequency count of the statements
in procedure Fibonacci (n)

The total frequency count is $5n + 3$, and therefore, the time complexity of the program is $T(n) = O(n)$.

## PROBLEM 2.5.–

Obtain the time complexity of the following program:

```
procedure whirlpool (m)

if (m ≤ 0) then print("eddy!"); exit();
else {
            swirl = whirlpool(m-1) + whirlpool(m-1);
            print("whirl");

        }
end whirlpool
```

## Solution:

We first obtain the recurrence relation for the time complexity of the procedure whirlpool. Let $T(m)$ be the time complexity of the procedure. The recurrence relation is formulated as given below:

$T(m) = a$, if $m \leq 0$

$\quad = 2T(m – 1) + b$, if $m > 0$.

Here, $2T(m – 1)$ expresses the total time complexity of the two calls to whirlpool $(m – 1)$. $a$ and $b$ indicate the constant time complexities to execute the rest of the statements when $m \leq 0$ and $m > 0$, respectively.

Solving for the recurrence relation yields the following steps:

$T(m) = 2T(m – 1) + b$ ………(step 1)

$\quad = 2(2T(m – 2)+b) + b$

$\quad = 2^2 T(m – 2) + b\ (1+2)$……….(step 2)

$\quad = 2^2(2T(m – 3)+b) +b(1+2)$

$\quad = 2^3(T(m – 3) + b(1+2+2^2)$…….(step 3)

In general, in the $i$th step

$T(m) = 2^i T(m-i) + b(1 + 2+ 2^2 +....2^{i-1})$……(step $i$)

When $i = m$,

$$T(m) = 2^m T(0) + b(1 + 2 + 2^2 + ....2^{m-1})$$

$$= a \cdot 2^m + b(2^m - 1)$$

$$= k \cdot 2^m + l \text{ where } k, l \text{ are positive constants}$$

$$= O(2^m)$$

The time complexity of the procedure `whirlpool` is therefore $O(2^m)$.

## PROBLEM 2.6.–

The frequency count of line 3 in the following program fragment is ___.

a) $\frac{4n^2 - 2n}{2}$    b) $\frac{i^2 - i}{2}$    c) $\frac{(i^2 - 3i)}{2}$    d) $\frac{(4n^2 - 6n)}{2}$

```
1.  i = 2n
2.  for j = 1 to i
3.      for k = 3 to j
4.          m = m+1;
5.      end
6.  end
```

**Solution:**

The frequency count of line 3 is given by $\sum_{j=1}^{i}(j - 3 + 1) + 1 = \sum_{j=1}^{2n}(j - 1) = \frac{4n^2 - 2n}{2}$. Hence, the correct option is *a*.

## PROBLEM 2.7.–

Find the frequency count and the time complexity of the following program fragment:

```
1.  for i = 20 to 30
2.      for j = 1 to n
3.          am = am+1;
4.      end
5.  end
```

## Solution:

The frequency count of the program fragment is shown in Table P2.7.

| Line number | Frequency count |
|:---:|:---:|
| 1 | $12$ |
| 2 | $\sum_{i=20}^{30} (n + 1) = 11(n + 1)$ |
| 3 | $\sum_{i=20}^{30} \sum_{j=1}^{n} 1 = 11n$ |
| 4 | $11n$ |
| 5 | $11$ |

**Table P2.7.** *Frequency count of the statements in the program fragment of Problem 2.7*

The total frequency count is $33n + 34$, and the time complexity is therefore $O(n)$.

## PROBLEM 2.8.–

State which of the following are true or false:

(i) $f(n) = 30n^2 2^n + 6n2^n + 8n^2 = O(2^n)$

(ii) $g(n) = 9.\,2^n + n^2 = \Omega(2^n)$

(iii) $h(n) = 9.\,2^n + n^2 = \Theta(2^n)$

## Solution:

i) False.

For $f(n) = O(2^n)$, it is essential that

$$|f(n)| \leq c.\,|2^n|$$

$$(\text{i. e.}) \left| \frac{30n^2 2^n + 6n2^n + 8n^2}{2^n} \right| \leq c$$

This is not possible since the left-hand side is an increasing function.

(ii) True.

(iii) True.

## PROBLEM 2.9.–

Solve the following recurrence relation assuming $n = 2^k$:

$$C(n) = 2, \qquad\qquad n = 2$$
$$= 2.\, C(n/2) + 3, \quad n > 2$$

## Solution:

The solution of the recurrence relation proceeds as given below:

$$
\begin{aligned}
C(n) &= 2.C(n/2) + 3 \text{........... (step 1)}\\
&= 2(2C(n/4) + 3) + 3\\
&= 2^2 C(n/2^2) + 3.(1+2) \text{...... (step 2)}\\
&= 2^2 (2.C(n/2^3) + 3) + 3.(1+2)\\
&= 2^3 C(n/2^3) + 3(1+2+2^2) \text{........ (step 3)}
\end{aligned}
$$

In the $i$th step,

$$C(n) = 2^i C(n/2^i) + 3(1 + 2 + 2^2 + \dots + 2^{i-1}) \text{........ (step i)}$$

Since $n = 2^k$, in the step when $i = (k-1)$,

$$C(n) = 2^{k-1} C(n/2^{k-1}) + 3(1 + 2 + 2^2 + \dots + 2^{k-2}) \text{........ (step k-1)}$$

$$= \frac{n}{2}.C(2) + 3(2^{k-1} - 1)$$

$$= \frac{n}{2}.2 + 3(\frac{n}{2} - 1)$$

$$= 5.\frac{n}{2} - 3$$

Hence, $C(n) = 5 \cdot n/2 - 3$.

## PROBLEM 2.10.–

Consider the following recursive function GUESS (n, m) written in pseudo-code. Hand trace the code to determine the output when the recursive function is called with $n = 6$ and $m = 3$.

```
function GUESS (n, m)
     if (m > n) then return (0);
     if (m = n) then return (1);
     if (n = 1) or (m = 0) then return (1);
     if (m < n) then return ((n-1)*GUESS(n-1, m-1));
end GUESS
```

## Solution:

It is convenient and effective to hand trace a recursive program or function with the help of what is called *a tree of recursive calls*. The tree grows with every call to the function and tracks the values returned when each of the functions that was called terminates and returns the output to the function that called it.

Figure P2.10 illustrates the tree of recursive calls for GUESS (6, 3). The solid arrows indicate the recursive calls to the function that is shown as a box. The broken arrows indicate the return of values to the point of call when the called functions terminate. The forward calls to the function and the return of values to the called function have been shown separately for the sake of clarity.

**Forward calls to function GUESS          Returning values to called functions**

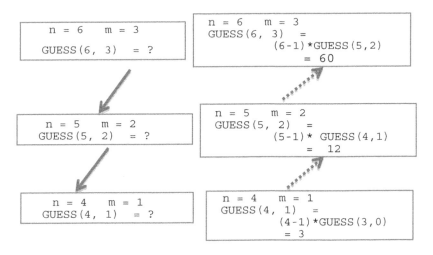

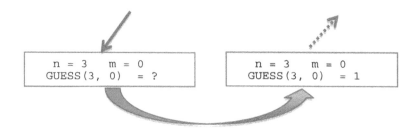

**Figure P2.10.** *Tree of recursive calls for the recursive function GUESS(6,3)*

GUESS (3,0), where $n = 3$ and $m = 0$, triggers one of the three base case conditions given, and hence, the function terminates returning the value 1. This further triggers the termination of the called functions one after another until the first call to the recursive function GUESS (6, 3) is terminated returning the output value of 60. It can be easily seen from the number of boxes that the number of calls made to the recursive function GUESS is 4.

## PROBLEM 2.11.–

What is the time complexity of a recursive program whose recurrence relation is as given below? Assume that the input size $n$ of the problem is a power of 4, that is, $n = 4^s$.

$$T(n) = 3.T\left(\frac{n}{4}\right) + c.n^2, n > 1$$
$$= a, \text{otherwise}$$

## Solution:

$$T(n) = 3.T\left(\frac{n}{4}\right) + c.n^2 \text{ ... step (1)}$$

$$= 3.\left[3.T\left(\frac{n}{4^2}\right) + c.\left(\frac{n}{4}\right)^2\right] + c.n^2$$

$$= 3^2.T\left(\frac{n}{4^2}\right) + c.n^2\left(1 + \frac{3}{4^2}\right) \text{ ... step (2)}$$

$$= 3^3 .T\left(\frac{n}{4^3}\right) + c.n^2 \left(1 + \frac{3}{4^2} + \frac{3^2}{4^4}\right) \dots \text{step (3)}$$

Generalizing, in the $k$th step,

$$T(n) = 3^k .T\left(\frac{n}{4^k}\right) + c.n^2 \left(1 + \frac{3}{4^2} + \frac{3^2}{4^4} + \frac{3^3}{4^6} + \dots \frac{3^{k-1}}{4^{2k-2}}\right) \dots \text{step (k)}$$

We try to obtain the sum S of the series as follows:

$$S = \left(1 + \frac{3}{4^2} + \frac{3^2}{4^4} + \frac{3^3}{4^6} + \dots \frac{3^{k-1}}{4^{2k-2}}\right)$$

$$4^{2k} .S = 4^{2k}\left(1 + \frac{3}{4^2} + \frac{3^2}{4^4} + \frac{3^3}{4^6} + \dots \frac{3^{k-1}}{4^{2k-2}}\right) = 4^{2k} + \left(3.4^{2k-2} + 3^2.4^{2k-4} + 3^3.4^{2k-6} + \dots 3^{k-1}.4^2\right) \quad (1)$$

$$3.4^{2k-2} .S = 3.4^{2k-2} + \left(3^2.4^{2k-4} + 3^3.4^{2k-6} + 3^4.4^{2k-8} \dots + 3^k\right) \quad \dots (2)$$

Subtracting (2) from (1) yields

$$4^{2k} .S - 3.4^{2k-2} .S = 4^{2k} - 3^k,$$

that is, $S = \dfrac{4^{2k} - 3^k}{4^{2k} - 3.4^{2k-2}} = \dfrac{4^{2k} - 3^k}{13.4^{2k-2}}$      $\dots$ (3)

Therefore, $T(n) = 3^k .T\left(\dfrac{n}{4^k}\right) + c.n^2 \left(\dfrac{4^{2k} - 3^k}{13.4^{2k-2}}\right)$      $\dots$ (4)

Since $n$ is a power of 4 ($n = 4^s$), in the $s$th step (putting $k = s$), we obtain

$$T(n) = 3^s .T\left(\frac{n}{4^s}\right) + c.n^2 \left(\frac{4^{2s} - 3^s}{13.4^{2s-2}}\right)$$

$$= 3^s .T(1) + c.n^2 .16\left(\frac{n^2 - 3^s}{13.n^2}\right)$$

$$= 3^s.a + b.\left(n^2 - 3^s\right), \text{ for constants } a \text{ and } b.$$

$$= b.n^2 + d.3^{\log_4 n}, \text{ for some constant } d.$$

Therefore, $T(n) = O\left(n^2\right)$.

### PROBLEM 2.12.–

What is the total frequency count and time complexity of the following pseudo-code, given $a$ and $n$ as inputs?

```
1. product = 1;
2. sum = 0;
3. for i =1 to n do
4.        product = product *a;
5.        sum = sum + a;
6. end
7. power = product;
8. summation = sum;
```

### Solution:

The frequency counts of the individual statements and the total frequency count of the statements in the pseudo-code are shown in the following table:

| Statement label | 1 | 2 | 3 | 4 | 5 | 6 | 7 | 8 |
|---|---|---|---|---|---|---|---|---|
| Frequency count | 1 | 1 | n + 1 | n | n | n | 1 | 1 |
| Total frequency count | | | | 4n + 5 | | | | |

Hence, the time complexity of the pseudo-code program is $O(n)$.

### Review questions

1) Frequency count of the statement

"**for** k = 3 **to** (m+2) **do** " is

a)  *(m+2)*    b) *(m-1)*        c) *(m+1)*    d) *(m+5)*

2) If functions $f(n)$ and $g(n)$, for a positive integer $n_0$ and a positive number $C$, are such that $|f(n)| \geq C|g(n)|$, for all $n \geq n_0$, then

a) $f(n) = \Omega(g(n))$   b) $f(n) = O(g(n))$   c) $f(n) = \Theta(g(n))$

d) $f(n) = o(g(n))$

3) For $T(n) = 167\, n^5 + 12\, n^4 + 89\, n^3 + 9n^2 + n + 1$,

a) $T(n) = O(n)$   b) $T(n) = O(n^5)$   c) $T(n) = O(1)$

d) $T(n) = O(n^2 + n)$

4) State whether true or false:

(i) Exponential functions have rapid growth rates when compared to polynomial functions.

(ii) Therefore, exponential time algorithms run faster than polynomial time algorithms.

a) (i) true (ii) true   b) (i) true (ii) false

c) (i) false (ii) false  d) (i) false (ii) true

5) Find the odd one out:    $O(n)$, $O(n^2)$, $O(n^3)$, $O(3^n)$

a) $O(n)$   b) $O(n^2)$   c) $O(n^3)$    d) $O(3^n)$

6) How does one measure the efficiency of algorithms?

7) Distinguish between best case, worst case and average case complexities of an algorithm.

8) Define $O$ and $\Omega$ notations of time complexity.

9) Compare and contrast exponential time complexity with polynomial time complexity.

10) How are recursive programs analyzed?

11) Analyze the time complexity of the following program:

```
...
for send =  1 to n do
   for receive = 1 to send do
      for ack = 2 to receive do
         message = send - (receive + ack);
      end
   end
end
```

12) Solve the recurrence relation:

$S(n) = 2 \cdot S(n-1) + b.n$, if $n > 1$

$\quad = a,$ \qquad\qquad if $n = 1$

13) Write a pseudo-code to obtain the maximum element given a set of elements. What is the time complexity of your program? Is it possible to discuss worst case or best case complexities for the pseudo code that you designed?

14) Write pseudo-code procedures to (i) add two matrices and (ii) multiply two matrices. Obtain the total frequency counts and the time complexities of the iterative procedures.

15) What is the time complexity of a recursive program whose recurrence relation is given as follows assuming that $n$ is a power of $(3/2)$:

$$T(n) = T\left(\frac{2n}{3}\right) + 1, \quad n > 1$$
$$= c, n = 1$$

# 3

# Arrays

## 3.1. Introduction

In Chapter 1, an abstract data type (ADT) was defined to be a set of data objects and the fundamental operations that can be performed on this set.

In this regard, an **array** is an ADT whose objects are a sequence of elements of the same type, and the two operations performed on it are **store** and **retrieve**. Thus, if $a$ is an array, the operations can be represented as STORE *(a, i, e)* and RETRIEVE *(a, i),* where $i$ is termed the **index** and $e$ is the **element** that is to be stored in the array. These functions are equivalent to the programming language statements $a[i]:= e$ and $a[i]$, where $i$ is termed **subscript** and $a$ is termed **array variable name** in programming language parlance.

Arrays can be **one-dimensional, two-dimensional, three-dimensional** or in general **multidimensional**. Figure 3.1 illustrates a one-dimensional and two-dimensional array. It may be observed that while one-dimensional arrays are mathematically likened to **vectors**, two-dimensional arrays are likened to **matrices**. In this regard, two-dimensional arrays also have the terminologies of **rows** and **columns** associated with them.

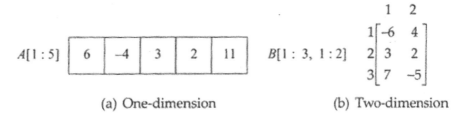

(a) One-dimension          (b) Two-dimension

**Figure 3.1.** *Examples of arrays*

In Figure 3.1, *A[1:5]* refers to a one-dimensional array where *1* and *5* are referred to as the **lower** and **upper indexes** or the **lower** and **upper bounds** of the index range, respectively. Similarly, *B[1:3, 1:2]* refers to a two-dimensional array where 1, 3 and 1, 2 are the lower and upper indexes of the rows and columns, respectively.

Additionally, each element of the array, namely, *A[i]* or *B[i, j]*, resides in a memory location also called a **cell**. Here, the cell refers to a unit of memory and is machine dependent.

## 3.2. Array operations

An array, when viewed as a data structure, supports only two operations, namely:

(i) storage of values, that is, writing into an array (STORE (*a, i, e*));

(ii) retrieval of values, that is, reading from an array (RETRIEVE (*a, i*)).

For example, if *A* is an array of five elements, then Figure 3.2 illustrates the operations performed on *A*.

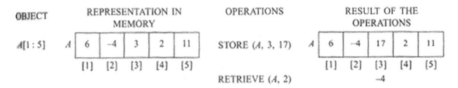

Figure 3.2. *Array operations: store and retrieve*

## 3.3. Number of elements in an array

In this section, the computation of the size of the array by way of the number of elements in the array is discussed. This is important since, when arrays are declared in a program, it is essential that the number of memory locations needed by the array is "booked" beforehand by the compiler.

### 3.3.1. *One-dimensional array*

Let *A[1:u]* be a one-dimensional array. The size of the array, as is evident, is *u*, and the elements are *A[1], A[2], ... A[u-1]*, and *A[u]*. In the case of the array *A[l: u]*, where *l* is the lower bound and *u* is the upper bound of the index range, the number of elements is given by $(u - l + 1)$.

## EXAMPLE 3.1.–

The number of elements in

i) A[1:26] = 26;

ii) A[5:53] = 49 (∵53 – 5+1);

iii) A[–1:26] = 28.

### 3.3.2. Two-dimensional array

Let $A[1{:}u_1,\ 1{:}u_2]$ be a two-dimensional array, where $u_1$ indicates the number of rows and $u_2$ the number of columns in the array.

Then, the number of elements in $A$ is $u_1.u_2$. Generalizing, $A[l_1 : u_1,\ l_2{:}u_2]$ has a size of $(u_1{-}l_1{+}1)\ (u_2{-}l_2{+}1)$ elements. Figure 3.3 illustrates a two-dimensional array and its size.

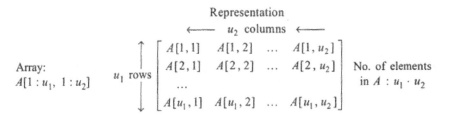

**Figure 3.3.** *Size of a two-dimensional array*

## EXAMPLE 3.2.–

The number of elements in

(i) A[1:10, 1:5] = 10 × 5 = 50;

(ii) A[–1:2, 2:6] = 4 × 5 = 20;

(iii) A[0:5, –1:6] = 6 × 8 = 48.

### 3.3.3. Multidimensional array

A multidimensional array $A[1{:}\ u_1,\ 1{:}u_2,\ \dots\ 1{:}\ u_n]$ has a size of $u_1.u_2\dots u_n$ elements, that is, $\prod_{i=1}^{n} u_i$.

Figure 3.4 illustrates a three-dimensional array and its size.

Generalizing, array A $[l_1:u_1, l_2:u_2, l_3:u_3 \ldots l_n:u_n]$ has a size of $\prod_{i=1}^{n}(u_i - l_i + 1)$ elements.

| Array: | Elements | Number of elements |
|---|---|---|
| $A[1:2 \quad 1:2 \quad 1:3]$ | $A[1, 1, 1] \; A[1, 1, 2] \; A[1, 1, 3]$ <br> $A[1, 2, 1] \; A[1, 2, 2] \; A[1, 2, 3]$ <br> $A[2, 1, 1] \; A[2, 1, 2] \; A[2, 1, 3]$ <br> $A[2, 2, 1] \; A[2, 2, 2] \; A[2, 2, 3]$ | $2 \times 2 \times 3 = 12$ |

**Figure 3.4.** *Size of a three-dimensional array*

EXAMPLE 3.3.–

The number of elements in

i) $A[-1:3, 3:4, 2:6] = (3 - (-1) + 1)(4 - 3 + 1)(6 - 2 + 1) = 50$;

ii) $A[0:2, 1:2, 3:4, -1:2] = 3 \times 2 \times 2 \times 4 = 48$.

## 3.4. Representation of arrays in memory

How are arrays represented in memory? This is an important question, at least from the compiler's point of view. In many programming languages, the name of the array is associated with the address of the starting memory location to facilitate efficient storage and retrieval. Additionally, while the computer memory is considered one dimensional (linear), it must accommodate multidimensional arrays. Hence, address calculation to determine the appropriate locations in memory becomes important.

In this aspect, it is convenient to imagine a two-dimensional array $A[1:u_1, 1:u_2]$ as $u_1$ number of one-dimensional arrays whose dimension is $u_2$. Again, in the case of three-dimensional arrays $A[1: u_1, 1: u_2, 1: u_3]$ it can be viewed as $u_1$ number of two-dimensional arrays of size $u_2, u_3$. Figure 3.5 illustrates this idea.

In general, a multidimensional array $A[1: u_1, 1: u_2, \ldots 1: u_n]$ is a colony of $u_1$ arrays, each of dimension $A[1: u_2, 1: u_3, \ldots 1: u_n]$.

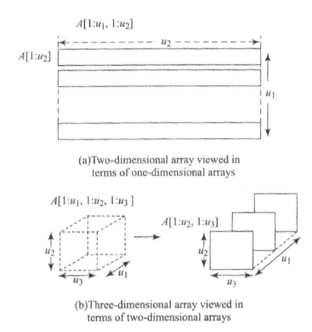

(a)Two-dimensional array viewed in
terms of one-dimensional arrays

(b)Three-dimensional array viewed in
terms of two-dimensional arrays

**Figure 3.5.** *Viewing higher dimensional arrays in
terms of their lower dimensional counterparts*

The arrays are stored in memory in one of the two ways, namely, **row major
order** or **column major order**. In the ensuing discussion, we assume a row major
order representation. Figure 3.6 distinguishes between the two methods of
representation.

### 3.4.1. One-dimensional array

Consider the array $A(1{:}u_1)$, and let $\alpha$ be the address of the starting memory
location referred to as the **base address** of the array. Here, as it is evident, $A[1]$
occupies the memory location whose address is $\alpha$, $A[2]$ occupies $\alpha + 1$ and so on. In
general, the address of $A[i]$ is given by $\alpha + (i - 1)$. Figure 3.7 illustrates the
representation of a one-dimensional array in memory.

In general, for a one-dimensional array $A(l_1{:}\ u_1)$, the address of $A[i]$ is given by
$\alpha + (i - l_1)$, where $\alpha$ is the base address.

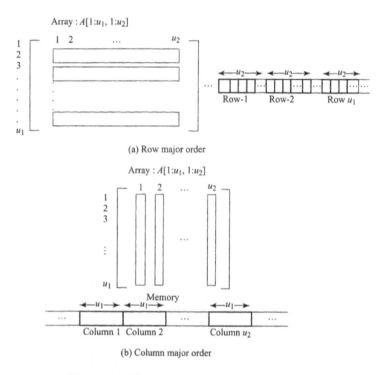

(a) Row major order

(b) Column major order

**Figure 3.6.** *Row-major order and column-major order of a two-dimensional array*

EXAMPLE 3.4.–

For the array given below with base address $\alpha = 100$, the addresses of the array elements specified are computed as given below:

| Array | Element | Address |
|---|---|---|
| (i) A[1:17] | A[7] | $\alpha + (7 - 1) = 100 + 6 = 106$ |
| (ii) A[–2:23] | A[16] | $\alpha + (16 - (-2)) = 100 + 18 = 118$ |

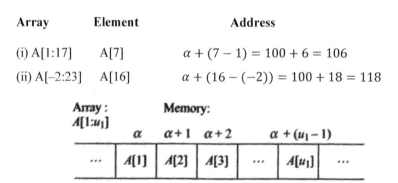

**Figure 3.7.** *Representation of one-dimensional arrays in memory*

### 3.4.2. *Two-dimensional arrays*

Consider the array $A[1:u_1, 1:u_2]$, which is to be stored in memory. It is helpful to imagine this array as $u_1$ number of one-dimensional arrays of length $u_2$. Thus, if $A[1,1]$ is stored in address $\alpha$, the base address, then $A[i,1]$ has address $\alpha + (i-1)u_2$, and $A[i, j]$ has address $\alpha + (i-1)u_2 + (j-1)$.

To understand this, let us imagine the two-dimensional array $A[i, j]$ to be a building with $i$ floors, each accommodating $j$ rooms. To access room $A[i, 1]$, the first room on the $i$th floor, one has to traverse $(i-1)$ floors, each having $u_2$ rooms. In other words, $(i-1).u_2$ rooms have to be left behind before one knocks at the first room on the $i$th floor. Since $\alpha$ is the base address, the address of $A[i,1]$ would be $\alpha + (i-1)u_2$. Again, extending a similar argument to access $A[i, j]$, the $j$th room on the $i$th floor, one has to leave behind $(i-1)u_2$ rooms and reach the $j$th room on the $i$th floor. This again, as before, computes the address of $A[i, j]$ as $\alpha + (i-1)u_2 + (j-1)$. Figure 3.8 illustrates the representation of two-dimensional arrays in memory.

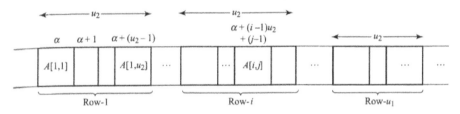

**Figure 3.8.** *Representation of a two-dimensional array in memory*

Observe that the addresses of array elements are expressed in terms of the cells, which hold the array elements.

In general, for a two-dimensional array $A[l_1: u_1, l_2: u_2]$, the address of A[i, j] is given by $\alpha + (i - l_1)(u_2 - l_2 + 1) + (j - l_2)$.

### EXAMPLE 3.5.–

For the arrays given below with $\alpha = 220$ as the base address, the addresses of the elements specified are computed as follows:

| Array | Element | Address |
|-------|---------|---------|
| $A[1:10,1:5]$ | $A[8,3]$ | $220 + (8-1).5 + (3-1) = 257$ |
| $A[-2:4,-6:10]$ | $A[3,-5]$ | $220 + (3-(-2)).(10-(-6)+1) + (-5-(-6)) = 306$ |

### 3.4.3. Three-dimensional arrays

Consider the three-dimensional array $A[1:u_1, 1:u_2, 1:u_3]$. As discussed before, we will imagine it to be $u_1$ number of two-dimensional arrays of dimension $u_2.u_3$. Reverting to the analogy of building - floor - rooms, the three-dimensional array $A[i, j, k]$ could be viewed as a colony of $i$ buildings, each having $j$ floors with each floor accommodating $k$ rooms. To access $A[i, 1, 1]$, the first room on the first floor of the $i$th building, one has to walk past $(i - 1)$ buildings, each comprising $u_2.u_3$ rooms, before climbing on to the first floor of the $i$th building to reach the first room! This means that the address of $A[i, 1, 1]$ would be $\alpha + (i - 1)u_2.u_3$. Similarly, the address of $A[i, j, 1]$ requires the first room on the $j$th floor of the $i$th building to be accessed, which works out to $\alpha + (i - 1)u_2u_3 + (j - 1)u_3$. Proceeding on similar lines, the address of $A[i, j, k]$ is given by $\alpha + (i - 1)u_2u_3 + (j - 1)u_3 + (k - 1)$.

Figure 3.9 illustrates the representation of three-dimensional arrays in memory.

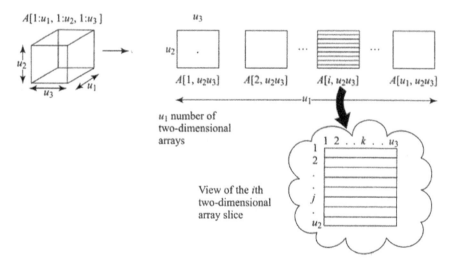

**Figure 3.9.** *Representation of three-dimensional arrays in the memory*

In general, for a three-dimensional array $A[l_1:u_1, l_2:u_2, l_3:u_3]$, the address of $A[i,j,k]$ is given by $\alpha + (i - l_1)(u_2 - l_2 + 1)(u_3 - l_3 + 1) + (j - l_2)(u_3 - l_3 + 1) + (k - l_3)$.

## EXAMPLE 3.6.–

For the arrays given below with base address $\alpha = 110$, the addresses of the elements specified are as follows:

| Array | Element | Address |
|---|---|---|
| $A[1:5, 1:2, 1:3]$ | $A[2,1,3]$ | $110+(2-1).6+(1-1).3+(3-1)=118$ |
| $A[-2:4, -6:10, 1:3]$ | $A[-1,-4,2]$ | $110+(-1-(-2)).17.3+(-4-(-6)).3+(2-1)=168$ |

### 3.4.4. N-dimensional array

Let $A[1:u_1, 1:u_2, 1:u_3, \dots 1:u_N]$ be an $N$-dimensional array. The address calculation for the retrieval of various elements is given as follows:

| Element | Address |
|---|---|
| $A[i_1,1,1,\dots.1]$ | $\alpha + (i_1 - 1)u_2 u_3 \dots u_N$ |
| $A[i_1,i_2,1,1,\dots1]$ | $\alpha + (i_1 - 1)u_2 u_3 .. u_N + (i_2 - 1)u_3.u_4 \dots u_N$ |
| $A[i_1,i_2,i_3,1,1,1,\dots1]$ | $\alpha + (i_1 - 1)u_2 u_3 .. u_N + (i_2 - 1)u_3 u_4 .. u_N + (i_3 - 1)u_4 u_5 \dots u_N$ |

.

.

.

$A[i_1,i_2,i_3,\dots i_N]$     $\alpha + (i_1 - 1)u_2 u_3 \dots u_N + (i_2 - 1)u_3 u_4 \dots u_N + \dots + (i_N - 1)$

$$= \alpha + \sum_{j=1}^{N}(i_j - 1)a_j \text{ where } a_j = \prod_{k=j+1}^{N} u_k, 1 \leq j < N$$

## 3.5. Applications

In this section, we introduce concepts that are applications of arrays and generally found to be useful in computer science, namely, **sparse matrices**, **ordered lists**, **strings** and **bit arrays**.

### 3.5.1. *Sparse matrix*

A matrix is a mathematical object that finds applications in various scientific problems. A matrix is an arrangement of *m.n* elements arranged as *m* rows and *n* columns. The **sparse matrix** is a matrix with **zeros as the dominating elements**. However, there is no precise definition for a sparse matrix. The term "sparseness", therefore, is relatively defined. Figure 3.10 illustrates a matrix and a sparse matrix.

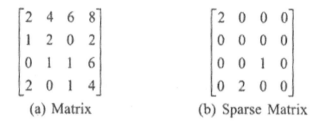

**Figure 3.10.** *Matrix and a sparse matrix*

A matrix consumes considerable memory space. Thus, a $1,000 \times 1,000$ matrix needs 1 million storage locations in memory. Imagine the situation when the matrix is sparse! To store a handful of non-zero elements, voluminous memory is allotted and thereby wasted!

In such a case, to save valuable storage space, we resort to a 3-tuple representation (*i, j, value*) to represent each non-zero element of the sparse matrix. Thus, a sparse matrix *A* is represented by another matrix *B[0:t, 1:3]* with *t* + 1 rows and three columns. Here, *t* refers to the number of non-zero elements in the sparse matrix. While rows 1 to *t* record the details pertaining to the non-zero elements as three tuples (i.e., three columns), the zeroth row, namely, *B[0,1], B[0,2]* and *B[0,3]*, records the number of rows, columns and non-zero elements of the original sparse matrix *A*, respectively. Figure 3.11 illustrates a sparse matrix representation.

$$A[1:7, 1:6]$$

$$\begin{bmatrix} 0 & 1 & 0 & 0 & 0 & 0 \\ 0 & 0 & 0 & 0 & 0 & 0 \\ -2 & 0 & 0 & 1 & 0 & 0 \\ 0 & 0 & 0 & 0 & 0 & 0 \\ 0 & 0 & 0 & 0 & 0 & 0 \\ 0 & -3 & 0 & 0 & 0 & 0 \\ 0 & 0 & 0 & 0 & 0 & 1 \end{bmatrix}$$

$$B[0:5, 1:3]$$

$$\begin{bmatrix} 7 & 6 & 5 \\ 1 & 2 & 1 \\ 3 & 1 & -2 \\ 3 & 4 & 1 \\ 6 & 2 & -3 \\ 7 & 6 & 1 \end{bmatrix}$$

**Figure 3.11.** *Sparse matrix representation*

A simple example of a sparse matrix can be found in the arrangement of choices of let us say five elective courses, from the specified list of 100 elective courses, by 20,000 students of a university. The arrangement of choices would turn out to be a matrix with 20,000 rows and 100 columns with just five non-zero entries per row, indicative of the individual student choices. Such a matrix could definitely be classified as sparse!

### 3.5.2. Ordered lists

One of the simplest and most useful data objects in computer science is an *ordered list* or *linear list*. An ordered list can be either empty or non-empty. In the latter case, the elements of the list are known as **atoms** and are chosen from a set $D$. The ordered lists provide a variety of operations, such as retrieval, insertion, deletion and update. The most common way to represent an ordered list is by using a one-dimensional array. Such a representation is termed **sequential mapping**, although better forms of representation have been presented in the literature.

### EXAMPLE 3.7.–

The following are ordered lists:

i) (sun, mon, tue, wed, thu, fri, sat);

ii) $(a_1, a_2, a_3, a_4, \ldots a_n)$;

iii) (Unix, CP/M, Windows, Linux).

The ordered lists shown above have been represented as one-dimensional arrays WEEK, VARIABLE and OS, as given below.

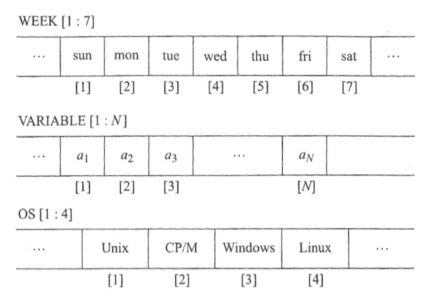

WEEK [1 : 7]

| ... | sun | mon | tue | wed | thu | fri | sat | ... |
|-----|-----|-----|-----|-----|-----|-----|-----|-----|
|     | [1] | [2] | [3] | [4] | [5] | [6] | [7] |     |

VARIABLE [1 : $N$]

| ... | $a_1$ | $a_2$ | $a_3$ | ... | $a_N$ |   |
|-----|-------|-------|-------|-----|-------|---|
|     | [1]   | [2]   | [3]   |     | [$N$] |   |

OS [1 : 4]

| ... | Unix | CP/M | Windows | Linux | ... |
|-----|------|------|---------|-------|-----|
|     | [1]  | [2]  | [3]     | [4]   |     |

Below, we illustrate some of the operations performed on ordered lists, with examples.

| Operation | Original ordered list | Resultant ordered list after the operation |
|-----------|----------------------|--------------------------------------------|
| Insertion (**Insert** $a_6$) | $(a_1, a_2, a_7, a_9)$ | $(a_1, a_2, a_6, a_7, a_9)$ |
| Deletion (**Delete** $a_9$) | $(a_1, a_2, a_7, a_9)$ | $(a_1, a_2, a_7)$ |
| Update (**Update** $a_2$ to $a_5$) | $(a_1, a_2, a_7, a_9)$ | $(a_1, a_5, a_7, a_9)$ |

### 3.5.3. Strings

A **string** is a data type used in many programming languages and represents text rather than numbers. String represents alphanumeric data and can therefore be made up of alphabet, numbers and spaces, in addition to other appropriate characters, typically enclosed within quotation marks.

EXAMPLE 3.8.–

The following are some examples of strings:

(i) "Newspaper",  (ii) "Coffee mug", (iii) "New Delhi 110092", (iv) "PARIS".

A string is defined as an array of characters. Thus, each character comprising the string resides in a cell belonging to the one-dimensional array. However, some implementations of strings in programming languages insist on terminating the array of characters belonging to a string with the special character "\0", also known as the *null character*. Figure 3.12 illustrates a one-dimensional array of characters *S[1:13]* that holds the string "INDIAN OCEAN".

| S | [1] | [2] | [3] | [4] | [5] | [6] | [7] | [8] | [9] | [10] | [11] | [12] | [13] |
|---|-----|-----|-----|-----|-----|-----|-----|-----|-----|------|------|------|------|
|   | I | N | D | I | A | N |   | O | C | E | A | N | \0 |

**Figure 3.12.** *String as an array of characters*

A collection of strings can be stored using a two-dimensional array. In other words, an array of strings can be represented using an array of characters. Needless to say, the maximum number of characters that comprise the string has to be the same for all the strings. Figure 3.13 illustrates a collection of strings stored in a two-dimensional array RIVER[1:4, 1:9].

String as a data type is built over the concept of *string* defined in *formal language theory*. Thus, a *formal string* is simply defined to be a sequence of characters or *alphabet,* and a *formal language* denotes any set of strings over some fixed alphabet. In formal languages, strings are also referred to as *words* or *sentences.* An *empty string* denoted by $\varepsilon$ contains zero characters. Strings are endowed to support a suite of operations such as (i) *Length,* (ii) *concatenation,* (iii) *prefix,* (iv) *suffix,* (v) *substring,* (vi) *equality* and (vii) *subsequence,* to list a few.

| RIVER | [1] | [2] | [3] | [4] | [5] | [6] | [7] | [8] | [9] |
|-------|-----|-----|-----|-----|-----|-----|-----|-----|-----|
| [1] | G | A | N | G | E | S | \0 |   |   |
| [2] | A | M | A | Z | O | N | \0 |   |   |
| [3] | S | E | I | N | E | \0 |   |   |   |
| [4] | N | I | L | E | \0 |   |   |   |   |

**Figure 3.13.** *Array of strings*

The length of a string $x$, denoted as $|x|$, computes the number of characters in the string. Concatenation of two strings $x$ and $y$, denoted $x + y$, yields a string in which $y$ is appended to $x$. Prefix and suffix are a consecutive set of characters that are a leading contiguous part of a string or a trailing contiguous part of string, respectively. A string obtained by deleting a prefix and a suffix from the original string is called a substring. While prefixes and suffixes of a given string are substrings of the original string, not every substring is a suffix or a prefix. Equality, denoted by "=", tests if two given strings are one and the same. A subsequence is any string formed by deleting zero or more characters without changing the order of the remaining elements in the original string.

## EXAMPLE 3.9.–

Given strings $x$ = "Deep", $y$ = "Learning" and an empty string $\varepsilon$, the following are some operations undertaken on the strings:

i) Lengths of $x$, $y$, $\varepsilon$ are $|x|$ = |"Deep"| = 4, $|y|$ = |"Learning"| = 8 and $|\varepsilon|$ = 0.

ii) The concatenation operation applied over $x$, $y$ and $\varepsilon$ as follows yields the resulting strings and results:

$x + y$ = "DeepLearning"   $y + x$ = "LearningDeep"   $x + \varepsilon$ = "Deep"

$\varepsilon + y$ = "Learning"   $|x + y|$ = 12   $|\varepsilon + y|$ = 8

iii) "Learn" is a prefix of string $y$, and "Deep" is a prefix of string $x + y$.

iv) "earning" is a suffix of string $y$, and "Learning" is a suffix of string $x + y$.

v) "earn" is a substring of string $y$.

vi) $x = y$ is false; $x = x + \varepsilon$ is true.

vii) "Lenin" is a subsequence of string $y$.

Most programming languages that have accommodated strings either as a data type or as a character array also provide a collection of library functions that implement a variety of useful string operations as mentioned above.

### 3.5.4. Bit array

A **bit array**, also known as **bit vector**, **bit map**, **bit string** or **bit set**, is a one-dimensional array that compactly stores **bits** (0 or 1). A bit array supports the following operations:

i) *NOT* or **Complement**: This is a unary operation that performs *logical negation* on each bit of the bit array, thereby transforming 1s to 0s and 0s to 1s.

ii) *AND*: This is a binary operation that takes two equal length bit arrays and performs *logical AND* operation on each pair of the bits of the two bit arrays. A logical AND of two input bits is 1 if both bits are 1 and 0 otherwise.

iii) *OR*: This is a binary operation that takes two equal length bit arrays and performs *logical OR* operation on each pair of bits of the two bit arrays. A logical OR of two input bits is 0 if both bits are 0 and 1 otherwise.

iv) *XOR*: This is a binary operation that takes two equal length bit arrays and performs *logical XOR* operations on each pair of bits of the two bit arrays. A logical *XOR* of two input bits is 1 if either of the two bits is 1 (not both) and 0 otherwise.

EXAMPLE 3.10.–

Given two bit arrays $A = [0\ 1\ 0\ 1]$ and $B = [1\ 1\ 0\ 0]$, the following are the results of the bit array operations.

*NOT A*: [1 0 1 0],        *A AND B*: [0 1 0 0],

*A OR B*: [1 1 0 1],        *A XOR B*: [1 0 0 1]

ADT for arrays

**Data objects:**
A set of elements of the same type stored in a sequence.

**Operations:**
- Store value VAL  in the *i*th element of the array ARRAY

        ARRAY[i] = VAL

- Retrieve the value in the *i*th element of array ARRAY as VAL

        VAL = ARRAY[i]

## Summary

– An array as an ADT supports only two operations: STORE and RETRIEVE.

– Arrays may be one-dimensional, two-dimensional or multidimensional and stored in memory in consecutive memory locations, either in the row major order or column major order.

– Since memory is considered one-dimensional and arrays may be multi dimensional, it is essential to know the representations of arrays in memory and their address calculations, especially from the compiler's point of view.

– Sparse matrices, ordered lists, strings and bit arrays are some significant applications of array data structure.

## 3.6. Illustrative problems

### PROBLEM 3.1.–

The following details are available about an array RESULT. Find the address of RESULT[17].

| | |
|---|---|
| Base address | : 520 |
| Index range | : 1:20 |
| Array type | : Real |
| Size of the memory location | : 4 bytes |

### Solution:

Since RESULT[1:20] is a one-dimensional array, the address for RESULT[17] is given by base address + (17 – lower index). However, the cell is made of 4 bytes; hence, the address is given by base address + (17 – lower index).4 = 520 + (17 – 1).4 = 584.

The array RESULT may be visualized as follows.

RESULT [1:20]

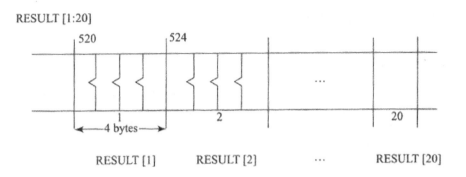

RESULT [1]          RESULT [2]          ...          RESULT [20]

## PROBLEM 3.2.–

For the following array B, compute:

i) the dimension of B;

ii) the space occupied by B in the memory;

iii) the address of B[7,2].

Array: B                          Column index:  0:5

Base address: 1003                Size of the memory location: 4 bytes

Row index: 0:15

## Solution:

i) The number of elements in B is $16 \times 6 = 96$.

ii) The space occupied by B is $96 \times 4 = 384$ bytes.

iii) The address of B[7,2] is given by

$$1003 + [(7 - 0) \cdot 6 + (2 - 0)] \cdot 4 = 1003 + 176 = 1179.$$

## PROBLEM 3.3.–

A programming language permits indexing of arrays with character subscripts; for example, CHR_ARRAY['A':'D']. In such a case, the elements of the array are CHR_ARRAY['A'], CHR_ARRAY['B'], and so on, and the ordinal number (ORD) of the characters, namely, ORD('A') = 1, ORD('B') = 2, ORD('Z') = 26 and so on, is used to denote the index.

Now, two arrays TEMP[1:5, -1:2] and CODE['A':'Z', 1:2] are stored in memory beginning from address 500. Additionally, CODE succeeds TEMP in storage. Calculate the addresses of (i) TEMP[5, -1], (ii) CODE['N',2] and (iii) CODE['Z',1].

## Solution:

From the details given, the representation of TEMP and CODE arrays in memory is as follows:

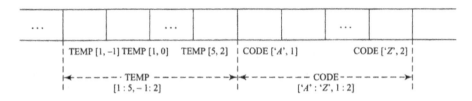

i) The address of TEMP[5, -1] is given by

base-address + $(5 - 1)(2 - (-1) + 1) + (-1 - (-1))$

$= 500 + 16$

$= 516.$

ii) To obtain the addresses of CODE elements, it is necessary to obtain the base address, which is the immediate location after TEMP[5,2], the last element of array TEMP.

Hence, the TEMP [5,2] is computed as

$500 + (5 - 1)(2 - (-1) + 1) + (2 - (-1))$

$= 500 + 16 + 3$

$= 519.$

Therefore, the base address of CODE is given by 520.

Now, the address of CODE ['N', 2] is given by

base address of CODE + $[(ORD('N') - ORD('A')).(2 - 1 + 1)] + (2 - 1)$

$= 520 + (14 - 1)\,2 + 1$

$= 547.$

iii) The address of CODE['Z',1] is computed as

base address of CODE $+ ((ORD('Z') - ORD('A')).(2 - 1 + 1)) + (1 - 1)$

$= 520 + (26 - 1)(2) + 0$

$= 570.$

NOTE.– The base address of CODE may also be computed as

base address of TEMP + (number of elements in TEMP – 1) + 1

$= 500 + (5.4 - 1) + 1$

$= 520.$

## PROBLEM 3.4.–

Given a $= 10$, b $= 5$, c $= 3$ and the array arr[1:5] $=$ [ 9 6 8 5 7], what does the following pseudo-code do to the array arr and the variables a, b, c?

```
for i = 1 to 5
  arr[i] = a
  a = b
  b = c
  c = arr[i]
end
```

## Solution:

Since each step of the loop modifies the values of the variables and the array, it is easy to track the variables and the array concerned with each step of the iteration by constructing the following table:

| Loop counter i | a | b | c | arr[1] | arr[2] | arr[3] | arr[4] | arr[5] |
|---|---|---|---|---|---|---|---|---|
| Initialization | 10 | 5 | 3 | 9 | 6 | 8 | 5 | 7 |
| 1 | 5 | 3 | 10 | 10 | 6 | 8 | 5 | 7 |
| 2 | 3 | 10 | 5 | 10 | 5 | 8 | 5 | 7 |
| 3 | 10 | 5 | 3 | 10 | 5 | 3 | 5 | 7 |
| 4 | 5 | 3 | 10 | 10 | 5 | 3 | 10 | 7 |
| 5 | 3 | 10 | 5 | 10 | 5 | 3 | 10 | 5 |

Thus, at the end of the loop, the modified array and variables are, a = 3, b = 10, c = 5 and the array `arr[1:5]` = [ 10 5 3 10 5].

## PROBLEM 3.5.–

What does the following pseudo-code do to the array `A[1: n, 1: n]`, which is already provided as input to the code?

```
B = 5
for i = 1 to n
  for j = 1 to n
    temp = A[i,j] - B
    A[i, j] = A[j, i]
    A[j, i] = temp + B
  end
end
```

## Solution:

The array A, going by the statements in the body of the innermost loop of the code, seems to swap its *i*th row *j*th column element with the *j*th row *i*th column element. However, since this swapping is attempted for each element of the array (note the two **for** loops that work over the rows and columns of A), each element undergoes two swaps, and therefore, array A remains the same when the loops terminate.

## PROBLEM 3.6.–

Given a bit array A = [ 0 0 1 1 0 1] on which the operations discussed in section 3.5.4 are workable:

i) Can you use OR to change any desired bit of A to 1?

ii) Can you use AND to change any desired bit of A to 0?

iii) Can you use XOR to invert or toggle any desired bit of A?

## Solution:

i) Let us suppose the fifth bit of A needs to be changed to 1. Choose a bit array B = [0 0 0 0 1 0] of the same length as A, with the fifth bit set to 1 and all else set to 0. A OR B yields

[0 0 1 1 0 1] OR [0 0 0 0 1 0] = [0 0 1 1 1 1], which is the desired result.

ii) Let us suppose the third bit of A needs to be changed to 0. Choose a bit array C = [1 1 0 1 1 1] of the same length as A, with its third bit set to 0 and all else set to 1. A AND B yields

[0 0 1 1 0 1] AND [1 1 0 1 1 1] = [0 0 0 1 0 1], which is the desired result.

iii) Let us suppose the fourth bit of A needs to be toggled. Choose a bit array

D = [0 0 0 1 0 0] of the same length as A and with the fourth bit set to 1 and all else set to 0. A XOR B yields

[ 0 0 1 1 0 1] XOR [0 0 0 1 0 0] = [0 0 1 0 0 1 ], which is the desired result.

## PROBLEM 3.7.–

Here is a pseudo-code that works over two strings, STRING1 and STRING2, represented as an array of characters with sufficient sizes. length is a function that computes the length of a string. What does the code do to the input strings?

```
1. LENGTH1 = length(STRING1);
2. LENGTH2 = length(STRING2);
3. for POSITION = 1 to LENGTH2
4.    LENGTH1 = LENGTH1+1;
5.    STRING1[LENGTH1]=STRING2[POSITION];
6. end
```

## Solution:

The pseudo-code performs a concatenation operation over STRING1 and STRING2. STRING1 holds the concatenated string, while STRING2 remains the same. LENGTH1 holds the length of the concatenated string and LENGTH2 the same for STRING2.

## Review questions

1) Which of the following pairs of operations is supported by an array ADT?

  i) Store and retrieve.

  ii) Insert and delete.

  iii) Copy and delete.

  iv) Append and copy.

  a) (i)          b) (ii)              c) (iii)              d) (iv)

2) The number of elements in an array $ARRAY[l_1 : u_1, l_2:u_2]$ is given by

  a) $(u_1 - l_1 - 1)(u_2 - l_2 - 1)$          b) $(u_1.u_2)$          c) $(u_1 - l_1)(u_2 - l_2)$

  d) $(u_1 - l_1 + 1)(u_2 - l_2 + 1)$

3) A multidimensional array OPEN[0:2, 10:20, 3:4, -10:2] contains _____ elements.

  a) 240                  b) 858                  c) 390                  d) 160

4) For array $A[1:u_1, 1:u_2]$, where $\alpha$ is the base address, $A[i,1]$ has its address given by

  a) $(i-1)u_2$      b) $\alpha + (i-1)u_2$      c) $\alpha + i.u_2$      d) $\alpha + (i-1).u_1$

5) For the array $A[1:u_1, 1:u_2, 1:u_3]$, where $\alpha$ is the base address, the address of $A[i,j,1]$ is given by

  a) $\alpha + (i-1)u_2 u_3 + (j-1)u_3$          b) $\alpha + i.u_2 u_3 + j.u_3$

  c) $\alpha + (i-1)u_1 u_2 + (j-1)u_2$          d) $\alpha + i.u_1 u_2 + j.u_2$

6) Distinguish between the row major and column major ordering of an array.

7) For an $n$-dimensional array $A[1:u_1, 1:u_2, \ldots 1:u_N]$, obtain the address of the element $A[i_1, i_2, i_3, \ldots i_N]$ given $\beta$ as the home address.

8) For the following sparse matrix, obtain an array representation.

$$\begin{bmatrix} 0 & 0 & 0 & -7 & 0 \\ 0 & -5 & 0 & 0 & 0 \\ 3 & 0 & 6 & 0 & -1 \\ 0 & 0 & 0 & 0 & 0 \\ 5 & 0 & 0 & 0 & 0 \\ 0 & 0 & 0 & 0 & 0 \\ 9 & 0 & 0 & 4 & 0 \end{bmatrix}$$

9) For a string STRNG whose length $|STRNG| = 11$ and is stored as an array of characters STRNG[1:12], where STRNG[12] = "\0", the null character can be ignored for this problem, match the following:

| | |
|---|---|
| STRNG[1:5] | Subsequence |
| | Substring |
| STRNG[9:11] | Prefix |
| STRNG[3:7] | Suffix |

10) What are the operations that when undertaken on a bit array can (i) toggle or invert a specific bit and (ii) toggle or invert all the bits in the bit array?

## Programming assignments

1) Declare a one-dimensional, two-dimensional and a three-dimensional array in a programming language (C, for example) that has the capability to display the addresses of array elements. Verify the various address calculation formulae that you have learnt in this chapter against the arrays that you have declared in the program.

2) For the matrix A given below, obtain a sparse matrix representation B. Write a program to

i) obtain B given matrix A as input;

ii) obtain the transpose of A using matrix B.

$A: 10 \times 12$

|    | 1 | 2 | 3 | 4 | 5 | 6 | 7 | 8 | 9 | 10 | 11 | 12 |
|----|---|---|---|---|---|---|---|---|---|----|----|----|
| 1  | 0 | 0 | 0 | 0 | 0 | 0 | 0 | 0 | 0 | 0 | 0 | 0 |
| 2  | 0 | -1 | 0 | 0 | 0 | 2 | 0 | 0 | 0 | 0 | 0 | 0 |
| 3  | 0 | 0 | 0 | 0 | 0 | 0 | 0 | 0 | 0 | 0 | 0 | 0 |
| 4  | 0 | 0 | 0 | 0 | 0 | 0 | 0 | 0 | 0 | 0 | 0 | 0 |
| 5  | 4 | 0 | 0 | -3 | 0 | 0 | 0 | 0 | 0 | 1 | 0 | 0 |
| 6  | 0 | 0 | 0 | 0 | 0 | 0 | 0 | 0 | 0 | 0 | 0 | 0 |
| 7  | 0 | 0 | 0 | 0 | 0 | 0 | 0 | 0 | 0 | 0 | 0 | 0 |
| 8  | -1 | 0 | 0 | 0 | 5 | 0 | 0 | 0 | 0 | 0 | 0 | 0 |
| 9  | 0 | 0 | 0 | 0 | 0 | 0 | 2 | 0 | 0 | 4 | 0 | 0 |
| 10 | 0 | 0 | 0 | 0 | 0 | 0 | 0 | 1 | 1 | 0 | 0 | 0 |

3) Open an ordered list $L = (d_1, d_2, \ldots d_n)$, where each $d_i$ is the name of a peripheral device, and the list is maintained in alphabetical order.

Write a program to

i) insert a device $d_k$ into the list $L$;

ii) delete an existing device $d_i$ from $L$. In this case, the new ordered list should be $L^{new} = (d_1, d_2, \ldots d_{i-1}, d_{i+1}, \ldots d_n)$ with $(n-1)$ elements;

iii) find the length of $L$;

iv) update device $d_j$ to $d_l$ and print the new list.

4) If an element in the array is greater than all the elements to its right, then such an element is designated as a *leader*. Given an array of elements, find all the leaders.

Example: For the array A = [ 1 8 6 7 3 1 5 2], 8, 7 and 5 are leaders.

5) Given an array, find the next greater element for each element in the array, if available. If not available, print the element itself. The next greater element y for an element x in the array is the first element that is greater than x and occurs on its right side. The next greater element of the right most element in an array is the element itself.

Example:  Given A = [ 6 8 4 3 9] the next greater element list

B = [8 9 9 9 9].

6) Given an array, arrange the elements in an array in such a way that the first maximum element is succeeded by the first minimum element, the second maximum element is succeeded by the second minimum element and so on.

Example: Given A = [ 8 5 1 3 9 7 6] the rearranged array

B = [ 9 1 8 3 7 5 6].

7) Implement the string operations of length, concatenation and equality illustrated in example 3.9 as functions, using a programming language that allows you to declare a string as a character array.

8) Given a string *s* that is input as a character array, (i) reverse the string and (ii) check if it is a *palindrome*. A palindrome is a string that reads the same forward and backward, for example, "MADAM".

9) Implement a library of bit array functions that will perform the operations of AND, OR, NOT and XOR on a given set of bit arrays.

# 4

# Stacks

In this chapter, we introduce the stack data structure, the operations supported by it and their implementations. Additionally, we illustrate two of its useful applications in computer science, namely, recursive programming and evaluation of expressions, among the innumerable available.

## 4.1. Introduction

A **stack** is an ordered list with the restriction that elements are added or deleted from only one end of the list termed the **top of stack**. The other end of the list that lies "inactive" is termed the **bottom of stack**.

Thus, if S is a stack with three elements $a, b, c$ where $c$ occupies the top of stack position, and if $d$ were to be added, the resultant stack contents would be $a, b, c, d$. Note that $d$ occupies the top of stack position. Again, initiating a delete or remove operation would automatically throw out the element occupying the top of the stack, namely, $d$. Figure 4.1 illustrates this functionality of the stack data structure.

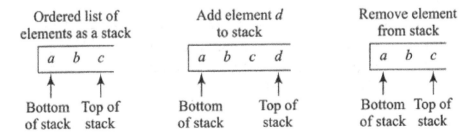

**Figure 4.1.** *Stack and its functionality*

It needs to be observed that during the insertion of elements into the stack, it is essential that their identities be specified, whereas for removal, no identity needs to be specified, since by virtue of its functionality, the element that occupies the top of the stack position is automatically removed.

The stack data structure therefore obeys the principle of **Last In First Out (LIFO)**. In other words, elements inserted or added into the stack join last, and those that joined last are the first to be removed.

Some common examples of a stack occur during the serving of slices of bread arranged as a pile on a platter or during the usage of an elevator (see Figure 4.2). It is obvious that when a slice is added to a pile or removed when serving, it is the top of the pile that is affected. Similarly, in the case of an elevator, the last person to board the cabin must be the first person to alight from it (at least to make room for the others to alight!).

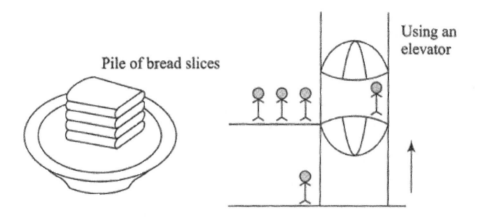

**Figure 4.2.** *Common examples of a stack*

## 4.2. Stack operations

The two operations that support the stack data structure are

i) insertion or addition of elements known as *Push*;

ii) deletion or removal of elements known as *Pop*.

Before we discuss the operations supported by the stack in detail, it is essential to know how stacks are implemented.

### 4.2.1. *Stack implementation*

A common and basic method of implementing stacks is to make use of another fundamental data structure, namely, arrays. While arrays are *sequential data structures,* the other alternative of employing *linked data structures* has been successfully attempted and applied. We discuss this elaborately in Chapter 7. In this chapter, we confine our discussion to the implementation of stacks using arrays.

Figure 4.3 illustrates an array-based implementation of stacks. This is fairly convenient considering the fact that stacks are one-dimensional ordered lists and so are arrays, which, despite their multidimensional structure, are inherently associated with a one-dimensional consecutive set of memory locations (Chapter 3).

Figure 4.3 shows a stack of four elements $R$, $S$, $V$, and $G$ represented by an array STACK[1:7]. In general, if a stack is represented as an array STACK[1:$n$], then $n$ elements and not one more can be stored in the stack. It therefore becomes essential to issue a signal or warning termed **STACK_FULL** when elements whose number is over and above $n$ are pushed into the stack.

Again, during a pop operation, it is essential to ensure that one does not delete an empty stack! Hence, the necessity for a signal or a warning termed **STACK_EMPTY** during the implementation of the pop operation. While implementation of stacks using arrays necessitates checking for STACK_FULL/ STACK_EMPTY conditions during push/pop operations, the implementation of stacks with linked data structures dispenses with these testing conditions.

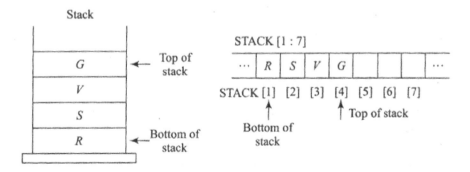

**Figure 4.3.** *Array implementation of stacks*

### 4.2.2. *Implementation of push and pop operations*

Let STACK[1:n] be an array implementation of a stack and top be a variable recording the current top of the stack position. top is initialized to 0. item is the element to be pushed into the stack. n is the maximum capacity of the stack.

Algorithm 4.1 illustrates the push operation in pseudo-code.

```
procedure  PUSH(STACK, n, top, item)
    if (top = n) then STACK_FULL;
    else
    { top = top + 1;
      STACK[top] = item; /* store item as top
                             element of  STACK */
    }
end  PUSH
```

**Algorithm 4.1.** *Implementation of push operation on a stack*

In the case of the pop operation, as previously mentioned, no element identity needs to be specified since, by default, the element occupying the top of the stack position is deleted. Algorithm 4.2 illustrates the pop operation in pseudo-code. Note that in Algorithm 4.2, item is used as an output variable only to store a copy of the element removed.

```
procedure  POP(STACK, top, item)
    if (top = 0) then STACK_EMPTY;

    else
        { item = STACK[top];

          top = top - 1;

        }
    end  POP
```

**Algorithm 4.2.** *Implementation of pop operation on a stack*

It is evident from the algorithms that to perform a single push/pop operation, the time complexity is $O(1)$.

## EXAMPLE 4.1.–

Consider a stack DEVICE[1:3] of peripheral devices. The insertion of the four items PEN, PLOTTER, JOY STICK and PRINTER into DEVICE and a deletion are illustrated in Table 4.1.

| Stack operation | Stack before operation | Algorithm invocation | Stack after operation | Remarks |
|---|---|---|---|---|
| 1. Push 'PEN' into DEVICE[1:3] | DEVICE[1:3] <br> [1][2][3] | PUSH(DEVICE, 3,0,'PEN') | DEVICE[1:3] <br> PEN <br> [1] [2] [3] <br> ↑ Top | Push 'PEN' successful. |
| 2. Push 'PLOTTER' into DEVICE[1:3] | DEVICE[1:3] <br> 'PEN' <br> ↑ Top | PUSH(DEVICE,3, 1, 'PLOTTER') | DEVICE[1:3] <br> PEN PLOTTER <br> [1] [2] [3] <br> ↑ Top | Push 'PLOTTER' successful. |
| 3. Push 'JOY STICK' into DEVICE[1:3] | DEVICE[1:3] <br> PEN PLOTTER <br> [1] [2] [3] <br> ↑ Top | PUSH(DEVICE, 3, 2, 'JOY STICK') | DEVICE[1:3] <br> PEN PLOTTER JOY STICK <br> [1] [2] [3] <br> ↑ Top | Push 'JOY STICK' successful. |
| 4. Push 'PRINTER' into DEVICE[1:3] | DEVICE[1:3] <br> PEN PLOTTER JOY STICK <br> [1] [2] [3] <br> ↑ Top | PUSH(DEVICE, 3, 3, 'PRINTER') | DEVICE[1:3] <br> PEN PLOTTER JOY STICK <br> [1] [2] [3] <br> ↑ Top | Push 'PRINTER' failure! STACK-FULL condition invoked. |
| 5. Pop from DEVICE[1:3] | DEVICE[1:3] <br> PEN PLOTTER JOY STICK <br> [1] [2] [3] <br> ↑ Top | POP(DEVICE, 3, ITEM) | DEVICE[1:3] <br> PEN PLOTTER JOY STICK <br> [1] [2] <br> ↑ Top | ITEM = 'JOY STICK' Pop operation successful. |

Table 4.1. *Push/pop operations on stack DEVICE[1:3]*

Note that in operation 5, which is a pop operation, the top pointer is merely decremented as a mark of deletion. No physical erasure of data is carried out.

## 4.3. Applications

Stacks have found innumerable applications in computer science and other allied areas. In this section, we introduce two applications of stacks that are useful in computer science, namely,

i) recursive programming;

ii) evaluation of expressions.

### 4.3.1. *Recursive programming*

The concepts of recursion and recursive programming are introduced in Chapter 2. In this section, we demonstrate through a sample recursive program how stacks are helpful in handling recursion.

Consider the recursive pseudo-code for factorial computation shown in Figure 4.4. Observe the recursive call in Step 3. It is essential that during the computation of $n!$, the procedure does not lead to an endless series of calls to itself! Hence, the need for a base case, $0! = 1$, which is written in Step 1.

The spate of calls made by procedure FACTORIAL() to itself based on the value of $n$ can be viewed as FACTORIAL() replicating itself as many times as it calls itself with varying values of $n$. Additionally, all of these procedures await normal termination before the final output of $n!$ is completed and displayed by the very first call made to FACTORIAL(). A procedural call would have a normal termination only when either the base case is executed (Step 1) or the recursive case has successfully ended, that is, Steps 2–5 have completed their execution.

During the execution, to keep track of the calls made to itself and to record the status of the parameters at the time of the call, a stack data structure is used. Figure 4.5 illustrates the various snap shots of the stack during the execution of FACTORIAL(5). Observe how the values of the three parameters of the procedure FACTORIAL(), namely, n, x and y, are kept track of in the stack data structure.

```
procedure   FACTORIAL(n)
Step 1:     if (n = 0) then FACTORIAL = 1;
Step 2:     else {x = n - 1;
Step 3:            y = FACTORIAL(x);
Step 4:              FACTORIAL = n * y;}
Step 5:     end FACTORIAL
```

**Figure 4.4**. *Recursive procedure to compute n!*

When the procedure FACTORIAL(5) is initiated (see Figure 4.5(a)) and executed (see Figure 4.5(b)), x obtains the value 4, and the control flow moves to Step 3 in the procedure FACTORIAL(5). This initiates the next call to the procedure as FACTORIAL(4). Observe that the first call (FACTORIAL(5)) has not yet finished its execution when the next call (FACTORIAL(4)) to the procedure has been issued. Therefore, there is a need to preserve the values of the variables used, namely, n, x and y, in the preceding calls. Hence, there is a need for a stack data structure.

Every new procedure call pushes the current values of the parameters involved into the stack, thereby preserving the values used by the earlier calls. Figures 4.5(c) and (d) illustrate the contents of the stack during the execution of FACTORIAL(4) and subsequent procedure calls. During the execution of FACTORIAL(0) (see Figure 4.5(e)), Step 1 of the procedure is satisfied, and this terminates the procedure call yielding the value FACTORIAL = 1. Since the call for FACTORIAL(0) was initiated in Step 3 of the previous call (FACTORIAL(1)), y acquires the value of FACTORIAL(0), that is, 1, and the execution control moves to Step 4 to compute FACTORIAL = n * y (i.e.) FACTORIAL = 1 * 1 = 1. With this computation, FACTORIAL(1) terminates its execution. As previously mentioned, FACTORIAL(1) returns the computed value of 1 to Step 3 of the previous call FACTORIAL(2)). Once again, it yields the result FACTORIAL = n * y = 2 * 1 = 2, which terminates the procedure call to FACTORIAL(2) and returns the result to Step 3 of the previous call FACTORIAL(3) and so on.

Observe that the stack data structure grows due to a series of push operations during the procedure calls and unwinds itself by a series of pop operations until it reaches the step associated with the first procedure call to complete its execution and display the result.

During the execution of FACTORIAL(5), the first and oldest call to be made, y in Step 3 computes y = FACTORIAL(4) = 24 and proceeds to obtain FACTORIAL = n * y = 5 * 24 = 120, which is the desired result.

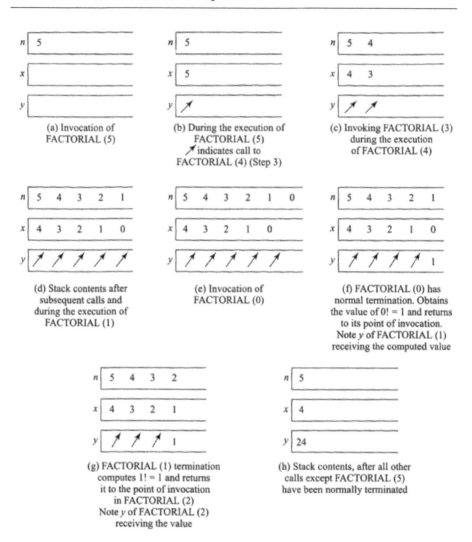

**Figure 4.5.** *Snapshots of the stack data structure during the execution of the procedural call* `FACTORIAL (5)`

### 4.3.1.1. *Tail recursion*

**Tail recursion** or **tail end recursion** is a special case of recursion where a recursive call to the function turns out to be the last action in the calling function. Note that the recursive call needs to be the **last executed statement** in the function and not necessarily the last statement in the function.

Generally, in a stack implementation of a recursive call, all of the local variables of the function that are to be "remembered" are pushed into the stack when the call is made. Upon termination of the recursive call, the local variables are popped out and restored to their previous values. Now for tail recursion, since the recursive call turns out to be the last executed statement, there is no need for the local variables to be pushed into a stack for them to be "remembered" and "restored" on termination of the recursive call. This is because when the recursive call ends, the calling function itself terminates, at which all local variables are automatically discarded.

Tail recursion is considered important in many high-level languages, especially functional programming languages. These languages rely on tail recursion to implement iteration. It is known that compared to iterations, recursions need more stack space, and tail recursions are ideal candidates for transformation into iterations.

### 4.3.2. Evaluation of expressions

#### 4.3.2.1. Infix, prefix and postfix expressions

The evaluation of expressions is an important feature of compiler design. When we write or understand an arithmetic expression, for example, $-(A + B) \uparrow C * D + E$, we do so by following the scheme of $\langle operand \rangle \langle operator \rangle \langle operand \rangle$ (i.e. an $\langle operator \rangle$ is preceded and succeeded by an $\langle operand \rangle$). Such an expression is termed **infix expression**. It is already known how infix expressions used in programming languages have been accorded rules of **hierarchy**, **precedence** and **associativity** to ensure that the computer does not misinterpret the expression but computes its value in a unique way.

In reality, the compiler reworks on the infix expression to produce an equivalent expression that follows the scheme of $\langle operand \rangle \langle operand \rangle \langle operator \rangle$ and is known as the **postfix expression**. For example, the infix expression $a + b$ would have the equivalent postfix expression $a\ b+$.

A third category of expression follows the scheme of $\langle operator \rangle \langle operand \rangle$ $\langle operand \rangle$ and is known as **prefix expression.** For example, the equivalent prefix expression corresponding to $a + b$ is $+a\ b$.

Examples 4.2 and 4.3 illustrate the hand computation of prefix and postfix expressions from a given infix expression.

## EXAMPLE 4.2.–

Consider an infix expression $a + b * c - d$. The equivalent postfix expression can be hand computed by decomposing the original expression into subexpressions based on the usual rules of hierarchy, precedence and associativity.

| Expression | Subexpression chosen based on rules of hierarchy, precedence and associativity | Postfix expression |
|---|---|---|
| (i) $a + b * c - d$ ①  | $b * c$ | ① : $bc *$ |
| (ii) $a + ① - d$ ② | $a + ①$ | $a ① +$ (i.e) ② : $abc * +$ |
| (iii) $② - d$ ③ | $② - d$ | $② d -$ (i.e) ③ : $abc * + d -$ |

Hence, $abc * + d -$ is the equivalent postfix expression of $a + b * c - d$.

## EXAMPLE 4.3.–

Consider the infix expression $(a * b - f * h) \uparrow d$. The equivalent prefix expression is hand computed as follows:

| Expression | Subexpression chosen based on rules of hierarchy, precedence and associativity | Equivalent prefix expression |
|---|---|---|
| (i) $(a * b - f * h) \uparrow d$ ① | $a * b$ | ① $* ab$ |
| (ii) $(① - f * h) \uparrow d$ ② | $f * h$ | ② : $* fh$ |

| (iii) | $(① - ②) \uparrow d$ <br> ③ | $(① - ②)$ | $③ : - ① ②$ <br> (i.e) <br> $- *ab * fh$ |
|---|---|---|---|
| (iv) | $③ \uparrow d$ <br> ④ | $③ \uparrow d$ | $④ : \uparrow ③ d$ <br> (i.e) <br> $\uparrow - *ab * fhd$ |

Hence, the equivalent prefix expression of $(a * b - f * h) \uparrow d$ is $\uparrow - * ab * fhd$.

### 4.3.2.2. *Evaluation of postfix expressions*

As discussed earlier, the compiler finds it convenient to evaluate an expression in its postfix form. The virtues of postfix form include elimination of parentheses, which signify priority of evaluation, and the elimination of the need to observe rules of hierarchy, precedence and associativity during evaluation of the expression. This implies that the evaluation of a postfix expression is done by merely undertaking a left-to-right scan of the expression, pushing operands into a stack and evaluating the operator with the appropriate number of operands popped out from the stack, and finally placing the output of the evaluated expression into the stack.

Algorithm 4.3 illustrates the evaluation of a postfix expression. Here, the postfix expression is terminated with $ to signal the end of the input.

**Procedure**   EVAL_POSTFIX(E)

```
    X = get_next_character(E);        /* get the next
                              character of expression E */
    case x of
    :x is an operand:  Push x into stack S;

    :x is an operator: Pop out required number of
                       operands from the stack S,
                       evaluate the operator and
                       push the result into the
                       stack S;

    :x = "$":          Pop out the result from
                       stack S;
    end case
end EVAL-POSTFIX.
```

**Algorithm 4.3.** *Procedure to evaluate a postfix expression E*

The evaluation of a postfix expression using Algorithm EVAL_POSTFIX is illustrated in example 4.4.

### EXAMPLE 4.4.–

To evaluate the postfix expression of $A + B * C \uparrow D$ for A = 2, B = −1, C = 2 and D = 3, using Algorithm EVAL_POSTFIX the equivalent postfix expression can be computed to be $ABCD \uparrow * +$.

The evaluation of the postfix expression using the algorithm is illustrated below. The values of the operands pushed into stack S are given within parentheses, e.g., A(2), B(-1), etc.

| X | Stack S | Action |
|---|---|---|
| A | A(2) | Push A into S |
| B | A(2) B(-1) | Push B into S |
| C | A(2) B(-1) C(2) | Push C into S |
| D | A(2) B(-1) C(2) D(3) | Push D into S |
| ↑ | A(2) B(-1) 8 | Pop out two operands from stack S, namely C(2) and D(3). Compute C↑D and push the result $C \uparrow D = 2 \uparrow 3 = 8$ into stack S. |
| * | A(2) - 8 | Pop out B(-1) and 8 from stack S. Compute $B * 8 = -1 * 8 = -8$ and push the result into stack S. |
| + | -6 | Pop out A(2), −8 from stack S. Compute $A - 8 = 2 - 8 = -6$ and push the result into stack S |
| ∮ |  | Pop out −6 from stack S and output the same as the result. |

**ADT for stacks**

**Data objects:**
A finite set of elements of the same type.

**Operations:**
Create an empty stack and initialize top of stack
        CREATE(STACK)
Check if stack is empty
        CHK_STACK_EMPTY(STACK) (Boolean function)
Check if stack is full
        CHK_STACK_FULL(STACK) (Boolean function)
Push ITEM into stack STACK
        PUSH(STACK, ITEM)
Pop element from stack STACK and output the element
popped in ITEM
        POP(STACK, ITEM)

## Summary

– A stack data structure is an ordered list with insertions and deletions done at one end of the list known as top of stack.

– An insert operation is called a push operation and a delete operation is called a pop operation.

– A stack can be commonly implemented using the array data structure. However, in such a case it is essential to take note of stack full/stack empty conditions during the implementation of push and pop operations, respectively.

– Handling recursive programming and evaluation of postfix expressions are applications of stack data structure.

## 4.4. Illustrative problems

### PROBLEM 4.1.–

The following is a pseudo-code of a series of operations on a stack S. PUSH(S, X) pushes an element X into S, POP(S,X) pops out an element from stack S as X, PRINT(X) displays the variable X and EMPTYSTACK(S) is a Boolean function that returns true if S is empty and false otherwise. What is the output of the code?

```
1.    X:=30;
2.    Y:=15;
3.    Z:=20;
4.    PUSH(S, X);
5.    PUSH(S, 40);
6.    POP(S, Z);
7.    PUSH(S, Y);
8.    PUSH(S, 30);
9.    PUSH(S, Z);
10.   POP(S, X);
11.   PUSH(S, 20);
12.   PUSH(S, X);
13.   while not EMPTYSTACK(S) do
14.       POP(S, X);
15.       PRINT(X);
16.   end
```

**Solution:**

We track the contents of the stack S and the values of the variables X, Y, Z as follows:

| Steps | Stack S | Variables X Y Z | | |
|:---:|:---|:---:|:---:|:---:|
| 1 – 3 | | 30 | 15 | 20 |
| 4 | 30 | 30 | 15 | 20 |
| 5 | 30  40 | 30 | 15 | 20 |
| 6 | 30 | 30 | 15 | 40 |
| 7 | 30  15 | 30 | 15 | 40 |
| 8 | 30  15  30 | 30 | 15 | 40 |

| 9 | `30 15 30 40` | 30   15   40 |
| 10 | `30 15 30` | 40   15   40 |
| 11 | `30 15 30 20` | 40   15   40 |
| 12 | `30 15 30 20 40` | 40   15   40 |

The execution of Steps 13–16 repeatedly pops out the elements from S displaying each element. The output would therefore be

$$40 \qquad 20 \qquad 30 \qquad 15 \qquad 30$$

with the stack S empty.

## PROBLEM 4.2.–

Use procedures PUSH(S,X), POP(S,X), PRINT(X) and EMPTY_STACK(S) (as described in illustrative problem 4.1) and TOP_OF_STACK(S), which returns the top element of stack S, to write pseudo codes to

i) assign X to the bottom element of stack S, leaving the stack empty;

ii) assign X to the bottom element of the stack, leaving the stack unchanged;

iii) assign X to the $n$th element in the stack (from the top), leaving the stack unchanged.

## Solution:

(i)      **while not** EMPTYSTACK(S) **do**

     POP(S,X)
  **end**
  PRINT(X);

X holds the element at the bottom of stack.

(ii) Since the stack S has to be left unchanged, we make use of another stack T to temporarily hold the contents of S.

```
while not EMPTYSTACK(S) do
    POP(S,X)
    PUSH(T,X)
end          /* empty contents of S into T */

PRINT(X);        /* output X */


while not EMPTYSTACK(T) do
    POP(T, Y)
    PUSH(S, Y)
end    /* empty contents of T back into S */
```

(iii) We make use of a stack T to remember the top *n* elements of stack S before replacing them back into S.

```
for i:=1 to n do
 POP(S,X)
 PUSH(T,X)
end        /* Push top n elements of S into T */
PRINT(X);    /* display X */
for i = 1 to n do
 POP(T, Y);
 PUSH(S,Y);
end      /* Replace back the top n elements
            available in T into  S */
```

## PROBLEM 4.3.–

What is the output produced by the following segment of code, where for a stack S, PUSH(S,X), POP(S, X), PRINT(X), EMPTY_STACK(S) are procedures as described in illustrative problem 4.1 and CLEAR(S) is a procedure that empties the contents of the stack S?

```
1.     TERM = 3;
2.     CLEAR(STACK);
3.     repeat
4.       if TERM <=12 then {PUSH(STACK, TERM);
5.                          TERM = 2 * TERM;}
6.       else
7.         {POP(STACK, TERM);
8.          PRINT(TERM);
9.          TERM = 3 * TERM + 2;}
10.    until EMPTY_STACK(STACK) and TERM > 15.
```

## Solution:

Let us keep track of the stack contents and the variable TERM as follows:

| Steps | Stack STACK | TERM | Output displayed |
|---|---|---|---|
| 1-2 | | 3 | |
| 3, 4, 5, 10 | 3 | 6 | |
| 3, 4, 5, 10 | 3   6 | 12 | |
| 3, 4, 5, 10 | 3   6   12 | 24 | |
| 3, 6, 7 | 3   6 | 12 | |
| 8 | 3   6 | 12 | 12 |
| 9, 10 | 3   6 | 38 | |
| 3, 6, 7 | 3 | 6 | |
| 8 | 3 | 6 | 6 |
| 9, 10 | 3 | 20 | |
| 3, 6, 7 | | 3 | |

| 8 | [_____] | 3 | 3 |
|---|---|---|---|
| 9, 10 | [_____] | 11 | |
| 3, 4, 5, 10 | [11_____] | 22 | |
| 3, 6, 7 | [_____] | 11 | |
| 8 | [_____] | 11 | 11 |
| 9, 10 | [_____] | 35 | |

The output is 12, 6, 3 and 11.

## PROBLEM 4.4.–

For the following pseudo-code of a recursive program *mod* that computes *a mod b* given *a, b* as inputs, trace the stack contents during the execution of the call *mod* (23, 7).

```
procedure mod (a, b)
  if (a < b) then mod := a
  else
          { x₁ := a − b
            y₁ := mod(x₁, b)
          mod := y₁
          }
  end mod
```

$$x_1 := a - b$$
$$y_1 := \mod(x_1, b)$$
$$\mod := y_1$$

## Solution:

We open a stack structure to track the variables a, b, $x_1$ and $y_1$ as shown below. The snap shots of the stack during recursion are shown.

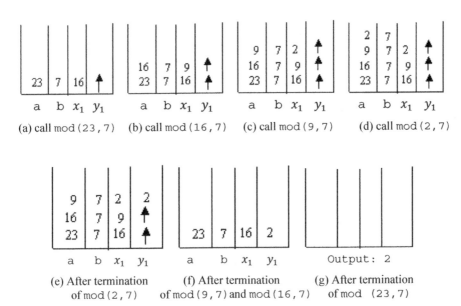

(a) call mod (23, 7)    (b) call mod (16, 7)    (c) call mod (9, 7)    (d) call mod (2, 7)

(e) After termination         (f) After termination         (g) After termination
    of mod (2, 7)         of mod (9, 7) and mod (16, 7)    of mod (23, 7)

## PROBLEM 4.5.–

For the infix expression given below, obtain (i) the equivalent postfix expression, (ii) the equivalent prefix expression and (iii) evaluate the equivalent postfix expression obtained in (i) using the Algorithm EVAL_POSTFIX() (Algorithm 4.3), with $A = 1, B = 10, C = 1, D = 2, G = -1$ and $H = 6$.

$$(-(A + B + C) \uparrow D) * (G + H)$$

## Solution:

(i) and (ii): We demonstrate the steps to compute the prefix expression and postfix expression in parallel in the following table:

| Expression | Subexpression chosen based on rules of hierarchy, precedence and associativity | Equivalent postfix expression | Equivalent prefix expression |
|---|---|---|---|
| $(-(A+B+C)\uparrow D)*(G+H)$ ①  | $(A + B + C)$ Note: $(A + B + C)$ is equivalent to the two sub expressions $(A + B + C')$ ①' $((①+C))$ ①" | ①: $AB+C+$ | ①: $++ABC$ |
| $(-①\uparrow D)*(G+H)$ ② | $-①$ | ②: $AB+C+-$ | ②: $-++ABC$ |
| $(②\uparrow D)*(G+H)$ | $(②\uparrow D)$ | ③: $AB+C+-D\uparrow$ | ③: $\uparrow-++ABCD$ |
| $③*(G+H)$ ④ | $(G + H)$ | ④ $GH +$ | ④:$+GH$ |
| $③ * ④$ ⑤ | $③ * ④$ | ⑤: $AB+C+-D\uparrow GH+*$ | ⑤: $*\uparrow-++ABCD+GH$ |

The equivalent postfix and prefix expressions are $AB + C + -D \uparrow GH +*$ and $*\uparrow - + +ABCD + GH$, respectively.

(iii) To evaluate $AB + C + -D \uparrow GH +* \$$ for $A = 1$, $B = 10$, $C = 1$, $D = 2$, $G = -1$ and $H = 6$, using Algorithm EVAL_POSTFIX(), the steps are listed in the following table:

| x | Stack S | Action |
|---|---------|--------|
| A | A(1) | Push A into S |
| B | A(1)  B(10) | Push B into S |
| + | 11 | Evaluate A+B and push result into S |
| C | 11  C(1) | Push C into S |
| + | 12 | Evaluate 11+C and push result into S |
| − ## | − 12 | Evaluate (unary minus) −12 and push result into S |
| D | − 12  D(2) | Push D into S |
| ↑ | 144 | Evaluate (−12) ↑ D and push result into S |
| G | 144  G(-1) | Push G into S |
| H | 144  G(-1)  H(6) | Push H into S |
| + | 144    5 | Evaluate G+H and push result into S |
| * | 720 | Evaluate 144 ∗ 5 and push result into S |
| $ | | Output 720 |

---

## A compiler basically distinguishes between a unary "−" and a binary "−" by generating different tokens. Hence, there is no ambiguity regarding the number of operands to be popped out from the stack when the operator is "−". In the case of a unary "−", a single operand is popped out, and in the case of binary "−", two operands are popped out from the stack.

## PROBLEM 4.6.–

Two stacks S1 and S2 are to be stored in a single array *A[1:n]*, with PushS1(x) and PushS2(x) handling their respective push operations with regard to element x and PopS1(x) and PopS2(x) handling their respective pop operations, with the output variable x indicating the element popped out from the stack. Let TopS1 and TopS2 be their respective top-of-stack variables. The stacks share their storage space in such a way that their respective *bottom of stacks are positioned in the middle of the array,* as shown in Figure P4.1, and the stacks grow in the opposite directions.

Array A:

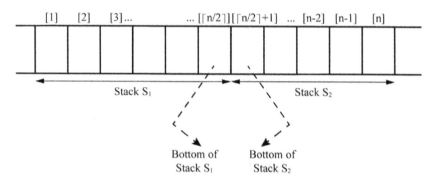

**Figure P4.1.** *Two stacks are stored in a single array A with the bottom of stacks positioned in the middle of the array*

i) For *n* = 5, if S1 = *{a, b}* and S2 = *{m, n}*, how would array A look after all of the elements of stacks S1 and S2 were pushed into it invoking PushS1(x) and PushS2(x)?

ii) How would array A look if the following operations were carried out in a sequence? What values do the variables w and y represent at the end of the operations?

> PopS1(w)
>
> PopS2(y)
>
> PushS1(y)
>
> PushS2(w)
>
> PopS2(y)
>
> PopS2(w)

iii) For $n = 5$, if S1 = *{a, b, c, d}* and S2 = *{m}*, what are your observations regarding the representation of stacks in the array?

iv) What are the stack full conditions for the two stacks?

v) Is such a method of storing two stacks in a single array efficient?

## Solution:

i) Array A would look as shown in Figure P4.2(a) after elements of S1 and S2 were pushed into the respective stacks stored in array A.

ii) Figure P4.2(b) illustrates array A after the operations have been performed. The values of the variables are w = "m" and y = "b".

iii) From Figure P4.2(c), it can be seen that stack S1 reports stack overflow, and therefore element "d" could not find a place in stack S1, although array A had one memory location free.

iv) The stack full condition for stack S1 is (TopS1 = 1), and the condition for stack S2 is (TopS2 = n).

v) No. As illustrated in illustrative problem 4.6(ii), there is the possibility of one stack signaling overflow when there are free memory locations available in array A that could have accommodated the elements concerned. Hence, this method is not storage efficient.

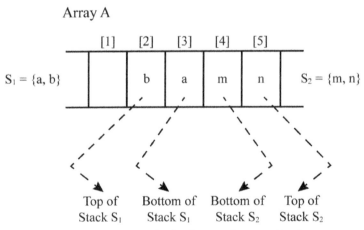

Array A

$S_1 = \{a, b\}$          b    a    m    n          $S_2 = \{m, n\}$

Top of        Bottom of     Bottom of     Top of
Stack $S_1$     Stack $S_1$    Stack $S_2$    Stack $S_2$

(a) Array A after the operations mentioned
in illustrative problem 4.6(i) are executed.

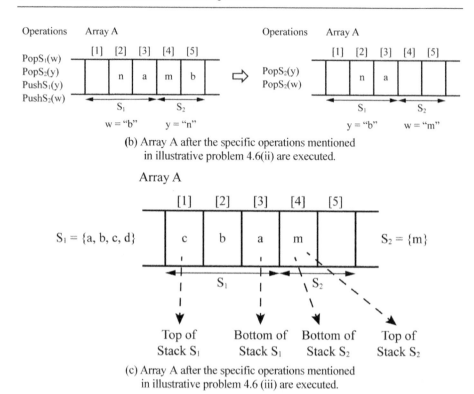

(b) Array A after the specific operations mentioned
in illustrative problem 4.6(ii) are executed.

(c) Array A after the specific operations mentioned
in illustrative problem 4.6 (iii) are executed.

**Figure P4.2.** *Snapshots of array A in illustrative problem 4.6*

## PROBLEM 4.7.–

If the stacks S1 and S2 discussed in illustrative problem 4.6, with their respective push and pop procedures, were stored with their respective *bottom of stacks positioned on the left and right extreme of the array, respectively,* and with the stacks growing toward the middle of the array, as shown in Figure P4.3, redo questions (i)–(v) of illustrative problem 4.6 over the new configuration of stacks in array $A(1:n)$.

## Solution:

i) See Figure P4.4(a).

ii) See Figure P4.4(b). The values of the variables are $w = b$ and $y = m$.

iii) See Figure P4.4(c). Unlike the configuration shown in Figure P4.2(c), no stack over flow is reported by S1 since element "*d*" finds a place in the stack making use of the memory space available.

iv) The stack overflow conditions are (TopS1+1) = TopS2 for stacks S1 and S2.

v) Yes. It is a space-efficient method when compared to the one discussed in illustrative problem 4.6, since it is possible to avoid stack full conditions of the kind illustrated in illustrative problem 4.6(iii) and elements can be pushed into the stacks as long as the memory locations are free in array A.

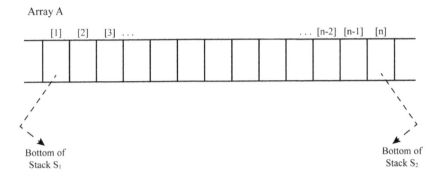

**Figure P4.3.** *Two stacks stored in a single array A with their bottom of stacks positioned at the extreme ends of the array*

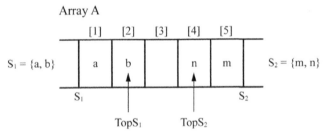

(a) Array A after the operations mentioned
in illustrative problem 4.7(i) are executed.

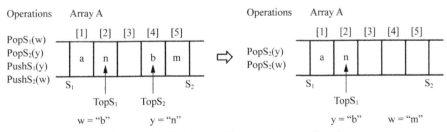

(b) Array A after the specific operations mentioned
in illustrative problem 4.7(ii) are executed.

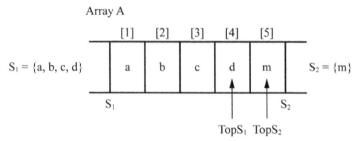

(c) Array A after the specific operations mentioned
in illustrative problem 4.7(iii) are executed.

**Figure P4.4.** *Snapshots of array A in illustrative problem 4.7*

## PROBLEM 4.8.–

You are allowed to operate on a stack WORK and a temporary stack TEMP (if needed) supporting their ADT operations of PUSH (S,X), POP (S, X) and EMPTYSTACK (S) only, where X represents an element/variable to be pushed in or popped out of the stack and S represents a stack. You are also permitted to use one variable if needed to carry out the operations.

i) Given $n$ distinct random numbers that are to be pushed into WORK, how can you find the minimum element that was pushed into it? You are permitted to use a lone variable.

ii) Given $n$ distinct random numbers that are to be pushed into WORK, how can you find the maximum element that was pushed into it, all the while ensuring that the elements stored in WORK are in their descending order with the maximum element beginning at the bottom of stack? You are permitted to use a lone variable and a temporary stack TEMP.

iii) Given an array $A[1: n]$ of distinct random numbers how can you obtain the sorted list in the array, making use of stacks alone?

## Solution:

i) Let $x_1, x_2, \ldots x_n$ be the $n$ distinct random numbers to be pushed into WORK, and let MIN be the variable that will record the minimum number. Set MIN = $x_1$ and execute PUSH (WORK, $x_1$). Next, consider $x_2$; if $x_2$ is greater than MIN, simply execute PUSH (WORK, $x_2$). On the other hand, if $x_2$ is less than MIN, set MIN = $x_2$ and PUSH (WORK $x_2$).

In general, if the current element $x_i$ to be pushed into WORK is less than MIN, set MIN = $x_i$ and PUSH (WORK, $x_i$); otherwise, simply execute PUSH (WORK, $x_i$). After all the elements have been pushed into WORK, MIN records the minimum element in the input list.

ii) Let $x_1$, $x_2$, ...$x_n$ be the $n$ distinct random numbers to be pushed into WORK, and let MAX be the variable that will record the maximum element. Set MAX = $x_1$ and execute PUSH (WORK, $x_1$). Now consider $x_2$; if $x_2$ is less than MAX, PUSH (WORK, $x_2$) and move on to the next element in the input list. If $x_2$ is larger than MAX, then set MAX = $x_2$, POP (WORK, X) where X = $x_1$, PUSH (TEMP, X), PUSH (WORK, $x_2$), POP (TEMP, X), PUSH (WORK, X). The set of operations puts the elements in WORK in descending order, making use of the stack TEMP while preserving the maximum element in MAX.

In general, if the current input element $x_i$ is greater than MAX, then set MAX = $x_i$, and repeatedly execute POP (WORK, X) and PUSH (TEMP, X) for every element X in WORK until EMPTYSTACK (WORK) is true. Now do PUSH (WORK, $x_i$) and repeatedly POP (TEMP, X), PUSH (WORK, X) until EMPTYSTACK (TEMP) is true. TEMP serves to hold the elements in WORK so that the elements in WORK are put in descending order after the current maximum element has been input into WORK as the bottom most element in WORK.

If the current input element $x_i$ is less than MAX but greater than the top element of WORK, then pop out elements from WORK that are less than $x_i$, push them into TEMP to hold them, PUSH ($x_i$, WORK) and pop out all elements from TEMP until EMPTYSTACK (TEMP) is true and push them back into WORK.

Thus, the elements in WORK arrange themselves in descending order with the help of stack TEMP, while MAX reports the maximum element in the stack WORK.

iii) This only requires a minor refinement of the process discussed in illustrative problem 4.8(ii) to obtain the sorted list of elements in WORK. After the sorted list of elements is available in WORK, pop out the elements in WORK and store them in array A. Storing it from the first memory location will yield an ascending order of array elements, and storing it from the last memory location will yield a descending order of array elements in $A[1:n]$.

## Review questions

1) Which among the following properties does not hold true in a stack?

   (i) A stack supports the principle of Last In First Out.

(ii) A push operation decrements the top pointer.

(iii) A pop operation deletes an item from the stack.

(iv) A linear stack has limited capacity.

a) (i)                    b) (ii)                    c) (iii)                    d) (iv)

2) A linear stack S is implemented using an array as shown below. The TOP pointer that points to the top most element of the stack is set as shown.

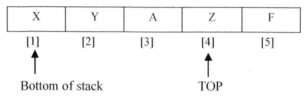

| X | Y | A | Z | F |
|---|---|---|---|---|
| [1] | [2] | [3] | [4] | [5] |

Bottom of stack                    TOP

Execution of the operation PUSH(S, "W") would result in

a) TOP = 4    b) TOP = 5        c) Stack full condition        d) TOP = 3

3) For the linear stack shown in review question 2, execution of the operations POP (S), POP(S), PUSH(S, "U"), and POP(S) in a sequential fashion would leave the element —————on top of the stack with the TOP pointer set to the value ————.

a) Y, 2        b) U, 3            c) U, 1                        d) U, 4

4) The equivalent post fix expression for the infix expression a + b + c is

a) a b c + +    b) a b + c +      c) a b + + c                  d) a + + b c

5) The equivalent postfix expression for the infix expression a↑b ↑c ↑d is

a) ab↑cd↑↑ b) abc↑↑↑d    c) ab↑c↑d↑                  d) abcd↑↑↑

6) How are insert operations carried out in a stack?

7) What are the demerits of a linear stack?

8) If a stack S[1:n] was to be implemented with the bottom of the stack at S[n], write a procedure to undertake the push operation on S.

9) For stack S[1:n] introduced in review question 8, write a procedure to undertake the pop operation on S.

10) For the following logical expression

(a and b and c) or d or e or (not h)

i) obtain the equivalent postfix expression;

ii) evaluate the postfix expression for $a$ = true, $b$ = false, $c$ = true, $d$ = true, $e$ = true, $h$ = false.

11) **Multiple stacks**: A single one-dimensional array $A[1:n]$ can accommodate multiple stacks. If $m$ stacks are to be accommodated in the array, then the array can be equally segmented to hold the $m$ stacks sequentially, each with its bottom of stack and top of stack variables. The size of each stack could then approximately be $m / n$.

Design a multiple stack scheme over an array $A[1:10]$ with three stacks S1, S2 and S3. Assume that S1 = { $a$, $h$, $y$, $m$}, S2 = { $b$, $j$, $l$, $s$, $z$} and S3 = { $k$, $c$}. Attempt to store the stacks in array A. What are their individual bottom of stack and top of stack variables? What are the stack full and stack empty conditions for each of the stacks? Demonstrate push and pop operations on these stacks and show how the top of stack variables are manipulated to accommodate these operations.

## Programming assignments

1) Implement a stack S of $n$ elements using arrays. Write functions to perform PUSH and POP operations. Implement queries, using the push and pop functions to

i)  Retrieve the $m$th element of the stack S from the top ($m < n$), leaving the stack without its top $m-1$ elements.

ii) Retain only the elements in the odd position of the stack and pop out all even positioned elements. For example,

|  | Stack S | | | | | Output stack S | | |
|---|---|---|---|---|---|---|---|---|
| Elements: | a | b | c | d | | a | c | |
| Position: | 1 | 2 | 3 | 4 | | 1 | 2 | |

2) Write a recursive program to obtain the $n$th order Fibonacci sequence number. Include appropriate input/output statements to track the variables participating in recursion. Do you observe the "invisible" stack at work? Record your observations.

3) Implement a program to evaluate any given postfix expression. Test your program for the evaluation of the equivalent postfix form of the expression $(-(A * B)/D) \uparrow C + E - F * H * I$ for $A = 1, B = 2, D = 3, C = 14, E = 110, F = 220, H = 16.78, I = 364.621$.

4) Write a program that inputs a list of numbers already stored in a stack STACK and sorts them, making use of a temporary stack TEMP. The sorted list of numbers should be made available in STACK.

6) S1 and S2 are two sorted stacks comprising $n$ and $m$ integers sorted in descending order, respectively, with their top elements pointing to the smallest in their lists. Create a stack MERGE that merges the elements in stacks S1 and S2 such that at the end of the merge, all of the elements in S1 and S2 are available in MERGE in descending order, that is, with the largest element as its top element. Note that the number of elements in stack MERGE would be $(n + m)$.

# 5

## Queues

In this chapter, we discuss the queue data structure, its operations and its variants, namely, circular queues, priority queues and deques. The application of the data structure is demonstrated on the problem of job scheduling in a time-sharing system environment.

### 5.1. Introduction

A *queue* is a linear list in which all insertions are made at one end of the list known as the *rear* or *tail* of the queue, and all deletions are made at the other end known as the *front* or *head* of the queue. An *insertion* operation is also referred to as *enqueuing a queue*, and a *deletion* operation is referred to as *dequeuing a queue*.

Figure 5.1 illustrates a queue and its functionality. Here, Q is a queue of three elements *a, b,* and *c* (Figure 5.1(a)). When an element *d* is to join the queue, it is inserted at the rear end of the queue (Figure 5.1(b)), and when an element is to be deleted, the element at the front end of the queue, namely, *a*, is deleted automatically (Figure 5.1(c)). Thus, a queue data structure obeys the principle of *First In First Out* (FIFO) or *First Come First Served* (FCFS).

Many examples of queues occur in everyday life. Figure 5.2(a) illustrates a queue of customers waiting to be served by a clerk at the booking counter, and Figure 5.2(b) illustrates a trail of components moving down an assembly line to be processed by a robot at the end of the line. The FIFO principle of insertion at the rear end of the queue when a new client arrives or when a new component is added, and deletion at the front end of the queue when the service of the client or processing of the component is complete, is evident.

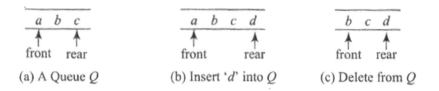

**Figure 5.1.** *A queue and its functionality*

## 5.2. Operations on queues

The queue data structure supports two operations, namely,

i) *insertion* or addition of elements to a queue;

ii) *deletion* or removal of elements from a queue.

Before we proceed to discuss these operations, it is essential to know how queues are implemented.

### 5.2.1. *Queue implementation*

As discussed for stacks, a common method of implementing a queue data structure is to use another sequential data structure, namely, arrays. However, queues have also been implemented using a linked data structure (Chapter 7). In this chapter, we confine our discussion to the implementation of queues using arrays.

Figure 5.3 illustrates an array-based implementation of a queue. A queue Q of four elements R, S, V and G is represented using an array Q [1:7]. Note how the variables FRONT and REAR keep track of the front and rear ends of the queue to facilitate execution of insertion and deletion operations, respectively.

However, just as in the stack data structure, the array implementation limits the capacity of the queue. In other words, the number of elements in the queue cannot exceed the maximum dimension of the one-dimensional array. Thus, a queue that is accommodated in an array Q[*1:n*] cannot hold more than *n* elements. Hence, every insertion of an element into the queue has to necessarily test for a **QUEUE-FULL** condition before executing the insertion operation. Again, each deletion has to ensure that it is not attempted on a queue that is already empty calling for the need to test for a **QUEUE-EMPTY** condition before executing the deletion operation. However, as said earlier with regard to stacks, the linked representation of queues dispenses with the need for QUEUE-FULL and QUEUE-EMPTY testing conditions and hence proves to be elegant and more efficient.

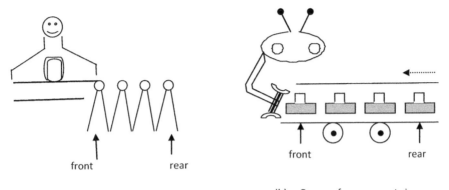

(a)   Queue before a booking counter.

(b)   Queue of components in an assembly line.

**Figure 5.2.** *Common examples of queues*

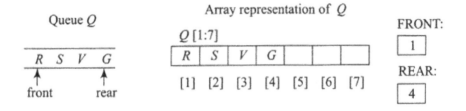

**Figure 5.3.** *Array implementation of a queue*

### 5.2.2. Implementation of insert and delete operations on a queue

Let Q[1:n] be an array implementation of a queue. Let FRONT and REAR be variables recording the front and rear positions of the queue. Observe that the FRONT *variable points to a position that is physically one less than the actual front of the queue.* ITEM is the element to be inserted into the queue. *n* is the maximum capacity of the queue. Both FRONT and REAR are initialized to 0.

Algorithm 5.1 illustrates the insert operation on a queue.

```
procedure INSERTQ (Q, n, ITEM, REAR)
/* insert item ITEM into Q with capacity n */
   if (REAR = n) then QUEUE_FULL;
   REAR = REAR + 1;        /* Increment REAR*/
   Q[REAR] = ITEM;         /* Insert ITEM as the rear
                              element*/
end INSERTQ
```

**Algorithm 5.1.** *Implementation of an insert operation on a queue*

Algorithm 5.1 shows that the addition of every new element into the queue increments the REAR variable. However, before insertion, the condition of whether the queue is full (QUEUE_FULL) is checked. This ensures that there is no overflow of elements in a queue.

The delete operation is illustrated in Algorithm 5.2. Although a deletion operation automatically deletes the front element of the queue, the variable ITEM is used as an output variable to store and perhaps display the value of the element removed.

```
procedure DELETEQ (Q, FRONT, REAR, ITEM )
   if (FRONT =REAR) then QUEUE_EMPTY;
   FRONT = FRONT +1;
   ITEM = Q[FRONT];
end DELETEQ.
```

**Algorithm 5.2.** *Implementation of a delete operation on a queue*

In Algorithm 5.2, observe that to perform a delete operation, the participation of both the FRONT and REAR variables is essential. Before deletion, the condition (FRONT = REAR) checks for the emptiness of the queue. If the queue is non-empty, FRONT is incremented by 1 to point to the element to be deleted, and subsequently, the element is removed through ITEM. Note how this leaves the FRONT variable remembering the position which is one less than the actual front of the queue. This helps in the usage of (FRONT = REAR) as a common condition for testing whether a queue is empty, which occurs either after its initialization or after a sequence of insert and delete operations when the queue has just emptied itself.

Soon after the queue Q has been initialized, FRONT = REAR = 0. Hence, the condition (FRONT = REAR) ensures that the queue is empty. Again, after a sequence of operations when Q has become partially or completely full and delete operations are repeatedly invoked to empty the queue, it may be observed how FRONT increments itself in steps of one with every deletion and begins moving toward REAR. During the final deletion, which renders the queue empty, FRONT coincides with REAR satisfying the condition (FRONT = REAR = k), k ≠ 0. Here, k is the position of the last element that was deleted.

Hence, we observe that in an array implementation of queues, with every insertion, REAR moves away from FRONT, and with every deletion, FRONT moves toward REAR. When the queue is empty, FRONT = REAR is satisfied, and when full, REAR = n (the maximum capacity of the queue) is satisfied.

Queues whose insert/deletion operations follow the procedures implemented in Algorithms 5.1 and 5.2 are known as *linear queues* to distinguish them from *circular queues*, which will be discussed in section 5.3.

Example 5.1 demonstrates the operation of a linear queue. The time complexity to perform a single insert/deletion operation in a linear queue is $O(1)$.

## EXAMPLE 5.1.–

Let BIRDS [1:3] be a linear queue data structure. The working of Algorithms 5.1 and 5.2 demonstrated on the insertions and deletions performed on BIRDS is illustrated in Table 5.1.

### 5.2.3. *Limitations of linear queues*

Example 5.1 illustrates the implementation of insert and delete operations on a linear queue. In operation 4, when "SWAN" was inserted into BIRDS [1:3], the insertion operation was unsuccessful since the QUEUE_FULL condition was invoked. Additionally, one observes the queue BIRDS to be physically full, justifying the condition. However, after operations 5 and 6 were performed, when two elements, namely, DOVE and PEACOCK, were deleted, despite the space they had created to accommodate two more insertions, the insertion of "SWAN" attempted in operation 7 was rejected once again due to the invocation of the QUEUE_FULL condition. This is a gross limitation of a linear queue since the QUEUE_FULL condition does not check whether Q is "physically" full. It merely relies on the condition (REAR = n), which may turn out to be true even for a queue that is only partially full, as shown in operation 7 of example 5.1.

When one contrasts this implementation with the working of a queue that one sees around in everyday life, it is easy to see that with every deletion (after completion of service at one end of the queue), the remaining elements move forward toward the head of the queue, leaving no gaps in between. This obviously makes room for many insertions to be accommodated at the tail end of the queue depending on the space available.

However, attempting to implement this strategy during every deletion of an element is worthless since data movement is always computationally expensive and may render the process of queue maintenance highly inefficient.

In short, when a QUEUE_FULL condition is invoked, it does not necessarily imply that the queue is "physically" full. This leads to the limitation of rejecting insertions despite the space available to accommodate them. The rectification of this limitation leads to what are known as *circular queues*.

## 5.3. Circular queues

In this section, we discuss the implementation and operations on circular queues, which serve to rectify the limitation of linear queues.

As the name indicates, a *circular queue* is not linear in structure but instead *circular*. In other words, the FRONT and REAR variables, which displayed a linear (left to right) movement over a queue, display a circular movement (clockwise) over the queue data structure.

### 5.3.1. *Operations on a circular queue*

Let CIRC_Q be a circular queue with a capacity of three elements, as shown in Figure 5.4(a). The queue is obviously full, with FRONT pointing to the element at the head of the queue and REAR pointing to the element at the tail end of the queue.

Let us now perform two deletions and then attempt insertions of "d" and "e" into the queue.

Observe the circular movement of the FRONT and REAR variables. After two deletions, FRONT moves toward REAR and points to "c" as the current front element of CIRC_Q (Figure 5.4(b)). When "d" is inserted, unlike linear queues,

REAR curls back in a clockwise fashion to accommodate "d" in the vacant space available. A similar procedure follows for the insertion of "e" as well (Figure 5.4(c)).

| Operation | Queue before operation | Algorithm invocation | Queue after operation | Remarks |
|---|---|---|---|---|
| 1.  Insert 'DOVE' into BIRDS [1:3] | BIRDS [1:3]<br><br>[1]  [2]  [3]<br>FRONT: 0  REAR: 0 | INSERTQ ( BIRDS 3, 'DOVE', 0 ) | BIRDS [1:3]<br>DO VE<br>[1]  [2]  [3]<br>FRONT: 0  REAR: 1 | Insert 'DOVE' successful. |
| 2.  Insert 'PEACOCK' into BIRDS [1:3] | BIRDS [1:3]<br>DO VE<br>[1]  [2]  [3]<br>FRONT: 0  REAR: 1 | INSERTQ (BIRDS, 3, 'PEACOCK', 1) | BIRDS [1:3]<br>DO VE | PEAC OCK<br>[1]  [2]  [3]<br>FRONT: 0  REAR: 2 | Insert 'PEACOCK' successful. |
| 3.  Insert 'PIGEON' into BIRDS [1:3] | BIRDS [1:3]<br>DO VE | PEAC OCK<br>[1]  [2]  [3]<br>FRONT: 0  REAR: 2 | INSERTQ( BIRDS 3, 'PIGEON', 2 ) | BIRDS [1:3]<br>DO VE | PEAC OCK | PIGE ON<br>[1]  [2]  [3]<br>FRONT: 0  REAR: 3 | Insert 'PIGEON' successful. |
| 4.  Insert 'SWAN' into BIRDS [1:3] | BIRDS [1:3]<br>DO VE | PEAC OCK | PIGE ON<br>[1]  [2]  [3]<br>FRONT: 0  REAR: 3 | INSERTQ (BIRDS 3, 'SWAN', 3) | BIRDS [1:3]<br>DO VE | PEAC OCK | PIGE ON<br>[1]  [2]  [3]<br>FRONT: 0  REAR: 3 | Insert 'SWAN' failure!<br><br>QUEUE_FULL condition invoked. |
| 5.  Delete | BIRDS [1:3]<br>DO VE | PEAC OCK | PIGE ON<br>[1]  [2]  [3]<br>FRONT: 0  REAR: 3 | DELETEQ (BIRDS, 0, 3, ITEM) | BIRDS [1:3]<br>PEAC OCK | PIGE ON<br>[1]  [2]  [3]<br>FRONT: 1  REAR: 3 | Delete successful.<br><br>ITEM = DOVE |
| 6.  Delete | BIRDS [1:3]<br>PEAC OCK | PIGE ON<br>[1]  [2]  [3]<br>FRONT: 1  REAR: 3 | DELETEQ (BIRDS, 1, 3, ITEM) | BIRDS [1:3]<br>PIGE ON<br>[1]  [2]  [3]<br>FRONT: 2  REAR: 3 | Delete successful.<br><br>ITEM = PEACOCK |

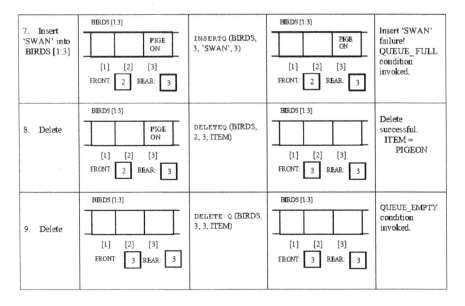

**Table 5.1.** *Insert/delete operations on the queue BIRDS [1:3]*

Figure 5.5 emphasizes this circular movement of FRONT and REAR variables over a general circular queue during a sequence of insertions/deletions.

A circular queue, when implemented using arrays, is non-different from linear queues in their physical storage. In other words, a linear queue is conceptually viewed to have a circular form to understand the clockwise movement of FRONT and REAR variables, as shown in Figure 5.6.

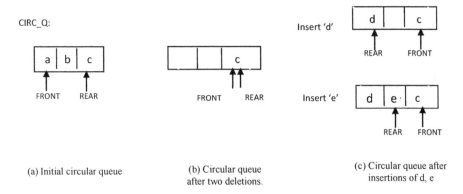

**Figure 5.4.** *Working of a circular queue*

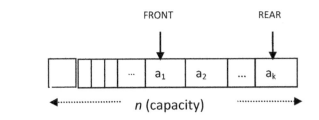

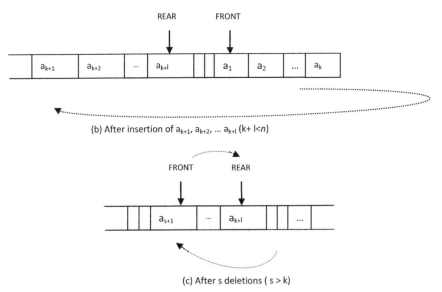

(a) A circular queue at some instance

(b) After insertion of $a_{k+1}, a_{k+2}, \dots a_{k+l}$ (k+ l<n)

(c) After s deletions ( s > k)

**Figure 5.5.** *Circular movement of FRONT and REAR variables in a circular queue*

### 5.3.2. Implementation of insertion and deletion operations in circular queue

Algorithms 5.3 and 5.4 illustrate the implementation of insert and delete operations in a circular queue, respectively. The circular movement of FRONT and REAR variables is implemented using the *mod* function, which is cyclical in nature. Additionally, the array data structure CIRC_Q to implement the queue is declared to be CIRC_Q [*0: n-1*] to facilitate the circular operation of FRONT and REAR variables. As in linear queues, FRONT points to a position that is *one less than the actual front of the circular queue*. Both FRONT and REAR are initialized to 0. Note that $(n - 1)$ is the actual physical capacity of the queue despite the array declaration as $[0: n - 1]$.

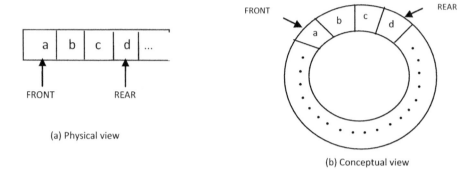

(a) Physical view

(b) Conceptual view

**Figure 5.6.** *Physical and conceptual view of a circular queue*

```
procedure INSERT_CIRCQ(CIRC_Q, FRONT,REAR, n, ITEM)
    REAR=(REAR + 1) mod n;
    If (FRONT = REAR) then CIRCQ_FULL; /* Here CIRCQ_FULL
                    tests for the queue full condition
                    and if so, retracts REAR to its
                    previous value*/
    CIRC_Q [REAR]= ITEM;
end INSERT_CIRCQ.
```

**Algorithm 5.3.** *Implementation of insert operation in a circular queue*

```
procedure DELETE_CIRCQ(CIRC_Q, FRONT,REAR, n, ITEM)
    If (FRONT = REAR) then CIRCQ_EMPTY;
                        /* CIRC_Q is physically empty*/
    FRONT = (FRONT+1) mod n;
    ITEM = CIRC_Q [FRONT];
end DELETE_CIRCQ
```

**Algorithm 5.4.** *Implementation of a delete operation in a circular queue*

The time complexity of Algorithms 5.3 and 5.4 is $O(1)$. The working of the algorithms is demonstrated on an illustration given in example 5.2.

## EXAMPLE 5.2.–

Let COLOURS [0:3] be a circular queue data structure. Note that the actual physical capacity of the queue is only three elements despite the declaration of the array as [0:3]. The operations illustrated in Table 5.2 demonstrate the working of Algorithms 5.3 and 5.4.

| Circular Queue operation | Circular queue before operation | Algorithm Invocation | Circular queue after operation | Remarks |
|---|---|---|---|---|
| 1. Insert 'ORANGE' into COLOURS [0:3] | COLOURS [0:3]<br>[0] [1] [2] [3]<br>FRONT: 0  REAR: 0 | INSERT _CIRCQ (COLOURS, 0, 0, 4, 'ORANGE') | COLOURS [0:3]<br>ORANGE ([1])<br>[0] [1] [2] [3]<br>FRONT: 0  REAR: 1 | Insert 'ORANGE' successful. |
| 2. Insert 'BLUE' into COLOURS [0:3] | COLOURS [0:3]<br>ORANGE ([1])<br>[0] [1] [2] [3]<br>FRONT: 0  REAR: 1 | INSERT _CIRCQ (COLOURS, 0, 1, 4, 'BLUE') | COLOURS [0:3]<br>ORANGE ([1]) BLUE ([2])<br>[0] [1] [2] [3]<br>FRONT: 0  REAR: 2 | Insert 'BLUE' successful. |
| 3. Insert 'WHITE' into COLOURS [0:3] | COLOURS [0:3]<br>ORANGE ([1]) BLUE ([2])<br>[0] [1] [2] [3]<br>FRONT: 0  REAR: 2 | INSERT _CIRCQ (COLOURS, 0, 2, 4, 'WHITE') | COLOURS [0:3]<br>ORANGE ([1]) BLUE ([2]) WHITE ([3])<br>[0] [1] [2] [3]<br>FRONT: 0  REAR: 3 | Insert 'WHITE' successful. |
| 4. Insert 'RED' into COLOURS [0:3] | COLOURS [0:3]<br>ORANGE ([1]) BLUE ([2]) WHITE ([3])<br>[0] [1] [2] [3]<br>FRONT: 0  REAR: 3 | INSERT _CIRCQ (COLOURS, 0, 3, 4, 'RED') | COLOURS [0:3]<br>ORANGE ([1]) BLUE ([2]) WHITE ([3])<br>[0] [1] [2] [3]<br>FRONT: 0  REAR: 3 | CIRCQ_FULL condition is invoked. Insert 'RED' failure!<br>Note: REAR retracts to its previous value of 3. |
| 5,6: Delete twice from COLOURS [0:3] | COLOURS [0:3]<br>ORANGE ([1]) BLUE ([2]) WHITE ([3])<br>[0] [1] [2] [3]<br>FRONT: 0  REAR: 3 | DELETE_CIRCQ (COLOURS ,0,3,4,ITEM)<br><br>DELETE_CIRCQ (COLOURS ,1,3,4,ITEM) | COLOURS [0:3]<br>WHITE ([3])<br>[0] [1] [2] [3]<br>FRONT: 2  REAR: 3 | DELETE operations successful.<br>ITEM = ORANGE<br>ITEM = BLUE |

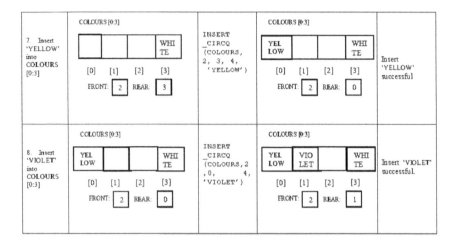

**Table 5.2.** *Insert and delete operations on the circular queue COLOURS [0:3]*

## 5.4. Other types of queues

### 5.4.1. *Priority queues*

A ***priority queue*** is a queue in which insertion or deletion of items from any position in the queue are done based on some property (such as ***priority*** of task)

For example, let P be a priority queue with three elements *a, b and c* whose priority factors are 2, 1 and 1, respectively. Here, the larger the number is, the higher the priority accorded to that element (Figure 5.7(a)). When a new element *d* with higher priority, namely, 4, is inserted, *d* joins at the head of the queue superseding the remaining elements (Figure 5.7(b)). When elements in the queue have the same priority, then the priority queue behaves like an ordinary queue following the principle of FIFO among such elements.

The working of a priority queue may be likened to a situation when a file of patients who have fixed an appointment with the doctor wait for their turn in a queue. All patients are accorded equal priority and follow an FCFS scheme by the date and time of their appointments. However, when a patient with bleeding injuries is brought in, they are accorded high priority and are immediately moved to the head of the queue for immediate attention by the doctor. This is priority queue at work!

A common method of implementing a priority queue is to open as many queues as there are priority factors. A low priority queue will be operated for deletion only when all its high priority predecessors are empty. In other words, deletion of an element in a priority queue $q_i$ with priority $p_i$ is possible only when those queues $q_j$ with priorities $p_j$ $(p_j > p_i)$ are empty. However, with regard to insertions, an element $e_k$ with priority $p_l$ joins the respective queue $q_l$ obeying the scheme of FIFO with regard to the queue $q_l$ alone.

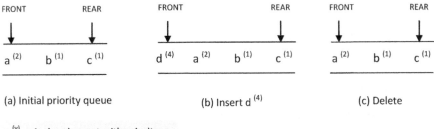

(a) Initial priority queue            (b) Insert d $^{(4)}$                (c) Delete

$x^{(y)}$ : x is the element with priority y

**Figure 5.7.** *A priority queue*

Another method of implementation could be to sort the elements in the queue according to the descending order of priorities every time an insertion takes place. The top priority element at the head of the queue is the element to be deleted.

The choice of implementation depends on a time-space trade-off-based decision made by the user. While the first method of implementation of a priority queue using a cluster of queues consumes space, the time complexity of an insertion is only $O(1)$. In the case of deletion of an element in a specific queue with a specific priority, it calls for the checking of all other queues preceding it in priority to be empty.

On the other hand, the second method consumes less space since it handles just a single queue. However, the insertion of every element calls for sorting all the queue elements in descending order, the most efficient of which reports a time complexity of $O(n.\log n)$. With regard to deletion, the element at the head of the queue is automatically deleted with a time complexity of $O(1)$.

The two methods of implementation of a priority queue are illustrated in example 5.3.

## EXAMPLE 5.3.–

Let JOB be a queue of jobs to be undertaken at a factory shop floor for service by a machine. Let high (2), medium (1) and low (0) be the priorities accorded to jobs. Let $J_i(k)$ indicate a job $J_i$ to be undertaken with priority $k$. The implementations of a priority queue to keep track of the jobs, using the two methods of implementation discussed above, are illustrated for a sample set of job arrivals (insertions) and job service completions (deletion).

Opening JOB queue: $J_1(1)$    $J_2(1)$    $J_3(0)$

Operations on the JOB queue in chronological order:

1) $J_4(2)$ arrives;

2) $J_5(2)$ arrives;

3) execute job;

4) execute job;

5) execute job.

The front and rear positions of the queues have been denoted using a solid $\uparrow$ arrow and a dashed arrow $\uparrow$, respectively.

A variant of the implementation of a priority queue using multiple queues is to make use of a single two-dimensional array to represent the list of queues and their contents. The number of rows in the array is equal to the number of priorities accorded to the data elements, and the columns are equal to the maximum number of elements that can be accommodated in the queues corresponding to the priority number. Thus, if PRIO_QUE $[1:m, 1:n]$ is an array representing a priority queue, then the data items joining the queue may have priority numbers ranging from 1 to $m$ and corresponding to each queue representing a priority, and a maximum of $n$ elements can be accommodated. Illustrative problem 5.4 demonstrates the implementation of a priority queue as a two-dimensional array.

| Implementation of a priority queue as a cluster of queues. | Implementation of a priority queue by sorting queue elements. | Remarks |
|---|---|---|
| **Initial configuration** — High priority (2) Job Queue; Medium priority (1) Job Queue: $J_1(1)$, $J_2(1)$; Low priority (0) Job Queue: $J_3(0)$; Machine service | **Initial configuration** — $J_1(1)$  $J_2(1)$  $J_3(0)$ | Opening Job queue. |
| **1. $J_4(2)$ arrives** — High priority (2) Job Queue: $J_4(2)$; Medium priority (1) Job Queue: $J_1(1)$, $J_2(1)$; Low priority (0) Job Queue: $J_3(0)$; Machine service | **1. $J_4(2)$ arrives** — $J_4(2)$  $J_1(1)$  $J_2(1)$  $J_3(0)$ | Insert $J_4(2)$ |
| **2. $J_5(2)$ arrives** — High priority (2) Job Queue: $J_4(2)$, $J_5(2)$; Medium priority (1) Job Queue: $J_1(1)$, $J_2(1)$; Low priority (0) Job Queue: $J_3(0)$; Machine service | **2. $J_5(2)$ arrives** — $J_4(2)$  $J_5(2)$  $J_1(1)$  $J_2(1)$  $J_3(0)$ | Insert $J_5(2)$ |

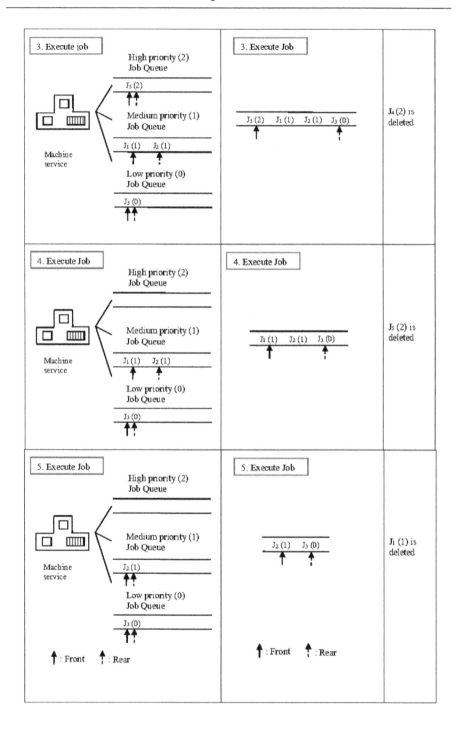

### 5.4.2. Deques

A *deque* (double-ended queue) is a linear list in which all insertions and deletions are made at the end of the list. A deque is pronounced as "deck" or "de queue".

A deque is therefore more general than a stack or queue and is a sort of **FLIFLO (First In Last In Or First Out Last Out)**. Thus, while one speaks of the top or bottom of a stack, or front or rear of a queue, one refers to the *right end* or *left end* of a deque. The fact that deque is a generalization of a stack or queue is illustrated in Figure 5.8.

A deque has two variants, namely, *input restricted deque* and *output restricted deque*. An input restricted deque is one where insertions are allowed at one end only while deletions are allowed at both ends. On the other hand, an output restricted deque allows insertions at both ends of the deque but permits deletions only at one end.

A deque is commonly implemented as a circular array with two variables LEFT and RIGHT taking care of the active ends of the deque. Example 5.4 illustrates the working of a deque with insertions and deletions permitted at both ends.

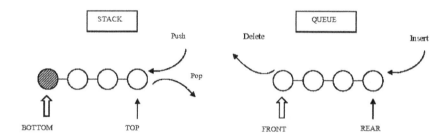

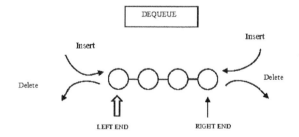

**Figure 5.8.** *A stack, queue and a deque – a comparison*

## EXAMPLE 5.4.–

Let DEQ[1:6] be a deque implemented as a circular array. The contents of DEQ and those of LEFT and RIGHT are given below:

DEQ:                                                    LEFT: 3        RIGHT: 5

| [1] | [2] | [3] | [4] | [5] | [6] |
| --- | --- | --- | --- | --- | --- |
|     |     | R   | T   | S   |     |

The following operations demonstrate the working of the deque DEQ, which supports insertions and deletions at both ends.

i) Insert X at the left end and Y at the right end

DEQ:                                                    LEFT: 2        RIGHT: 6

| [1] | [2] | [3] | [4] | [5] | [6] |
| --- | --- | --- | --- | --- | --- |
|     | X   | R   | T   | S   | Y   |

ii) Delete twice from the right end

DEQ:                                                    LEFT: 2        RIGHT: 4

| [1] | [2] | [3] | [4] | [5] | [6] |
| --- | --- | --- | --- | --- | --- |
|     | X   | R   | T   |     |     |

iii) Insert G, Q and M at the left end

DEQ:                                                    LEFT: 5        RIGHT: 4

| [1] | [2] | [3] | [4] | [5] | [6] |
| --- | --- | --- | --- | --- | --- |
| G   | X   | R   | T   | M   | Q   |

iv) Insert J at the right end

Here, no insertion is possible since the deque is full. Observe the condition LEFT = RIGHT+1 when the deque is full.

v) Delete twice from the left end

DEQ:                                                    LEFT: 1          RIGHT: 4

[1]    [2]    [3]    [4]    [5]    [6]

| G | X | R | T | | |
|---|---|---|---|---|---|

It is easy to observe that for insertions at the left end, LEFT is decremented in steps of 1 and for insertions at the right end RIGHT is incremented in steps of 1. For deletions at the left end, LEFT is incremented in steps of 1, and for deletions at the right end, RIGHT is decremented in steps of 1. Again, before performing a deletion if LEFT = RIGHT, then it implies that there is only one element and in such a case after deletion set LEFT = RIGHT = NIL to indicate that the deque is empty.

LEFT and RIGHT undertake anticlockwise and clockwise movements across the circular array during insertions and deletions.

## 5.5. Applications

In this section, we discuss the application of a linear queue and a priority queue in the scheduling of jobs by a processor in a time-sharing system.

### 5.5.1. *Application of a linear queue*

Figure 5.9 shows a naive diagram of a time-sharing system. A CPU (processor) endowed with memory resources is to be shared by $n$ number of computer users. The sharing of the processor and memory resources is done by allotting a definite time slice of the processor's attention to the users and in a round robin fashion. In a system such as this, the users are unaware of the presence of other users and are led to believe that their job receives the undivided attention of the CPU. However, to keep track of the jobs initiated by the users, the processor relies on a queue data structure recording the active user-ids. Example 5.5 demonstrates the application of a queue data structure for this job scheduling problem.

EXAMPLE 5.5.–

The following is a table of three users A, B and C with their job requests $J_i(k)$, where $i$ is the job number and $k$ is the time required to execute the job.

| User | Job requests and the execution time in µs |
|------|-------------------------------------------|
| A | $J_1$ (4), $J_2$ (3) |
| B | $J_3$ (2), $J_4$(1), $J_5$ (1) |
| C | $J_6$ (6) |

Thus, $J_1$ (4), a job request initiated by A needs 4 µs for its execution before the user initiates the next request of $J_2$(3). Throughout the simulation, we assume a uniform user delay period of 5 µs between any two sequential job requests initiated by a user. Thus, B initiates $J_4$(1), 5 µs after the completion of $J_3$ (2) and so on. Additionally, to simplify the simulation, we assume that the CPU gives whole attention to the completion of a job request before moving to the next job request. In other words, all the job requests complete their execution well within the time slice allotted to them.

To initiate the simulation, we assume that A logged in at time 0, B at time 1 and C at time 2. Figure 5.10 shows a graphical illustration of the simulation. Note that at time 2 while A's $J_1$ (4) is being executed, B is in the wait mode with $J_3$ (2) and C has just logged in. The objective is to ensure the CPU's attention to all the jobs logged in according to the principle of FIFO.

To tackle such a complex scenario, a queue data structure is developed. As soon as a job request is made by a user, the user id is inserted into a queue. A job that is to be processed next would be the one at the head of the queue. A job until its execution is complete remains at the head of the queue. Once the request has been processed and execution is complete, the user id is deleted from the queue.

A snapshot of the queue data structure at times 5, 10 and 14 is shown in Figure 5.11. It can be observed that during the time period 16-21, the CPU is left idle.

### 5.5.2. Application of priority queues

Assume a time-sharing system in which job requests by users are of different categories. For example, some requests may be real time, and the others online and the last may be batch processing requests. It is known that real-time job requests carry the highest priority, followed by online processing and batch processing in that order. In such a situation, the job scheduler needs to maintain a priority queue to execute the job requests based on their priorities. If the priority queue were to be implemented using a cluster of queues of varying priorities, the scheduler had to maintain one queue for real-time jobs (R), one for online processing jobs (O) and the third for batch processing jobs (B). The CPU proceeds to execute a job request in O only when R is empty. In other words, all real-time jobs awaiting execution in R have to be completed and cleared before execution of a job request from O. In the case of queue B, before executing a job in queue B, queues R and O should be empty. Example 5.6 illustrates the application of a priority queue in a time-sharing system with priority-based job requests.

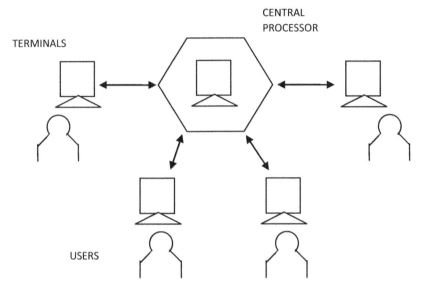

**Figure 5.9.** *A naive diagram of a time-sharing system*

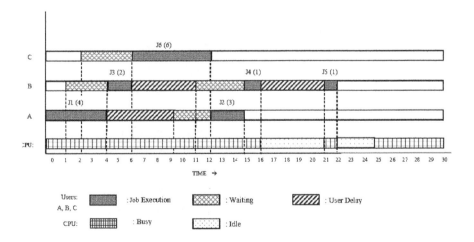

**Figure 5.10.** *Time-sharing system simulation – non-priority-based job requests*

| | B | C | Job Queue |
|---|---|---|---|
| Time 5 | $(J_3 (2))$ | $(J_6 (6))$ | |

| | C | A |
|---|---|---|
| Time 10 | $(J_6 (6))$ | $(J_2 (3))$ |

| | A | B |
|---|---|---|
| Time 14 | $(J_2 (3))$ | $(J_4 (1))$ |

**Figure 5.11.** *Snapshot of the queue at time 5, 10 and 14*

**EXAMPLE 5.6.–**

The following is a table of three users A, B and C with their job requests. $R_i (k)$ indicates a real-time job $R_i$ whose execution time is $k$ μs. Similarly, $B_i(k)$ and $O_i(k)$ indicate batch processing and online processing jobs, respectively.

| User | Job requests and their execution time in μs |
|---|---|
| A | $R_1 (4)$    $B_1 (1)$ |
| B | $O_1 (2)$    $O_2 (3)$    $B_2 (3)$ |
| C | $R_2 (1)$    $B_3 (2)$    $O_3 (3)$ |

As before, we assume a user delay of 5 μs between any two sequential job requests by the user and assume that the CPU gives undivided attention to a job request until its completion. Additionally, A, B and C login at times 0, 1 and 2, respectively.

Figure 5.12 illustrates the simulation of the job scheduler for priority-based job requests. Figure 5.13 shows a snapshot of the priority queue at times 4, 8 and

12. Observe that the processor while scheduling jobs and executing them falls into idle modes during time periods 7–9 and 15–17.

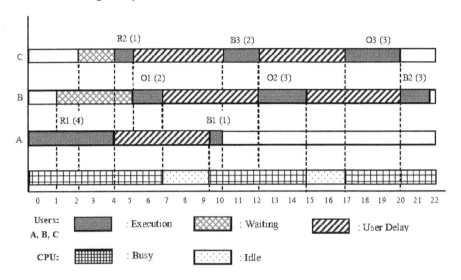

**Figure 5.12.** *Simulation of the time-sharing system for priority-based jobs*

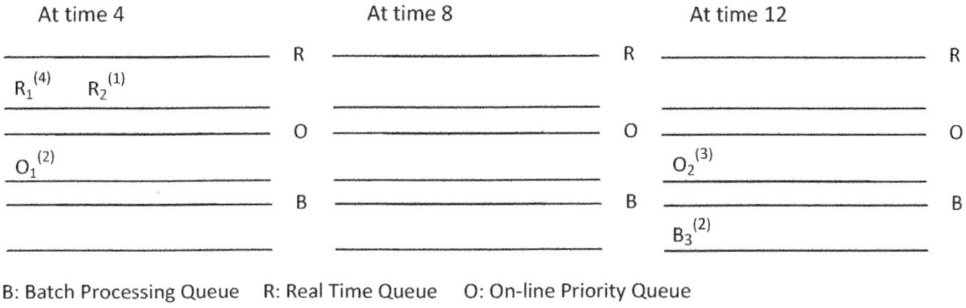

At time 4                    At time 8                    At time 12

_____ R   _____ R   _____ R

$R_1^{(4)}$    $R_2^{(1)}$

_____      _____      _____

_____ O   _____ O   _____ O

$O_1^{(2)}$                                              $O_2^{(3)}$

_____ B   _____ B   _____ B

                                                        $B_3^{(2)}$

_____      _____      _____

B: Batch Processing Queue    R: Real Time Queue    O: On-line Priority Queue

**Figure 5.13.** *Snapshots of the priority queue at times 4, 8 and 12*

## ADT for queues

**Data objects:**

A finite set of elements of the same type.

**Operations:**

- Create an empty queue and initialize front and rear variables of the queue

    CREATE (QUEUE, FRONT, REAR)
- Check if queue QUEUE is empty

    CHK_QUEUE_EMPTY (QUEUE) (Boolean function)
- Check if queue QUEUE is full

    CHK_QUEUE_FULL (QUEUE) (Boolean function)
- Insert ITEM into rear of queue QUEUE

    ENQUEUE (QUEUE, ITEM)
- Delete element from the front of queue QUEUE and output the element deleted in ITEM

    DEQUEUE (QUEUE, ITEM)

### Summary

– A queue data structure is a linear list in which all insertions are made at the rear end of the list and deletions are made at the front end of the list.

– A queue follows the principle of FIFO or FCFS and is commonly implemented using arrays. It therefore calls for the testing of QUEUE_FULL/QUEUE_EMPTY conditions during insert/delete operations, respectively.

– A linear queue suffers from the drawback of QUEUE_FULL condition invocation even when the queue in not physically full to its capacity. This limitation is over come to an extent in a circular queue.

– Priority queue is a queue structure in which elements are inserted or deleted from a queue based on some property known as priority.

– A deque is a double ended queue with insertions and deletions done at either ends or may be appropriately restricted at one of the two ends.

– Job scheduling in time-sharing system environments is an application of queues and priority queues.

## 5.6. Illustrative problems

### PROBLEM 5.1.–

Let INITIALISE (Q) be an operation that initializes a linear queue Q to be empty. Let ENQUEUE (Q, ITEM) insert an ITEM into Q and DEQUEUE (Q, ITEM) delete an element from Q through ITEM. EMPTY_QUEUE (Q) is a Boolean function that is true if Q is empty and false otherwise, and PRINT (ITEM) is a function that displays the value of ITEM.

What is the output of the following pseudo-code?

```
1.  X = Y = Z = 0;
2.  INITIALISE (Q)
3.  ENQUEUE (Q,10)
4.  ENQUEUE (Q, 70)
5.  ENQUEUE (Q, 88)
6.  DEQUEUE (Q, X)
7.  DEQUEUE (Q, Z)
8.  ENQUEUE (Q, X)
9.  ENQUEUE (Q, Y+18)
10. DEQUEUE (Q, X)
11. DEQUEUE (Q, Y)
12. while not EMPTY_QUEUE (Q) do
13.         DEQUEUE (Q, X)
14.         PRINT (X)
15. end
```

## Solution:

The contents of the queue Q and the values of the variables X, Y, Z are tabulated as follows:

| Steps | Queue Q | Variables | | |
|-------|---------|-----------|---|---|
| | | X | Y | Z |
| 1 - 2 | ———————— ———————— | 0 | 0 | 0 |

| 3 | 10 | 0 | 0 | 0 |
|---|---|---|---|---|
| 4 | 10   70 | 0 | 0 | 0 |
| 5 | 10   70   88 | 0 | 0 | 0 |
| 6 | 70   88 | 10 | 0 | 0 |
| 7 | 88 | 10 | 0 | 70 |
| 8 | 88   10 | 10 | 0 | 70 |
| 9 | 88   10   18 | 10 | 0 | 70 |
| 10 | 10   18 | 88 | 0 | 70 |
| 11 | 18 | 88 | 10 | 70 |
| 12–14 | | 18 | 10 | 70 |

The output of the program code is:  18

## PROBLEM 5.2.–

Given Q' to be a circular queue implemented as an array Q'[0:4] and using procedures declared in illustrative problem 5.1, but suitable for implementation on Q', what is the output of the following code?

[NOTE.– The procedures ENQUEUE (Q', X) and DEQUEUE (Q', X) may be assumed to be implementation of Algorithms 5.3 and 5.4.]

```
 1. INITIALISE (Q')
 2. X: = 56
 3. Y: = 77
 4. ENQUEUE (Q', X)
 5. ENQUEUE (Q', 50)
 6. ENQUEUE (Q', Y)
 7. DEQUEUE (Q', Y)
 8. ENQUEUE (Q', 22)
 9. ENQUEUE (Q', X)
10. ENQUEUE (Q', Y)
11. Z = X - Y
12. if (Z = 0)
13. then { while not EMPTY_QUEUE(Q')
14.           DEQUEUE (Q', X)
15.           PRINT (X)
16.         end }
17. else PRINT ("Process Complete");
```

## Solution:

The contents of the circular queue Q'[0:4] and the values of the variables X, Y, Z are illustrated below.

| Steps | Queue Q' | Variables | | |
|---|---|---|---|---|
| | | X | Y | Z |
| 1 | [0] [1] [2] [3] [4] | – | – | – |
| 2,3 | [0] [1] [2] [3] [4] | 56 | 77 | – |

| Step | [0] | [1] | [2] | [3] | [4] | | | |
|---|---|---|---|---|---|---|---|---|
| 4 | | 56 | | | | 56 | 77 | — |
| 5 | | 56 | 50 | | | 56 | 77 | — |
| 6 | | 56 | 50 | 77 | | 56 | 77 | — |
| 7 | | | 50 | 77 | | 56 | 56 | — |
| 8 | | | 50 | 77 | 22 | 56 | 56 | — |
| 9 | 56 | | 50 | 77 | 22 | 56 | 56 | — |
| 10 | 56 | | 50 | 77 | 22 | 56 | 56 | — <br> Queue full. <br> ENQUEUE(Q', Y) fails. |
| 11 | 56 | | 50 | 77 | 22 | 56 | 56 | 0 |
| 12 - 16 | | | | | | 50 <br> 77 <br> 22 <br> 56 | 56 <br> 56 <br> 56 <br> 56 | 0 <br> 0 <br> 0 <br> 0 |

Output of the program code:  50    77    22    56

## PROBLEM 5.3.–

S and Q are a stack and a priority queue of integers, respectively. The priority of an element C joining the priority queue Q is computed as C *mod* 3. In other words, the priority numbers of the elements are either 0 or 1 or 2. Given A, B, and C to be integer variables, what is the output of the following code? The procedures are similar to those used in illustrative problems 5.1 and 5.2. However, the queue procedures are modified to appropriately work on a priority queue.

```
1.A = 10
2.B = 11
3.C = A+B
4.while (C < 110) do
5.    if (C mod 3) = 0 then PUSH (S,C)
6.    else ENQUEUE (Q,C)
7.    A = B
8.    B = C
9.    C = A + B
10.end
11.while not EMPTY_STACK (S) do
12.    POP (S,C)
13.    PRINT (C)
14.end
15.while not EMPTY_QUEUE (Q) do
16.    DEQUEUE (Q, C)
17.    PRINT (C)
18.end
```

## Solution:

| Steps | Stack S | Queue Q | A | B | C |
|-------|---------|---------|---|---|---|
| 1–3 | 21 | | 10 | 11 | 21 |
| 4–6 | 21 | | 10 | 11 | 21 |
| 7–10 | 21 | | 11 | 21 | 32 |

| 4–6 | 21 | $32^{(2)}$ | 11 | 21 | 32 |
|---|---|---|---|---|---|
| 7–10 | 21 | $32^{(2)}$ | 21 | 32 | 53 |
| 4–6 | 21 | $32^{(2)}$  $53^{(2)}$ | 21 | 32 | 53 |
| 7–10 | 21 | $32^{(2)}$  $53^{(2)}$ | 32 | 53 | 85 |
| 4–6 | 21 | $32^{(2)}$  $53^{(2)}$  $85^{(1)}$ | 32 | 53 | 85 |
| 7–10 | 21 | $32^{(2)}$  $53^{(2)}$  $85^{(1)}$ | 53 | 85 | 138 |
| 11–14 | | $32^{(2)}$  $53^{(2)}$  $85^{(1)}$ | 53 85 21<br>Output: 21 | | |
| 15–18 | | | 53  85  32<br>53  85  53<br>53  85  85<br><br>Output: 32 53 85 | | |

The final output is:    21    32    53    85

## PROBLEM 5.4.–

TOKEN is a priority queue for organizing *n* data items with *m* priority numbers. TOKEN is implemented as a two-dimensional array TOKEN[*1:m, 1:p*], where *p* is the maximum number of elements with a given priority. Execute the following operations on TOKEN [1:3, 1:2]. Here, INSERT("xxx", m) indicates the insertion of item "xxx" with priority number *m,* and DELETE() indicates the deletion of the first among the high priority items.

i) INSERT("*not*", 1)

ii) INSERT("*and*", 2)

iii) INSERT("*or*", 2)

iv) DELETE()

v) INSERT ("*equ*", 3)

**Solution:**

The two-dimensional array TOKEN[1:3, 1:2] before the execution of operations is given as follows:

TOKEN:  [1] [2]

$$\begin{matrix} 1 \\ 2 \\ 3 \end{matrix} \begin{bmatrix} - & - \\ - & - \\ - & - \end{bmatrix}$$

After the execution of operations, TOKEN[1:3, 1:2] is as shown as follows:

| i) INSERT("*not*", 1)  ii) INSERT("*and*", 2)  iii) INSERT("*or*", 2) | $$\begin{matrix}  & [1] & [2] \\ 1 \\ 2 \\ 3 \end{matrix} \begin{bmatrix} 'not' & - \\ 'and' & 'or' \\ - & - \end{bmatrix}$$ |
|---|---|
| iv) DELETE() | $$\begin{matrix}  & [1] & [2] \\ 1 \\ 2 \\ 3 \end{matrix} \begin{bmatrix} - & - \\ 'and' & 'or' \\ - & - \end{bmatrix}$$  Note how "*not*" which is the first among the elements with the highest priority  is deleted |
| v) INSERT("*equ*", 3) | $$\begin{matrix}  & [1] & [2] \\ 1 \\ 2 \\ 3 \end{matrix} \begin{bmatrix} - & - \\ 'and' & 'or' \\ 'equ' & - \end{bmatrix}$$ |

**PROBLEM 5.5.–**

DEQ[0:4] is an output restricted deque implemented as a circular array, and LEFT and RIGHT indicate the ends of the deque, as shown below. INSERT("xx", [LEFT | RIGHT]) indicates the insertion of the data item at the left or right end as the case may be, and DELETE() deletes the item from the left end only.

DEQ:                                    LEFT: 2        RIGHT: 5

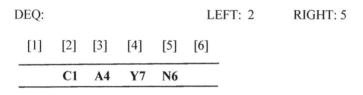

| [1] | [2] | [3] | [4] | [5] | [6] |
|-----|-----|-----|-----|-----|-----|
|     | C1  | A4  | Y7  | N6  |     |

Execute the following insertions and deletions on DEQ:

i) INSERT("**S5**", LEFT)

ii) INSERT("**K9**", RIGHT)

iii) DELETE()

iv) INSERT("**V7**", LEFT)

v) INSERT("**T5**", LEFT)

**Solution:**

– DEQ after the execution of operations

i) INSERT("S5", LEFT)

ii) INSERT("K9", RIGHT)

DEQ:                                    LEFT: 1        RIGHT: 6

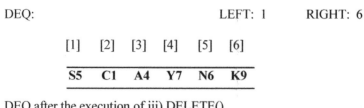

| [1] | [2] | [3] | [4] | [5] | [6] |
|-----|-----|-----|-----|-----|-----|
| S5  | C1  | A4  | Y7  | N6  | K9  |

DEQ after the execution of iii) DELETE()

DEQ:                                    LEFT: 2        RIGHT: 6

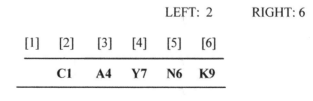

| [1] | [2] | [3] | [4] | [5] | [6] |
|-----|-----|-----|-----|-----|-----|
|     | C1  | A4  | Y7  | N6  | K9  |

– DEQ after the execution of operations

iv) INSERT("**V7**", LEFT)

v) INSERT("**T5**", LEFT)

DEQ:                                   LEFT: 1          RIGHT: 6

| [1] | [2] | [3] | [4] | [5] | [6] |
|-----|-----|-----|-----|-----|-----|
| **V7** | **C1** | **A4** | **Y7** | **N6** | **K9** |

After the execution of operation INSERT("**V7**", LEFT), the deque is full. Hence, "T5" is not inserted into the deque.


## PROBLEM 5.6.–

Implement a queue Q using two stacks S1 and S2 such that operations ENQUEUE(Q, X) and DEQUEUE(Q, Y), where Q is supposedly a queue and X is the element to be inserted into Q and Y the element deleted from Q, are worked upon by the stacks that operate together as a queue. Assume that the ADT operations of PUSH, POP and EMPTYSTACK are only available for the stacks.

Demonstrate the working of your method on a list {a, b, c}, which is to be operated upon as a queue by the stacks S1 and S2.


## Solution:

For the two stacks S1 and S2 to work as a queue, every time the ENQUEUE (Q, X) operation is invoked, the element X should join the rear of the queue, and every time DEQUEUE(Q, Y) is invoked, the first element in the queue should be deleted. One method to do this is to ensure that elements are stored in stack S1 in such a way that the top element of S1 is the first element of the queue. This can be accomplished by using stack S2.

Consider the list {a, b, c} to be stored as a queue. The operations undertaken by the stacks to accomplish this are shown in the following table:

| Queue operation | Operations on stacks S1 and S2 | Snapshots of the stacks S1 and S2 and their top of stack variables, TOP(S1) and TOP(S2) ("[" denotes bottom of stack) |
|---|---|---|
| ENQUEUE(Q, "a") | PUSH(S1, "a") | S1:[a<br><br>    TOP (S1) = "a"<br><br>S2:[<br><br>    TOP (S2) = Nil |
| ENQUEUE(Q, "b") | POP(S1, Y)<br>    where {Y = "a"}<br>PUSH(S2, Y)<br>PUSH(S1, "b")<br>POP(S2, Y)<br>PUSH(S1, Y) | S1: [b, a<br>    TOP (S1) = "a"<br><br>S2:[<br>    TOP (S2) = Nil |
| ENQUEUE(Q, "c") | **while not** EMPTYSTACK(S1) **do**<br>    POP(S1, Z)<br>    PUSH(S2, Z)<br>**end**<br>PUSH(S1, "c")<br><br><br>**while not** EMPTYSTACK(S2) **do**<br>    POP(S2, X)<br>    PUSH(S1, X)<br>**end** | S1:[c<br>    TOP (S1) = "c"<br>S2: [a, b<br>    TOP (S2) = "b"<br><br><br><br>S1: [c, b, a<br>    TOP (S1) = "a"<br>S2: [<br>    TOP (S2) = Nil |

The invocation of delete operations on the queue Q and the same executed by the stacks are shown in the following table:

| Queue operation | Operations on stacks S1 and S2 | Snapshots of the stacks S1 and S2 and their top of stack variables, TOP(S1) and TOP(S2) ("[" denotes the bottom of stack) |
|---|---|---|
| DEQUEUE(Q, X) | POP(S1, X) <br><br> Output: <br> X = {a} | S1: [c, b <br> TOP (S1) = "b" <br> S2: [ <br> TOP (S2) = Nil |
| DEQUEUE(Q, X) | POP(S1, X) <br><br> Output: <br> X = {b} | S1: [c <br> TOP (S1) = "c" <br> S2: [ <br> TOP (S2) = Nil |

## PROBLEM 5.7.−

Implement a stack S using two queues Q1 and Q2 so that operations PUSH (S, X) and POP(S, Y), where S is supposedly a stack and X is the element to be inserted into S and Y the element deleted from S, are worked upon by the queues that operate together as a stack. Assume that the ADT operations of ENQUEUE, DEQUEUE and EMPTYQUEUE are only available for the queues.

Demonstrate the working of your method on a list {a, b, c}, which is to be operated upon as a stack by the queues Q1 and Q2.

## Solution:

For the two queues Q1 and Q2 to work as a stack, every time PUSH(S, X) is invoked, element X should be stored as the front element in the queue so that when a POP(S, Y) operation is executed, the front element of the queue that is deleted stands for the last element to be popped out from the stack. A method to do this would be to delete all the existing elements in Q1 and insert them into Q2 in their respective order before inserting X as the front element of Q1. This is followed by deleting all elements from Q2 and inserting them into Q1 in their respective order, following the element X in Q1. Q1 now "behaves" like a stack when a pop operation on stack S is ordered by deleting X, which is the front element in queue Q1.

Consider the list {a, b, c} to be stored as a stack. The operations undertaken by the queues to accomplish this are shown in the following table:

| Stack operation on S | Operations on queues Q1 and Q2 | Snapshots of the queues Q1 and Q2 and the front and rear elements of the queues, FRONT() and REAR() |
|---|---|---|
| PUSH(S, "a") | ENQUEUE(Q1, "a") | Q1:[a]<br>  FRONT(Q1) = "a"<br>  REAR(Q1)  = "a"<br>Q2:[ ]<br>  FRONT(Q2) = Nil<br>  REAR(Q2)  = Nil |
| PUSH(S, "b") | DEQUEUE(Q1, Y)<br>  where {Y = "a"}<br>ENQUEUE(Q2, Y)<br>ENQUEUE(Q1, "b")<br>DEQUEUE(Q2, Y)<br>ENQUEUE(Q1, Y) | Q1: [b, a ]<br>  FRONT(Q1) = "b"<br>  REAR(Q1)  = "a"<br><br>Q2:[ ]<br>  FRONT(Q2) = Nil<br>  REAR(Q2)  = Nil |
| PUSH(S, "c") | **while not** EMPTYQUEUE(Q1) **do**<br>  DEQUEUE(Q1, Z)<br>  ENQUEUE(Q2, Z)<br>**end**<br>ENQUEUE(Q1, "c")<br><br><br><br>**while not** EMPTYQUEUE(Q2) **do**<br>  DEQUEUE(Q2, Y)<br>  ENQUEUE(Q1, Y)<br>**end** | Q1:[c]<br>  FRONT(Q1) = "c"<br>  REAR(Q1)  = "c"<br><br>Q2: [b, a]<br>  FRONT(Q1) = "b"<br>  REAR(Q1)  = "a"<br><br><br><br>Q1: [c, b, a]<br>  FRONT(Q1) = "c"<br>  REAR(Q1)  = "a"<br><br>Q2: []<br>  FRONT(Q2) = Nil<br>  REAR(Q2)  = Nil |

The invocation of delete operations on stack S and the same executed by the queues are shown in the following table:

| Stack operation | Operations on stacks S1 and S2 | Snapshots of the queues Q1 and Q2 and the front and rear elements of the queues, FRONT() and REAR() |
|---|---|---|
| POP(S, X) | DEQUEUE (Q1, X)<br>Output:<br>X = {c} | Q1: [b, a]<br>    FRONT(Q1) = "b"<br>    REAR(Q1)  = "a"<br><br>Q2: [ ]<br>    FRONT(Q2) = Nil<br>    REAR(Q2)  = Nil |
| POP(S, X) | DEQUEUE (Q1, X)<br>Output:<br>X = {b} | Q1: [a]<br>    FRONT(Q1) = "a"<br>    REAR(Q1)  = "a"<br><br>Q2: [ ]<br>    FRONT(Q2) = Nil<br>    REAR(Q2)  = Nil |

## Review questions

1) Which among the following properties does not hold good in a queue?

i) A queue supports the principle of first come first served.

ii) An enqueuing operation shrinks the queue length.

iii) A dequeuing operation affects the front end of the queue.

iv) An enqueuing operation affects the rear end of the queue

      a) (i)        b) (ii)        c) (iii)        d) (iv)

2) A linear queue Q is implemented using an array as shown below. The FRONT and REAR pointers, which point to the physical front and rear of the queue, are also shown.

FRONT: 2    REAR: 3

| X | Y | A | Z | S |
|---|---|---|---|---|
| [1] | [2] | [3] | [4] | [5] |

Execution of the operation ENQUEUE(Q, "W") would yield the FRONT and REAR pointers to carry the values shown in

  a) 2 and 4      b)  3 and 3      c)  3 and 4      d) 2 and 3

3) For the linear queue shown in review question 2, execution of the operation DEQUEUE(Q, M), where M is an output variable, would yield M, FRONT and REAR to, respectively, carry the values

  a) Z, 2, 3      b)  A, 2, 2      c)   Y, 3, 3      d) A, 2, 3

4) Given the following array implementation of a circular queue, with FRONT and REAR pointing to the physical front and rear of the queue,

FRONT: 3    REAR: 4

| X | Y | A | Z | S |
|---|---|---|---|---|
| [1] | [2] | [3] | [4] | [5] |

Execution of the operations ENQUEUE(Q, "H"), ENQUEUE(Q, "T") done in a sequence would result in

i) invoking queue full condition soon after ENQUEUE(Q, 'H') operation;

ii) aborting the ENQUEUE(Q, "T") operation;

iii) yielding FRONT = 1 and REAR = 4 after the operations;

iv) Yielding FRONT = 3 and REAR =1 after the operations.

  a) (i)      b) (ii)         c) (iii)         d) (iv)

5) State whether true or false:

For the following implementation of a queue, where FRONT and REAR point to the physical front and rear of the queue,

FRONT: 3    REAR: 5

| X | Y | A | Z | S |
|---|---|---|---|---|
| [1] | [2] | [3] | [4] | [5] |

Execution of the operation ENQUEUE(Q, "C"),

i) if Q is a linear queue, it would invoke the queue full condition;

ii) if Q is a circular queue, it would abort the enqueuing operation.

a) (i) true (ii) true                 b) (i) true (ii) false

c) (i) false (ii) false              d) (i) false (ii) true

6) What are the disadvantages of linear queues?

7) How do circular queues help overcome the disadvantages of linear queues?

8) If FRONT and REAR were pointers to the physical front and rear of a linear queue, comment on the condition, FRONT = REAR.

9) If FRONT and REAR were pointers to the physical front and rear of a circular queue,  comment on the condition, FRONT = REAR.

10) How are priority queues implemented using a single queue?

11) The following is a table of five users Tim, Shiv, Kali, Musa and Lobo, with their job requests $J_i(k)$, where $i$ is the job number and $k$ is the time required to execute the job. The time at which the users logged in is also shown in the following table.

| User | Job requests and the execution time in μs | Login time |
|---|---|---|
| Tim | $J_1$ (5), $J_2$ (4) | 0 |
| Shiv | $J_3$ (3), $J_4$(5), $J_5$ (1) | 1 |
| Kali | $J_6$ (6), $J_7$ (3), | 2 |
| Musa | $J_8$(5), $J_9$ (1) | 3 |
| Lobo | $J_9$ (3), $J_{10}$ (3), $J_{11}$ (6) | 4 |

Throughout the simulation, assume a uniform user delay period of 4 μs between any two sequential job requests initiated by a user. Additionally, to simplify the simulation, assume that the CPU gives whole attention to the completion of a job request before moving to the next job request. Trace a graphical illustration of the simulation to demonstrate a time-sharing system at work. Show snapshots of the linear queue used by the system to implement the FIFO principle of attending to jobs by the CPU.

12) For the time-sharing system discussed in review question 11, trace a graphical illustration of the simulation assuming that all job requests $J_i(k)$ where $i$ is even numbered have higher priority than those jobs $J_i(k)$ where $i$ is odd numbered. Show snapshots of the priority queue implementation.

## Programming assignments

1) Waiting line simulation in an Indian post office:

In an Indian post office that not only delivers mail but also functions as a savings bank carrying out specific transactions, a lone postal worker serves a single queue of customers. Every customer receives a token # (serial number) as soon as they enter the queue. After service, the token is returned to the postal worker, and the customer leaves the queue. At any point in time, the worker may want to know how many customers are yet to be served.

i) Implement the system using an appropriate queue data structure, simulating a random arrival and departure of customers after service completion.

ii) If a customer arrives to operate their savings account at the post office, then they are attended to first by permitting them to join a special queue. In such a case, the postal worker attends to them immediately before resuming their normal service of mail delivery. Modify the system to implement this addition in service.

2) Write a program to maintain a list of items as a circular queue, which is implemented using an array. Simulate insertions and deletions to the queue and display a graphical representation of the queue after every operation.

3) Let PQUE be a priority queue data structure and $a_1^{(p_1)}, a_2^{(p_2)}, \ldots a_n^{(p_n)}$ be $n$ elements with priorities $p_i$ $(0 \leq p_i \leq m - 1)$.

i) Implement PQUE using multiple circular queues one for each priority number.

ii) Implement PQUE as a two-dimensional array ARR_PQUE[$1{:}m, 1{:}d$], where $m$ is the number of priority values and $d$ is the maximum number of data items with a given priority.

iii) Execute insertions and deletions presented in a random sequence.

4) A deque DQUE is to be implemented using a circular one-dimensional array of size N. Execute procedures to:

i) insert and delete elements from DQUE at either end;

ii) implement DQUE as an output restricted deque;

iii) implement DQUE as an input restricted deque;

iv) for the procedures, what are the conditions used for testing whether DQUE is full (DQUE_FULL) and empty (DQUE_EMPTY)?

5) Execute a general data structure that is a deque supporting insertions and deletions at both ends but, depending on the choice input by the user, functions as a stack or a queue.

6) Write a program that checks if a string is a palindrome by making use of a single stack and a single queue. (Hint: Stack helps to read the string in its reverse order and a queue the same in the forward direction.)

# 6

---

# Linked Lists

---

In Chapters 3-5 we dealt with arrays, stacks and queues, which are linear sequential data structures (among the three, stacks and queues have a linked representation as well, which will be discussed in Chapter 7).

In this chapter, we detail linear data structures with a linked representation. We first list the demerits of the sequential data structure before introducing the need for a linked representation. Next, the linked data structures of singly linked list, circularly linked list, doubly linked list, multiply linked list, unrolled linked list and self-organizing linked list are elaborately presented. Finally, two problems, namely, polynomial addition and sparse matrix representation, demonstrating the application of linked lists are discussed.

## 6.1. Introduction

### 6.1.1. *Drawbacks of sequential data structures*

Arrays are fundamental sequential data structures. Even stacks and queues rely on arrays for their representation and implementation. However, arrays or sequential data structures in general suffer from the following drawbacks:

i) inefficient implementation of insertion and deletion operations;

ii) inefficient use of storage memory.

Let us consider an array A[1: 20]. This means a contiguous set of 20 memory locations have been made available to accommodate the data elements of A. As shown in Figure 6.1(a), let us suppose the array is partially full. Now, to insert a new element 108 in the position indicated, it is not possible to do so without affecting the neighboring data elements. Methods such as making use of a temporary array (B) to hold the data elements of A with 108 inserted at the appropriate position, or making use of B to hold the data elements of A that follow 108 before copying B into A, call for extensive data movement, which is computationally expensive. Again, attempting to delete 217 from A calls for the use of a temporary array B to hold the elements with 217 excluded before copying B to A (see Figure 6.1(b)).

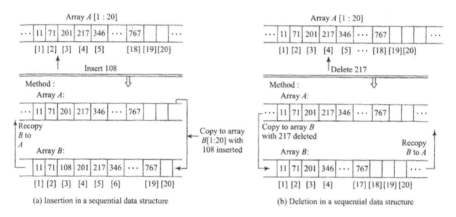

(a) Insertion in a sequential data structure            (b) Deletion in a sequential data structure

**Figure 6.1.** *Drawbacks of sequential data structures – inefficient implementation of insertion/deletion operations*

With regard to the second drawback of inefficient storage memory management, the need to allott contiguous memory locations for every array declaration is bound to leave fragments of free memory space unworthy of allotment for future requests. This may eventually lead to inefficient storage management. In fact, *fragmentation of memory* is a significant problem to be considered in computer science. Several methods have been proposed to counteract this problem.

Figure 6.2 shows a naïve diagram of a storage memory with fragmentation of free space.

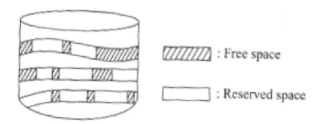

**Figure 6.2.** *Drawbacks of sequential data structures – inefficient storage memory management*

Note how fragments of free memory space, which when put together could be a huge chunk of free space, are rendered unworthy of accommodating sequential data structures due to lack of contiguity.

### 6.1.2. Merits of linked data structures

A linked representation serves to counteract the drawbacks of sequential representation by exhibiting the following merits:

i) Efficient implementation of insertion and deletion operations: Unlike sequential data structures, there is a complete absence of data movement of neighboring elements during the execution of these operations.

ii) Efficient use of storage memory: The operation and management of linked data structures are less prone to instigate memory fragmentation.

### 6.1.3. Linked lists – structure and implementation

A linked representation of a data structure known as a *linked list* is a collection of *nodes*. Each node is a collection of *fields* categorized as *data items* and *links*. The data item fields hold the information content or data to be represented by the node. The link fields hold the addresses of the neighboring nodes or of those nodes that are associated with the given node as dictated by the application.

Figure 6.3 illustrates the general node structure of a linked list. A node is represented by a rectangular box, and the fields are shown by partitions in the box. Link fields are shown to carry arrows to indicate the nodes to which the given node is linked or connected.

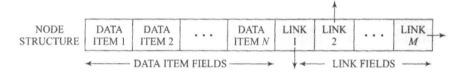

**Figure 6.3.** *A general structure of a node in a linked list*

This implies that unlike arrays, no two nodes in a linked list need to be physically contiguous. All the nodes in a linked list data structure may in fact be strewn across the storage memory, making effective use of what little space is available to represent a node. However, the link fields carry on the onerous responsibility of remembering the addresses of the other neighboring or associated nodes themselves to keep track of the data elements in the list.

In the programming language parlance, the link fields are referred to as ***pointers***. In this book, pointers and link fields will be interchangeably used in several contexts.

To implement linked lists, the following mechanisms are essential:

i) A mechanism to frame chunks of memory into nodes with the desired number of data items and fields. In most programming languages, this mechanism is implemented by making use of a "record" or "structure" or their look-alikes or even associated structures to represent the node and its fields.

ii) A mechanism to determine which nodes are free and which have been allotted for use.

iii) A mechanism to obtain nodes from the free storage area or storage pool for use. These are wholly provided and managed by the system. There is very little that an end user or a programmer can do to handle this mechanism themselves. This is made possible in many programming languages by the provision of inbuilt functions that help execute requests for a node with the specific fields. In this book, we make use of a function **GETNODE (X)** to implement this mechanism. The GETNODE (X) function allots a node of the desired structure and the address of the node, namely, X, is returned. In other words, X is an *output parameter* of the function GETNODE (X), whose value is determined and returned by the system.

iv) A mechanism to return or dispose nodes from the reserved area or pool to the free area after use. This is also made possible in many programming languages by providing an in-built function that helps return or dispose the node after use. In this book, we make use of the function **RETURN (X)** to implement this mechanism. The RETURN (X) function returns a node with address X from the reserved area of the pool to the free area of the pool. In other words, X is an *input parameter* of the function, the value of which is to be provided by the user.

Irrespective of the number of data item fields, a linked list is categorized as a ***singly linked list,*** a ***doubly linked list,*** a ***circularly linked list*** and a ***multiply linked list*** based on the number of link fields it owns and/or its intrinsic nature. Thus, a linked list with a ***single link field*** is known as a ***singly linked list,*** and the list with *circular connectivity* is known as a ***circularly linked list***. On the other hand, a linked list with *two links each pointing to the predecessor and successor* of a node is known as a ***doubly linked list,*** and the same with *multiple links* is known as a ***multiply linked list***. The following sections discuss these categories of linked lists in detail.

## 6.2. Singly linked lists

### 6.2.1. *Representation of a singly linked list*

A *singly linked list* is a linear data structure, each node of which has one or more data item fields (DATA), but only a *single link field* (LINK).

Figure 6.4 illustrates an example singly linked list and its node structure. Observe that the node in the list carries a single link that points to the node representing its immediate successor in the list of data elements.

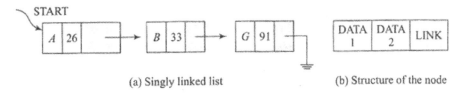

(a) Singly linked list                    (b) Structure of the node

**Figure 6.4.** *A singly linked list and its node structure*

Every node that is basically a chunk of memory carries an address. When a set of data elements to be used by an application are represented using a linked list, each data element is represented by a node. Depending on the information content of the data element, one or more data items may be opened in the node.

However, in a singly linked list, only a single link field is used to point to the node that represents its neighboring element in the list. The last node in the linked list has its link field empty. The empty link field is also referred to as *null link* or in programming language parlance – *null pointer*. The notation **NIL**, a ground symbol ( ⏚ ) or a zero (**0**) are commonly used to indicate null links.

The entire linked list is kept track of by remembering the address of the *start node*. This is indicated by START in the figure. Obviously, it is essential that the START pointer is carefully handled, otherwise it may result in losing the entire list.

#### EXAMPLE 6.1.–

Consider a list SPACE-MISSION of four data elements, as shown in Figure 6.5(a). This logical representation of the list has each node carrying three DATA fields, namely, name of the space mission, country of origin, the current status of the mission and a single link pointing to the next node. Let us suppose the nodes that house "Chandra", "INSAT-3A", "Mir" and "Planck" have addresses 1001, 16002,

0026 and 8456, respectively. Figure 6.5(b) shows the physical representation of the linked list. Note how the nodes are distributed all over the storage memory and not physically contiguous. Additionally, we observe how the LINK field of each node remembers the address of the node of its logical neighbor. The LINK field of the last node is NIL. The arrows in the logical representation represent the addresses of the neighboring nodes in its physical representation.

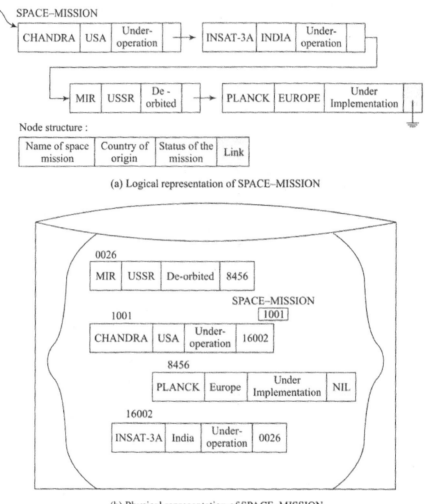

(a) Logical representation of SPACE–MISSION

(b) Physical representation of SPACE–MISSION

**Figure 6.5.** *A singly linked list – its logical and physical representation*

## 6.2.2. *Insertion and deletion in a singly linked list*

To implement insertion and deletion in a singly linked list, we need the two functions introduced in section 6.1.3, namely, GETNODE (X) and RETURN (X), respectively.

### 6.2.2.1. *Insert operation*

Given a singly linked list START, to insert a data element ITEM into the list to the right of node NODE (ITEM is to be inserted as the successor of the data element represented by node NODE), the steps to be undertaken are given below. Figure 6.6 illustrates the logical representation of the insert operation.

i) **Call GETNODE**(X) to obtain a node to accommodate ITEM. Node has address X.

ii) Set the DATA field of node X to ITEM, that is, DATA (X) = ITEM.

iii) Set the LINK field of node X to point to the original right neighbor of node NODE, that is, LINK(X) = LINK(NODE).

iv) Set LINK field of NODE to point to X, that is, LINK (NODE) = X. The resetting of the link is denoted by the rightwards arrow with stroke (↛) representing the removal of the old link and the rightwards arrow (→) showing the new/active link.

Algorithm 6.1 illustrates a pseudo-code procedure for insertion in a singly linked list that is non-empty.

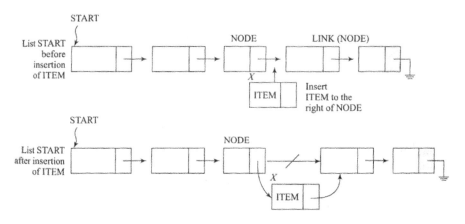

**Figure 6.6**. *Logical representation of insertion in a singly linked list*

```
procedure  INSERT_SL(START, ITEM, NODE)
/* Insert ITEM to the right of node  NODE in the list
START */
  Call GETNODE(X);
  DATA(X) = ITEM;
  LINK(X) = LINK(NODE);   /* Node X points to the
              original right neighbour of node NODE */
  LINK(NODE) = X;
end INSERT_SL.
```

**Algorithm 6.1.** *To insert a data element ITEM in a non-empty singly liked list START to the right of node NODE*

However, during the insert operation in a list, it is advisable to test whether the START pointer is null or non-null. If the START pointer is null (START = **NIL**), then the singly linked list is empty, and hence, the insert operation prepares to insert the data as the first node in the list. On the other hand, if the START pointer is non-null (START ≠ **NIL**), then the singly linked list is non-empty, and hence, the insert operation prepares to insert the data at an appropriate position in the list as specified by the application. Algorithm 6.1 works on a non-empty list. To handle empty lists, the algorithm must be appropriately modified, as illustrated in Algorithm 6.2.

In sheer contrast to an insert operation in a sequential data structure, observe the total absence of data movement in the list during insertion of ITEM. The insert operation merely calls for the update of two links in the case of a non-empty list.

```
procedure  INSERT_SL_GEN(START, NODE, ITEM)
/*  Insert ITEM as the first node in the list if START
is NIL. Otherwise insert ITEM after node  NODE */
  Call GETNODE(X);
  DATA(X) = ITEM;          /* Create node for ITEM */
  if (START = NIL) then
    {LINK(X) = NIL;                /* List is empty*/
     START = X;}/*Insert ITEM as the first node */
  else
      {LINK(X) = LINK(NODE);
       LINK(NODE) = X;} /* List is non empty. Insert
              ITEM to the right of node NODE */
end INSERT_SL_GEN.
```

**Algorithm 6.2.** *To insert ITEM after node NODE in a singly linked list START*

## EXAMPLE 6.2.–

In the singly linked list SPACE-MISSION illustrated in Figures 6.5(a) and (b), insert the following data elements:

| i) | APPOLLO | USA | Landed |
|---|---|---|---|
| ii) | SOYUZ 4 | USSR | Landed |

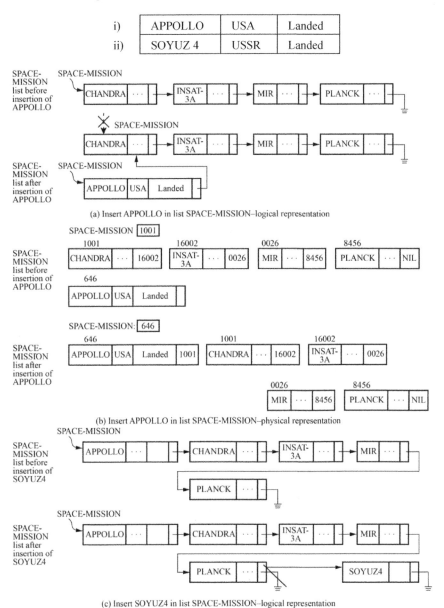

(a) Insert APPOLLO in list SPACE-MISSION–logical representation

(b) Insert APPOLLO in list SPACE-MISSION–physical representation

(c) Insert SOYUZ4 in list SPACE-MISSION–logical representation

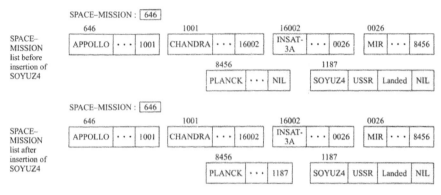

(d) Insert SOYUZ4 in list SPACE–MISSION—physical representation

**Figure 6.7.** *Insertion of APPOLLO and SOYUZ 4 in the SPACE_MISSION list shown in Figures 6.5(a) and (b)*

Let us suppose the **GETNODE**(X) function releases nodes with addresses X = 646 and X = 1187 to accommodate APPOLLO and SOYUZ 4 details, respectively. The insertion of APPOLLO is illustrated in Figures 6.7(a) and (b), and the insertion of SOYUZ 4 is illustrated in Figures 6.7(c) and (d).

### 6.2.2.2. Delete operation

Given a singly linked list START, the delete operation can acquire various forms, such as deletion of a node NODEY next to that of a specific node NODEX or, more commonly, deletion of a particular element in a list. We now illustrate the deletion of a node that is the successor of node NODEX.

The steps for the deletion of a node next to that of NODEX in a singly linked START are given below. Figure 6.8 illustrates the logical representation of the delete operation. The dashed rightward arrows with strokes (-/->) in the figure denote deleted links.

i) Set TEMP a temporary variable to point to the right neighbor of NODEX, that is, TEMP = LINK (NODEX). The node pointed to by TEMP is to be deleted.

ii) Set the LINK field of node NODEX to point to the right neighbor of TEMP, that is, LINK (NODEX) = LINK (TEMP).

iii) Dispose of node TEMP, that is, RETURN (TEMP).

Algorithm 6.3 illustrates a pseudo-code procedure for the deletion of a node that occurs to the right of a node NODEX in a singly linked list START. However, as always, it must be ensured that the delete operation is not undertaken over an empty list. Hence, it is essential to check if START is empty.

```
procedure  DELETE_SL(START, NODEX)
   if (START = NIL) then
      Call ABANDON_DELETE;/*ABANDON_DELETE terminates
                           the delete operation */
   else
      {TEMP = LINK(NODEX);
      LINK(NODEX) = LINK(TEMP);
      Call RETURN(TEMP);}

end DELETE_SL.
```

**Algorithm 6.3.** *Deletion of a node to the right*
*of node NODEX in a singly linked list START*

Observe how in contrast to deletion in a sequential data structure, which involves data movement, the deletion of a node in a linked list merely calls for the update of a single link.

Example 6.3 illustrates the deletion of a node in a singly linked list.

### EXAMPLE 6.3.–

The SPACE-MISSION list shown in Figures 6.5(a) and (b) undertakes the following deletions:

i) delete CHANDRA;

ii) delete PLANCK.

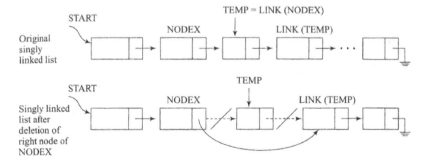

**Figure 6.8.** *Logical representation of deletion in a singly linked list*

The deletion of CHANDRA is illustrated in Figures 6.9(a) and (b), and the deletion of PLANCK is illustrated in Figures 6.9(c) and (d).

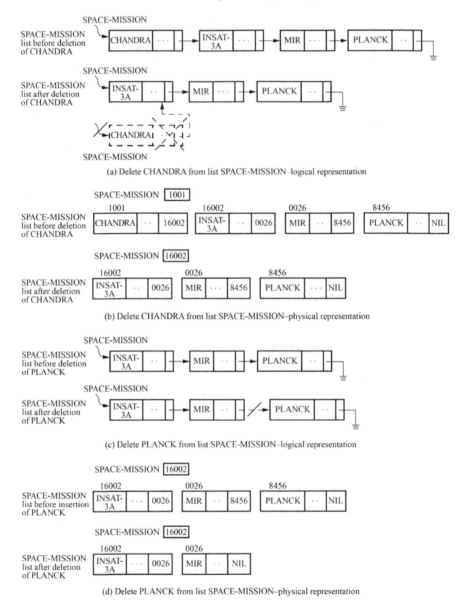

(a) Delete CHANDRA from list SPACE-MISSION–logical representation

(b) Delete CHANDRA from list SPACE-MISSION–physical representation

(c) Delete PLANCK from list SPACE-MISSION–logical representation

(d) Delete PLANCK from list SPACE-MISSION–physical representation

**Figure 6.9.** *Deletion of CHANDRA and PLANCK from the SPACE-MISSION list*

## 6.3. Circularly linked lists

### 6.3.1. *Representation*

A normal singly linked list has its last node carrying a null pointer. For further improvement in processing, we may replace the null pointer in the last node with the address of the first node in the list. Such a list is called a *circularly linked list*, a *circular linked list* or simply a *circular list*. Figure 6.10 illustrates the representation of a circular list.

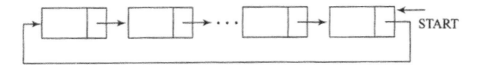

**Figure 6.10.** *Representation of a circular list*

### 6.3.2. *Advantages of circularly linked lists over singly linked lists*

i) The most important advantage pertains to the accessibility of a node. We can access any node from a given node due to the circular movement permitted by the links. We merely have to loop through the links to reach a specific node from a given node.

ii) The second advantage pertains to delete operations. Recall that for deletion of a node X in a singly linked list, the address of the preceding node (e.g. node Y) is essential to enable updating the LINK field of Y to point to the successor of node X. This necessity arises from the fact that in a singly linked list, we cannot access a node's predecessor due to the "forward" movement of the links. In other words, LINK fields in a singly linked list point to successors and not predecessors.

However, in the case of a circular list, to delete node X, we do not need to specify the predecessor. It can be easily determined by a simple "circular" search through the list before the deletion of node X.

iii) The third advantage is the relative efficiency in the implementation of list-based operations, such as concatenation of two lists, erasing a whole list, splitting a list into parts and so on.

### 6.3.3. *Disadvantages of circularly linked lists*

The only disadvantage of circularly linked lists is that during processing, we have to make sure that we do not enter an infinite loop owing to the circular nature of pointers in the list. This is liable to occur owing to the absence of a node that can help point out the end of the list and thereby terminate processing.

A solution to this problem is to designate a special node to act as the head of the list. This node, known as the *list head* or *head node,* has advantages other than pointing to the beginning of a list. The list can never be empty and represented by a "hanging" pointer (START = NIL), as was the case with empty singly linked lists. The condition for an empty circular list becomes (LINK (HEAD) = HEAD), where HEAD points to the head node of the list. Such a circular list is known as a *headed circularly linked list* or simply *circularly linked list with head node*. Figure 6.11 illustrates the representation of a headed circularly linked list.

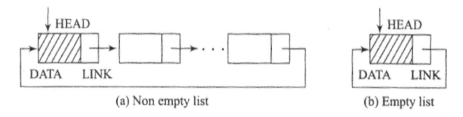

(a) Non empty list                    (b) Empty list

**Figure 6.11.** *A headed circularly linked list*

Although the head node has the same structure as the other nodes in the list, the DATA field of the node is unused and is indicated as a shaded field in the pictorial representation. However, in practical applications, these fields may be utilized to represent any useful information about the list relevant to the application, provided they are deftly handled and do not create confusion during the processing of the nodes.

Example 6.4 illustrates the functioning of circularly linked lists.

### EXAMPLE 6.4.–

Let CARS be a headed circularly linked list of four data elements, as shown in Figure 6.12(a). To insert MARUTI into the list CARS, the sequence of steps to be undertaken are as shown in Figures 6.12(b–d). To delete FORD from the list CARS shown in Figure 6.13(a), the sequence of steps to be undertaken is shown in Figures 6.13(b–d).

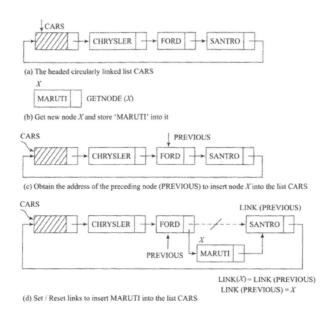

(a) The headed circularly linked list CARS

(b) Get new node *X* and store 'MARUTI' into it

(c) Obtain the address of the preceding node (PREVIOUS) to insert node *X* into the list CARS

LINK(*X*) = LINK (PREVIOUS)
LINK (PREVIOUS) = *X*

(d) Set / Reset links to insert MARUTI into the list CARS

**Figure 6.12.** *Insertion of MARUTI into the headed circularly linked list CARS*

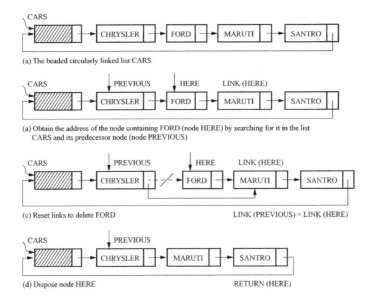

(a) The beaded circularly linked list CARS

(a) Obtain the address of the node containing FORD (node HERE) by searching for it in the list CARS and its predecessor node (node PREVIOUS)

(c) Reset links to delete FORD            LINK (PREVIOUS) = LINK (HERE)

(d) Dispose node HERE            RETURN (HERE)

**Figure 6.13.** *Deletion of FORD from the headed circularly linked list CARS*

### 6.3.4. *Primitive operations on circularly linked lists*

Some of the important primitive operations executed on a circularly linked list are detailed below. Here, P is a circularly linked list as illustrated in Figure 6.14(a).

i) Insert an element A as the left most element in the list represented by P.

The sequence of operations to execute the insertion is given as

```
Call GETNODE(X);
DATA(X) = A;
LINK(X) = LINK(P);
LINK(P) = X;
```

Figure 6.14(b) illustrates the insertion of A as the left most element in the circular list P.

ii) Insert an element A as the right most element in the list represented by P.

The sequence of operations to execute the insertion is the same as that of inserting A as the left most element in the list followed by the instruction.

```
P = X
```

Figure 6.14(c) illustrates the insertion of A as the right most element in list P.

iii) Set Y to the data of the left most node in list P and delete the node.

The sequence of operations to execute the deletion is given as

```
PTR = LINK(P);
Y = DATA(PTR);
LINK(P) = LINK(PTR);
Call RETURN(PTR);
```

Here, PTR is a temporary pointer variable. Figure 6.14(d) illustrates the deletion of the left most node in list P, setting Y to its data.

Observe that the primitive operations (i) and (iii), when combined, result in the circularly linked list working as a stack, and operations (ii) and (iii), when combined, result in the circularly linked list working as a queue.

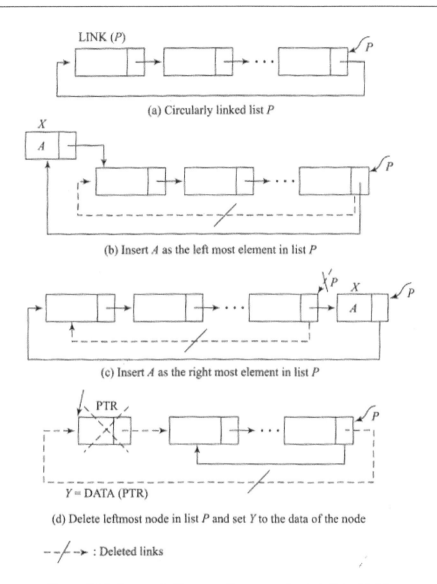

(a) Circularly linked list *P*

(b) Insert *A* as the left most element in list *P*

(c) Insert *A* as the right most element in list *P*

*Y* = DATA (PTR)

(d) Delete leftmost node in list *P* and set *Y* to the data of the node

$--\!\!\!/\!\!\rightarrow$ : Deleted links

**Figure 6.14.** *Some primitive operations on a circularly linked list P*

## 6.3.5. *Other operations on circularly linked lists*

The concatenation of two circularly linked lists L1 and L2, as illustrated in Figure 6.15, has the following sequence of instructions.

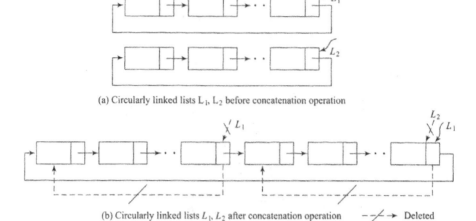

(a) Circularly linked lists $L_1$, $L_2$ before concatenation operation

(b) Circularly linked lists $L_1$, $L_2$ after concatenation operation    --⁄→ Deleted links

——→ Links after concatenation

**Figure 6.15.** *Concatenation of two circularly linked lists*

```
if L1 ≠ NIL then
      { if L2 ≠ NIL then
              {TEMP = LINK (L1)
               LINK(L1) = LINK(L2)
               LINK(L2) = TEMP
               L1 = L2
            }
      }
```

The other operations are, splitting a list into two parts (see programming assignment 2) and erasing a list.

## 6.4. Doubly linked lists

In sections 6.2 and 6.3, we discussed two types of linked representations, namely, singly linked list and circularly linked list, both making use of a single link. Additionally, the circularly linked list served to rectify the drawbacks of the singly linked list. To enhance greater flexibility of movement, the linked representation could include two links in every node, each of which points to the nodes on either side of the given node. Such a linked representation known as a *doubly linked list* is discussed in this section.

### 6.4.1. *Representation of a doubly linked list*

A *doubly linked list* is a linked linear data structure, each node of which has one or more data fields, but only two link fields termed the *left link* (LLINK) and *right link* (RLINK). The LLINK field of a given node points to the node on its left, and its RLINK field points to the node on its right. A doubly linked list may or may not have a head node. Again, it may or may not be circular.

Figure 6.16 illustrates the structure of a node in a doubly linked list and the various types of lists.

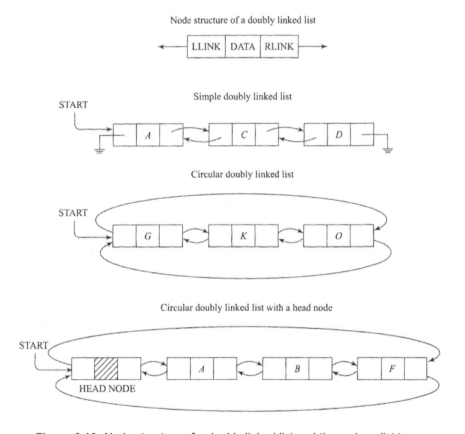

**Figure 6.16.** *Node structure of a doubly linked list and the various list types*

Example 6.5 illustrates a doubly linked list and its logical and physical representations.

## Example 6.5.–

Consider    a    list    FLOWERS    of    four    data    elements    LOTUS, CHRYSANTHEMUM, LILY and TULIP stored as a circular doubly linked list with a head node. The logical and physical representation of FLOWERS is illustrated in Figures 6.17(a) and (b). Observe how the LLINK and RLINK fields store the addresses of the predecessors and successors of the given node, respectively. In the case of FLOWERS being an empty list, the representation is shown in Figures 6.17(c) and (d).

### 6.4.2. Advantages and disadvantages of a doubly linked list

Doubly linked lists have the following advantages:

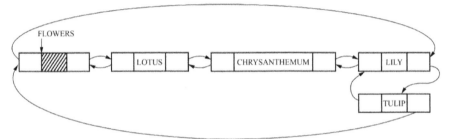

(a) Logical representation of a circular doubly linked list with a head node FLOWERS

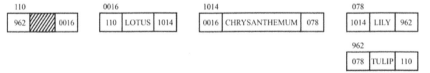

(b) Physical representation of a circular doubly linked list with a head node (FLOWERS)

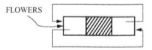

(c) Logical representation of an empty circular doubly linked list with a head node (FLOWERS)

(d) Physical representation of an empty circular doubly linked list with a head node

**Figure 6.17.** *The logical and physical representation of a circular doubly linked list with a head node, FLOWERS*

i) The availability of two links, LLINK and RLINK, permits forward and backward movement during the processing of the list.

ii) The deletion of a node X from the list calls only for the value X to be known. Note how in the case of a singly linked or circularly linked list, the delete operation necessarily needs to know the predecessor of the node to be deleted. While a singly linked list expects the predecessor of the node to be deleted to be explicitly known, a circularly linked list is endowed with the capability to move around the list to find the predecessor node. However, in the latter case, if the list is too long, it may render the delete operation inefficient.

The only disadvantage of the doubly linked list is its memory requirement. Each node needs two links, which could be considered expensive storagewise when compared to singly linked lists or circular lists. Nevertheless, the efficiency of operations due to the availability of two links more than compensates for the extra space requirement.

### 6.4.3. Operations on doubly linked lists

An insert and delete operation on a doubly linked list are detailed here.

#### 6.4.3.1. Insert operation

Let P be a headed circular doubly linked list that is non-empty. Algorithm 6.4 illustrates the insertion of a node X to the right of node Y. Figure 6.18(a) shows the logical representation of list P before and after insertion.

```
procedure  INSERT_DL(X, Y)
   LLINK(X)  = Y;
   RLINK(X)  = RLINK(Y);
   LLINK(RLINK(Y))  = X;
   RLINK(Y)  = X;
end INSERT_DL.
```

**Algorithm 6.4.** *To insert node X to the right
of node Y in a headed circular doubly linked list P*

Note how the four instructions in Algorithm 6.4 correspond to the setting/resetting of the four link fields, namely, links pertaining to node Y, its original right neighbor (RLINK(Y)) and node X.

### 6.4.3.2. *Delete operation*

Let P be a headed, circular doubly linked list. Algorithm 6.5 illustrates the deletion of a node X from P. The condition (X = P) that is checked ensures that the head node P is not deleted. Figure 6.18(b) shows the logical representation of list P before and after the deletion of node X from list P.

```
procedure  DELETE_DL(P, X)
   if (X = P) then  ABANDON_DELETE;
   else
        {RLINK(LLINK(X)) = RLINK(X);
         LLINK(RLINK(X)) = LLINK(X);
         Call RETURN(X); }
   end DELETE_DL.
```

**Algorithm 6.5.** *Delete node X from a headed circular doubly linked list P*

Note how the two instructions pertaining to links, in Algorithm 6.5, correspond to the setting/resetting of link fields of the two nodes, namely, the predecessor (LLINK(X)) and successor (RLINK(X)) of node X.

Example 6.6 illustrates the insert/delete operation on a doubly linked list PLANET.

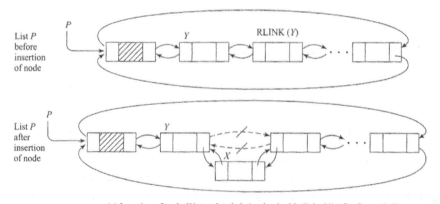

(a) Insertion of node *X* into a headed circular doubly linked list *P*, after node *Y*

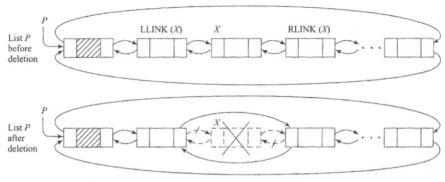

(b) Deletion of node $X$ from a headed circular doubly linked list $P$

**Figure 6.18.** *Insertion/deletion in a headed circular doubly linked list*

## EXAMPLE 6.6.–

Let PLANET be a headed circular doubly linked list with three data elements, namely, MARS, PLUTO and URANUS. Figure 6.19 illustrates the logical and physical representation of the list PLANET. Figure 6.20(a) illustrates the logical and physical representation of list PLANET after the deletion of PLUTO, and Figure 6.20(b) shows the same after the insertion of JUPITER.

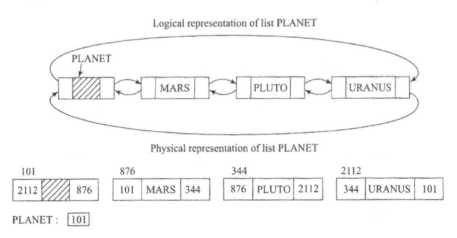

**Figure 6.19.** *Logical and physical representation of list PLANET*

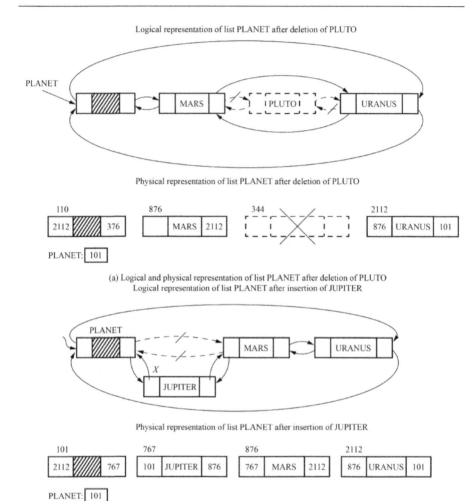

(a) Logical and physical representation of list PLANET after deletion of PLUTO

(b) Logical and physical representation of list PLANET after insertion of JUPITER

**Figure 6.20.** *Deletion of PLUTO and insertion of JUPITER in list PLANET*

## 6.5. Multiply linked lists

A multiply linked list, as its name suggests, is a linked representation with multiple data and link fields. A general node structure of a multiply linked list is shown in Figure 6.21.

Since each link field connects a group of nodes representing the data elements of a global list L, the multiply linked representation of the list L is a network of nodes that are connected to one another based on some association. The link fields may or may not render their respective lists to be circular, or may or may not possess a head node.

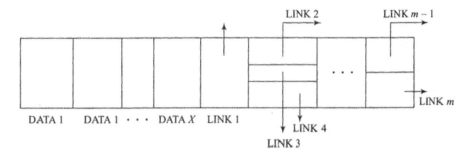

**Figure 6.21.** *The node structure of a multiply linked list*

Example 6.7 illustrates an example of multiple linked list.

## EXAMPLE 6.7.–

Let STUDENT be a multiply linked list representation whose node structure is as shown in Figure 6.22. Here, the SPORTS-CLUB-MEM link field links all student nodes who are members of the sports club, DEPT-ENROLL links all students enrolled with a given department and DAY-STUDENT links all students enrolled as day students.

Consider Table 6.1, which illustrates details pertaining to six students.

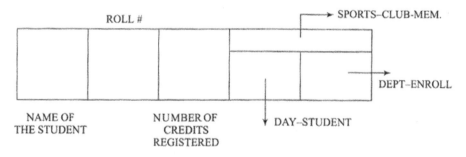

**Figure 6.22.** *Node structure of the multiply linked list STUDENT*

| Name of the student | Roll # | Number of credits registered | Sports club membership | Day student | Department |
|---|---|---|---|---|---|
| AKBAR | CS02 | 200 | Yes | Yes | Computer science |
| RAM | ME426 | 210 | No | Yes | Mechanical sciences |
| SINGH | ME927 | 210 | Yes | No | Mechanical sciences |
| YASSER | CE467 | 190 | Yes | No | Civil engineering |
| SITA | CE544 | 190 | No | Yes | Civil engineering |
| REBECCA | EC424 | 220 | Yes | No | Electronics and communication engineering |

**Table 6.1.** *Student details for representation as a multiply linked list*

The multiply linked structure of the data elements in Table 6.1 is shown in Figure 6.23. Here, S is a singly linked list of all sports club members, and DS is the singly linked list of all day students. Note how the DEPT-ENROLL link field maintains individual singly linked lists COMP-SC, MECH-SC, CIVIL ENGG and ECE to keep track of the students enrolled with the respective departments.

To insert a new node with the following details,

| ALI | CS108 | 200 | Yes | Yes | Computer Science |
|---|---|---|---|---|---|

into the list STUDENTS, the procedure is similar to that of insertion in singly linked lists. The point of insertion is to be determined by the user. The resultant list is shown in Figure 6.24. Here, we have inserted ALI in the alphabetical order of students enrolled with the computer science department.

To delete REBECCA from the list of sports club members of the multiply linked list STUDENT, we undertake a sequence of operations, as shown in Figure 6.25. Observe how the node for REBECCA continues to participate in the other lists despite its deletion from the list S.

A multiply linked list can be designed to accommodate much flexibility with respect to its links, depending on the needs and suitability of the application.

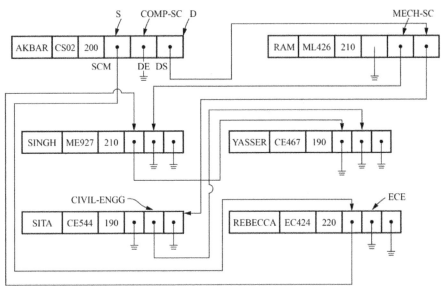

SCM: SPORTS-CLUB-MEME link field
DE: DEPT ENROLL link field
DS: DAY-STUDENT link field
S: List of sports club members
D: List of day students
Comp. SC: List of students enrolled with the
          Dept. of Computer Science

CIVIL-ENGG: List of students enrolled
          with the Dept. of Civil Engg.
MECH-SC: List of students enrolled with
          the Dept. of Mech Sc.
ECE: List of students enrolled with the
          the Dept. of E.C.E.

**Figure 6.23.** *Multiply linked list structure of list STUDENT*

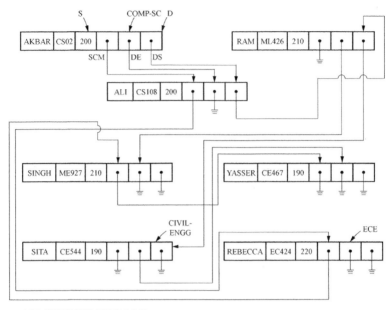

SCM: SPORTS-CLUB-MEM link field
DE: DEPT-ENTOLL link field
DS: DAY-STUDENT link field

**Figure 6.24.** *Insert ALI into the multiply linked list STUDENT*

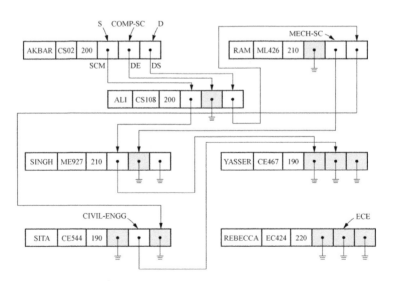

**Figure 6.25.** *Delete REBECCA from the sports club membership list of the multiply linked list STUDENTS*

## 6.6. Unrolled linked lists

*Unrolled linked lists* are "hybrid" data structures in that they combine the benefits of using an array data structure with those of the linked list data structure. As a result, they display the dual merits of small memory overheads of arrays coupled with efficient insert/delete operations of linked lists.

Unrolled linked lists are therefore variants of linked lists considering the fact that the nodes of an unrolled linked list hold an array of elements in addition to a link that helps to point to its neighboring node. The size of the array can even be large enough to fill a single cache line or its multiples thereof; therefore, unrolled linked lists can serve to improve cache performance while decreasing the memory overheads.

Since the operations of insert/delete undertaken on an unrolled linked list are sensitive to the number of elements stored in the array, it would be prudent to open an extra field in the node that keeps count of the number of elements currently stored in the node's array. Additionally, for efficient storage management, it is mandatory that each node in an unrolled linked list must have satisfied a *minimum level of storage utilization*. Thus, for example, at any point in time, a node in an unrolled linked list must be at least half full if the minimum storage utilization is set to 50%. In this discussion, we use half-full as the storage utilization factor.

Figure 6.26 shows the structure of a node in an unrolled linked list. An example unrolled linked list is shown in example 6.8.

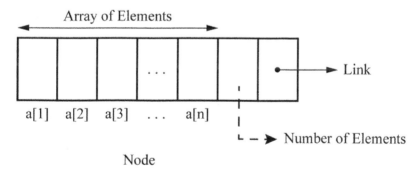

**Figure 6.26.** *Structure of a node in an unrolled linked list*

## EXAMPLE 6.8.–

T is an unrolled linked list with three nodes, NODE1, NODE2 and NODE3, and with each node storing an array of size 5. The field LINK points to the next node in the list, and the field NUMBER_OF_ELEMENTS stores the number of elements currently stored in the array. Figure 6.27 illustrates an example unrolled linked list T.

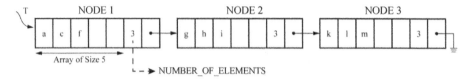

**Figure 6.27.** *An example unrolled linked list*

### 6.6.1. *Retrieval of an element*

To retrieve an element from an unrolled linked list, it is essential that the address of the node and the index of the array element, which determine the position of the element, are known. Thus, to retrieve an element, it may be essential to move down the list with the help of the link field to spot the node concerned and then retrieve the element from the array. For example, to retrieve element *k* whose address is (NODE 3 – [1]), we have to move down the list tracking NODE 3 and then access the element stored in index [1] of the array in the node concerned.

### 6.6.2. *Insert an element*

Given the position of insertion, the insertion operation in an unrolled linked list proceeds as if we are trying to retrieve the element from the list at the given position, but instead insert the element in the node at the position concerned. However, the following cases need to be considered during insertion.

If the node is half full, then simply store the element in the array in the first available empty cell available and increase the count in NUMBER_OF_ELEMENTS.

If the node is full and there is no space to insert the element, create a new node NEW_NODE that precedes or succeeds the node and move the appropriate half (lower half or upper half) of the elements in the current node to NEW_NODE before inserting the new element. Assuming that NEW_NODE was inserted as a successor to the current node, the upper half of the elements in the current node are first moved to NEW_NODE, and the new element to be inserted is stored in the first available empty cell of the array in NEW_NODE. The NUMBER_OF_ELEMENTS field in the current node is reset to NUMBER_OF_ELEMENTS/2, and the same in NEW_NODE is reset to (NUMBER_OF_ELEMENTS/2 +1).

### EXAMPLE 6.9.−

The insertion of elements p, q, r in NODE 3 of the unrolled linked list T shown in Figure 6.27 is demonstrated in Figure 6.28. The minimum level of storage utilization is fixed as ⌊5/2⌋=2, where the maximum size of the array in the node is 5. It can be seen that during the insertion of r, since NODE 3 is already full, the elements in the array of NODE 3 are split and accommodated in a new node NEW_NODE. Element r is inserted into NEW_NODE.

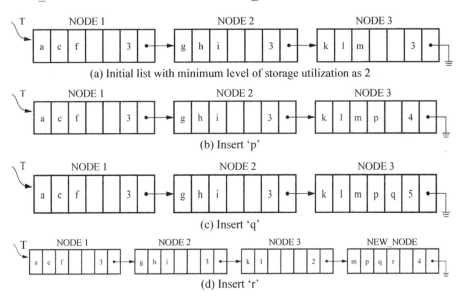

**Figure 6.28.** *Insertions in an unrolled linked list*

### 6.6.3. *Delete an element*

To delete an element, we proceed as if we were trying to retrieve the element, and once the location is reached, which is the node and the array cell concerned, the element is deleted. However, considering the minimum level of storage utilization insisted upon by unrolled linked lists, the following cases need to be considered for deletion:

i) if after deletion of the element from the node concerned, the minimum level of storage utilization does not fall below its stipulated level, then the deletion is done. Decrement the NUMBER_OF_ELEMENTS field in the node by 1;

ii) if after deletion of an element from the node concerned, the minimum level of storage utilization falls below its stipulated level, then the elements are transferred from its successor node NEXT_NODE to the current node until the minimum level of storage utilization is met. If this transfer, however, leaves NEXT_NODE short of its minimum level of storage utilization, then NEXT_NODE is merged with the current node. In both cases, the NUMBER_OF_ELEMENTS field is updated appropriately.

### EXAMPLE 6.10.–

The deletion of elements $i$ and $h$ demonstrated over the unrolled linked list shown in Figure 6.28(c) are shown in Figure 6.29. Observe how deletion of element $h$ results in NODE 2 falling below its minimum level and transferring element $k$ from NODE 3 to NODE 2 results in NODE 3 falling below its minimum level. Therefore, deletion of $h$ calls for the merging of the elements in the two nodes, namely, NODE 2 and NODE 3. The elements have been merged in NODE 2 and NODE 3 has been deleted.

It needs to be noted that while the generic retrieve, insert and delete operations on an unrolled linked list are as explained above, these operations could be fine-tuned to suit the application for which the data structure is used. Thus, the position that determines the point of insertion, the way elements are stored in the array and maintained during insertion/deletion of elements or the way the elements in the node are split or merged can all be determined based on the application or the user's needs.

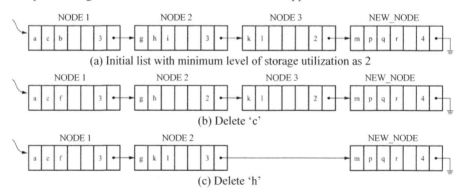

(a) Initial list with minimum level of storage utilization as 2

(b) Delete 'c'

(c) Delete 'h'

**Figure 6.29.** *Deletions in an unrolled linked list*

However, when compared to a singly linked list, the storage overheads for an unrolled linked list are undoubtedly higher. The time complexity of a retrieve or insert or delete operation turns out to be $O(n)$, where $n$ is the number of elements in the unrolled linked list, since all the operations involve moving down the list to spot their positions of execution, which in the worst case turns out to be $O(n)$. This includes the overheads of maintaining the array of elements in the node or splitting or merging nodes, as the case may be.

## 6.7. Self-organizing lists

In applications where frequent retrievals of data stored as a singly linked list are common, it pays well to organize the list in such a way that frequent data retrievals are efficiently handled. Maintaining the singly linked list as a sorted list yields a time complexity of $O(n)$ in the worst case, and the repeated retrievals of data only worsen the time complexity.

A prudent solution to this problem could be to adopt *self-organizing lists* that simply put, shift frequently accessed nodes to the beginning of the list. However, there needs to be a mechanism to prioritize nodes with frequent retrievals. The following are some methods that can be adopted to implement self-organizing lists.

i) *Count method*: Open a field COUNT in each node of the list. Every time a node is retrieved increment COUNT by 1. Reorganize the list according to the descending order of COUNT. However, this method incurs a storage overhead of an extra field in each node of the list and may involve frequent reorganization of the list.

ii) *Move to front method*: Every time a node is accessed move it to the front of the list, in the hope that further retrievals of the node would prove less expensive. The method does not require any extra storage and can be easily implemented. However, in the case of infrequently retrieved nodes, overrewarding such nodes by pushing them to the beginning of the list can severely affect the overall efficiency of retrievals in the list.

iii) *Transpose method*: Any node that is retrieved is swapped with its preceding node. The objective is to increase the priority of such nodes and keep them in the front portion of the list.

## 6.8. Applications

In this section, we discuss two applications of linked lists, namely,

i) addition of polynomials;

ii) representation of a sparse matrix.

The addition of polynomials is illustrative of the application of singly linked lists and sparse matrix representation is illustrative of the application of multiply linked lists.

## 6.8.1. Addition of polynomials

The objective of this application is to perform a symbolic addition of two polynomials, as illustrated below:

Let $P_1$: $2x^6 + x^3 + 5x + 4$;

$P_2$: $7x^6 + 8x^5 - 9x^3 + 10x^2 + 14$

be two polynomials over a variable $x$. The objective is to obtain the algebraic sum of $P_1$ and $P_2$, that is, $P_1 + P_2$ as,

$$P_1 + P_2 = 9x^6 + 8x^5 - 8x^3 + 10x^2 + 5x + 18$$

To perform this symbolic manipulation of the polynomials, we make use of a singly linked list to represent each polynomial. The node structure and the singly linked list representation for the two polynomials are given in Figure 6.30. Here, each node in the singly linked list represents a term of the polynomial.

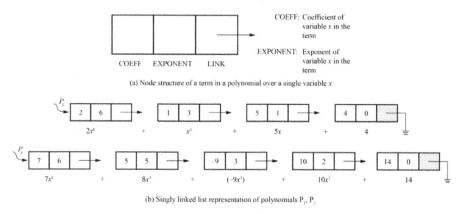

(a) Node structure of a term in a polynomial over a single variable $x$

(b) Singly linked list representation of polynomials $P_1$, $P_2$

**Figure 6.30.** *Addition of polynomials – node structure and singly linked list representation of polynomials*

To add the two polynomials, we presume that the singly linked lists have their nodes arranged in decreasing order of the exponents of the variable $x$.

The objective is to create a new list of nodes representing the sum $P_1 + P_2$. This is achieved by adding the COEFF fields of the nodes of similar powers of variable $x$ in lists $P_1$ and $P_2$ and adding a new node reflecting this operation in the resultant list $P_1 + P_2$. We present below the crux of the procedure.

Here, $P_1$ and $P_2$ are the starting pointers of the singly linked lists representing polynomials $P_1$ and $P_2$. Additionally, PTR1 and PTR2 are two temporary pointers initially set to $P_1$ and $P_2$, respectively.

```
if (EXPONENT(PTR1) = EXPONENT(PTR2)) then
            /*  PTR1 and PTR2 point to like terms */

if (COEFF(PTR1) + COEFF(PTR2)) ≠ 0 then
  {Call GETNODE(X);
  /* Perform the addition of terms and include  the
     result node as the last  node of list P₁ + P₂*/

  COEFF(X) = COEFF(PTR1) + COEFF(PTR2);
  EXPONENT(X)=EXPONENT(PTR1);
                            /*or EXPONENT(PTR2)*/

  LINK(X) = NIL;
  Add node X as the last node of the list P₁ + P₂'
  }

if  (EXPONENT(PTR1) <  EXPONENT(PTR2))  then
  /* PTR1 and PTR2 do not point to like terms */
            /* Duplicate  the node representing the
                highest power(i.e.) EXPONENT (PTR2) and
                insert it as the last node in P₁ + P₂*/

  {Call GETNODE(X);
  COEFF(X)  = COEFF(PTR2);
  EXPONENT(X) = EXPONENT(PTR2);
  LINK(X) = NIL;
  Add node X as the last node of list  P₁ + P₂;
  }
```

```
if   (EXPONENT (PTR1) > EXPONENT (PTR2)) then
/* PTR1 and PTR2 do not point to like terms. Hence
duplicate the node      representing the highest power
(i.e.) EXPONENT(PTR1) and insert it as the last node of
P₁ + P₂*/
   { Call GETNODE(X);
     COEFF(X)  = COEFF(PTR1);
     EXPONENT(X)  = EXPONENT(PTR1);
     LINK(X)  = NIL;
     Add node X as the last node of list P₁ + P₂;
   }
```

If any one of the lists during the course of the addition of terms has exhausted its nodes earlier than the other list, then the nodes of the other list are simply appended to list $P_1$ + $P_2$ in the order of their occurrence in their original list.

In the case of polynomials of two variables $x$ and $y$ or three variables $x$, $y$, and $z$, the node structures are as shown in Figure 6.31.

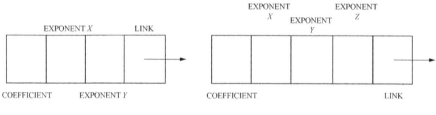

(a) Node structure of a polynomial in two variables          (b) Node structure of a polynomial in three variables

**Figure 6.31.** *Node structures of polynomials in two/three variables*

Here, COEFFICIENT refers to the coefficient of the term in the polynomial represented by the node. EXPONENT X, EXPONENT Y and EXPONENT Z are the exponents of variables $x$, $y$ and $z$, respectively.

### 6.8.2. *Sparse matrix representation*

The concept of sparse matrices is discussed in Chapter 3. An array representation for the efficient representation and manipulation of sparse matrices is discussed in section 3.5.1. In this section, we present a linked representation for the sparse matrix as an illustration of a multiply linked list.

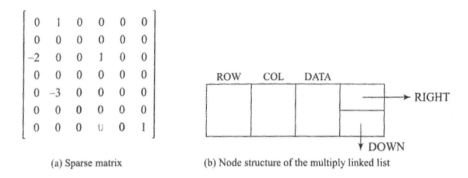

(a) Sparse matrix

(b) Node structure of the multiply linked list

**Figure 6.32.** *A sparse matrix and the node structure for its representation as a multiply linked list*

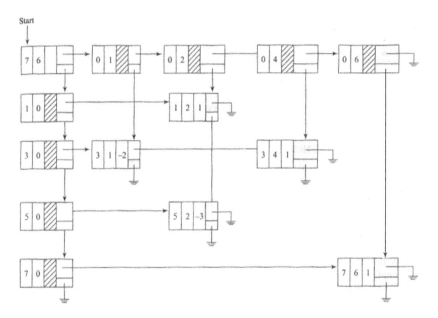

**Figure 6.33.** *Multiply linked representation of the sparse matrix shown in Figure 6.32(a)*

Consider the sparse matrix shown in Figure 6.32(a). The node structure for the linked representation of the sparse matrix is shown in Figure 6.32(b). Each non-zero element of the matrix is represented using the node structure. Here, the ROW, COL and DATA fields record the row, column and value of the non-zero element in the matrix. The RIGHT link points to the node holding the next non-zero value in the same row of the matrix. DOWN link points to the node holding the next non-zero value in the same column of the matrix. Thus, each non-zero value is linked to its rowwise and columnwise non-zero neighbors. The linked representation therefore ignores representing the zeros in the matrix.

Now, each of the fields connects together to form a singly linked list with a head node. Thus, all the nodes representing non-zero elements of a row in the matrix link themselves (through RIGHT LINK) to form a singly linked list with a head node. The number of such lists is equal to the number of rows in the matrix that contain at least one non-zero element. Similarly, all the nodes representing the non-zero elements of a column in the matrix link themselves (through the DOWN link) to form a singly linked list with a head node. The number of such lists is equal to the number of columns in the matrix that contain at least one non-zero element.

All the head nodes are also linked together to form a singly linked list. The head nodes of the row lists have their COL fields as zero, and the head nodes of the column lists have their ROW fields as zero. The head node of all head nodes, indicated by START, stores the dimension of the original matrix in its ROW and COL fields. Figure 6.29 shows the multiply linked list representation of the sparse matrix shown in Figure 6.28(a).

### ADT for links

**Data objects:**
Addresses of the nodes holding data and links

**Operations:**
- Allocate node (address X)  from Available Space to accommodate data
  GETNODE (X)
- Return node (address X) after use to   Available Space
  RETURN (X)
- Store a   value of  one  link  variable  LINK1  to another link variable LINK2
  STORE_LINK (LINK1, LINK2)
- Store  ITEM into  a node whose address is X
  STORE_DATA (X, ITEM)
- Retrieve  ITEM from  a node whose address is X
  RETRIEVE_DATA (X, ITEM)

## ADT for Singly Linked Lists

**Data objects:**
A list of nodes each holding   one (or more) data field(s) DATA and a  single link field LINK. LIST points to the start node of the list.

**Operations:**
- Check if  list LIST is empty
  CHECK_LIST_EMPTY (LIST)  (Boolean function)
- Insert ITEM into the list LIST as the first element
  INSERT_FIRST (LIST, ITEM)
- Insert ITEM into the list LIST as the last  element
  INSERT_LAST (LIST, ITEM)
- Insert ITEM into the list LIST in order
  INSERT_ORDER (LIST, ITEM)
- Delete the first node from the  list LIST
  DELETE_FIRST(LIST)
- Delete the last  node from the  list LIST
  DELETE_LAST(LIST)
- Delete ITEM from the  list LIST
  DELETE_ELEMENT (LIST, ITEM)
- Advance Link to traverse down the list
  ADVANCE_LINK (LINK)
- Store ITEM into a node whose address is X
  STORE_DATA(X, ITEM)
- Retrieve data of a node whose address is X  and return it in ITEM
  RETRIEVE_DATA(X, ITEM)
- Retrieve link of a node whose address is X and return the value in LINK1
  RETRIEVE_LINK (X, LINK1)

## Summary

– Sequential data structures suffer from the drawbacks of inefficient implementation of insert/delete operations and inefficient use of memory.

– A linked representation serves to rectify these drawbacks. However, it calls for the implementation of mechanisms such as GETNODE(X) and RETURN(X) to reserve a node for use and return the same to the free pool after use, respectively.

– A singly linked list is the simplest of a linked representation with one or more data fields, but with a single link field in its node structure that points to its successor. However, such a list has lesser flexibility and does not aid in an elegant performance of operation such as deletion.

– A circularly linked list is an enhancement of the singly linked list representation, in that the nodes are circularly linked. This not only provides better flexibility, but also results in a better rendering of the delete operation.

– A doubly linked list has one or more data items fields, but two links LLINK and RLINK pointing to the predecessor and successor of the node, respectively. Though the list exhibits the advantages of greater flexibility and efficient delete operation, it suffers from the drawback of increased storage requirement for the node structure in comparison to other linked representations.

– A multiply linked list is a linked representation with one or more data item fields and multiple link fields. A multiply linked list in its simplest form may represent a cluster of singly linked lists networked together.

– Unrolled linked lists are variants of linked lists that combine the best features of the array data structure with those of the linked list data structure.

– Self-organizing lists favor efficient handling of frequent data retrievals.

– The addition of polynomials and linked representation of a sparse matrix are two applications of linked lists.

## 6.9. Illustrative problems

### PROBLEM 6.1.–

Write a pseudo-code procedure to insert NEW_DATA as the first element in a singly linked list T.

## Solution:

We shall write a general procedure that will take care of the cases:

i) T is initially empty;

ii) T is non-empty.

The logical representation of list T before and after the insertion of NEW_DATA for the two cases listed above is shown in Figure P6.1.

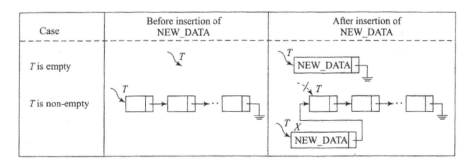

**Figure P6.1.** *Insertion of NEW_DATA as the first element in a singly linked list T*

The general procedure in pseudo-code:

```
procedure INSERT_SL_FIRST(T, NEW-DATA)
    Call GETNODE(X);
    DATA(X) = NEW_DATA;
    if (T = NIL) then { LINK(X) = NIL; }
    else {LINK(X) = T;}
    T:= X;
end INSERT_SL_FIRST.
```

## PROBLEM 6.2.–

Write a pseudo-code procedure to insert NEW_DATA as the k*th* element in a non-empty singly linked list T.

## Solution:

The logical representation of list T before and after the insertion of NEW_DATA as the *k*th element in the list is shown in Figure P6.2.

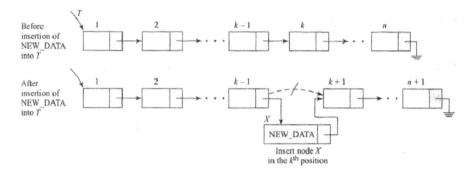

**Figure P6.2.** *Insertion of NEW_DATA as the kth element in a non-empty singly linked list T*

The pseudo-code procedure is as follows:

```
procedure INSERT_SL_K (T, k, NEW_DATA)
    Call GETNODE(X);
    DATA(X) = NEW_DATA;
    COUNT = 1;
    TEMP = T;
    while (COUNT ≠ k) do
      PREVIOUS_PTR = TEMP;/* Remember the address of
                                the predecessor node */
      TEMP = LINK(TEMP); /* TEMP slides down
                                        the list */
      COUNT = COUNT + 1;
    endwhile
    LINK(PREVIOUS_PTR) = X;
    LINK(X) = TEMP;
  end INSERT_SL_K
```

## PROBLEM 6.3.–

Write a pseudo-code procedure to delete the last element of a singly linked list T.

## Solution:

The logical representation of list T before and after deletion of the last element is shown in Figure P6.3.

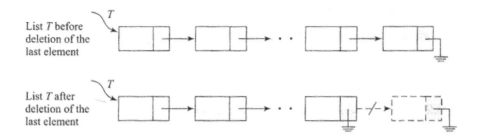

List *T* before deletion of the last element

List *T* after deletion of the last element

**Figure P6.3.** *Deletion of last element in a singly linked list T*

The pseudo-code procedure is given as

```
procedure DELETE_LAST(T)
    if (T = NIL) then    {call ABANDON_DELETE;}
    else
      { TEMP = T
        while (LINK(TEMP)  ≠ NIL)
            PREVIOUS_PTR = TEMP; /*slide down the list in
                                   search of the last node */
             TEMP = LINK(TEMP);
        endwhile
        LINK(PREVIOUS_PTR) = NIL;
        call RETURN(TEMP);
      }
end DELETE_LAST.
```

## PROBLEM 6.4.–

Write a pseudo-code procedure to count the number of nodes in a circularly linked list with a head node, representing a list of positive integers. Store the count of nodes as a negative number in the head node.

## Solution:

Let T be a circularly linked list with a head node, representing a list of positive integers. The logical representation of an example list T after execution of the pseudo-code procedure is shown in Figure P6.4.

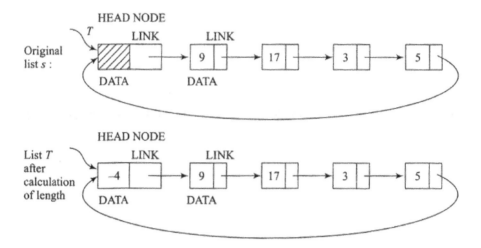

**Figure P6.4.** *Calculation of length of a circularly linked list T with a head node*

The pseudo-code procedure is as follows:

```
procedure LENGTH_CLL(T)
    COUNT = 0;
    TEMP = T;
    while (LINK(TEMP) ≠ T)
        TEMP = LINK(TEMP);
        COUNT = COUNT + 1;
    endwhile
    DATA(T) = - COUNT;
end LENGTH_CLL.
```

**PROBLEM 6.5.–**

For the circular doubly linked list T with a head node shown in Figure P6.5 with pointers X, Y, Z as illustrated, write a pseudo-code instruction to

i) express the DATA field of NODE 5;

ii) express the DATA field of NODE 1 referenced from head node T;

iii) express the left link of NODE 1 as referenced from NODE 2;

iv) express the right link of NODE 4 as referenced from NODE 5.

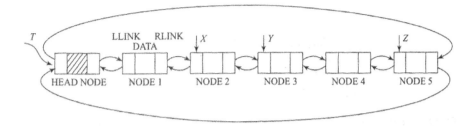

**Figure P6.5.** *A circular doubly linked list T with a head node*

## Solution:

i) DATA (Z);

ii) DATA (RLINK(T));

iii) LLINK(LLINK(X));

iv) RLINK(LLINK(Z)).

### PROBLEM 6.6.–

Given the circular doubly linked list of Figure P6.6(a), fill up the missing values in the DATA fields marked "?" using the clues given.

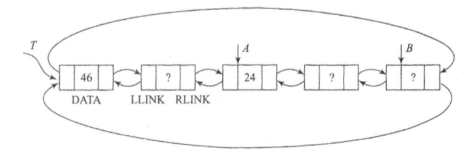

**Figure P6.6(a)** *A circular doubly linked list T with missing DATA field values*

i) DATA(B) = DATA(LLINK(RLINK(A)) + DATA(LLINK(RLINK(T)));

ii) DATA(LLINK(B)) = DATA(B) + 10;

iii) DATA (RLINK(RLINK(B)) = DATA(LLINK(LLINK(B))).

## Solution:

i) DATA(B) = DATA(A) + DATA(T)

(LLINK(RLINK(A)) = A and LLINK(RLINK(T))= T)

= 24 + 46

= 70

ii) DATA (LLINK(B)) = DATA(B) + 10

= 70 + 10

= 80

iii) DATA (RLINK(RLINK(B))) = DATA(A)

= 24

(LLINK(LLINK(B)) = A)

The updated list T is shown in Figure P6.6(b).

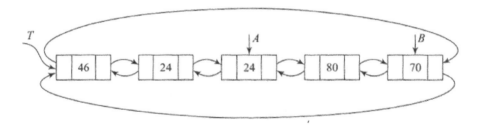

**Figure P6.6(b)** *Updated circular doubly linked list T*

## PROBLEM 6.7.–

In a programming language (Pascal), the declaration of a node in a singly linked list is shown in Figure P6.7(a). The list referred to for the problem is shown in Figure P6.7(b). Given P to be a pointer to a node, the instructions DATA(P) and LINK(P) referring to the DATA and LINK fields, respectively, of node P are equivalently represented by P↑. DATA and P↑. LINK in the programming language.

What do the following commands do to the logical representation of the list T?

```
TYPE
        POINTER =  ↑NODE;
        NODE = RECORD
                   DATA: integer;
                   LINK: POINTER
        END;
VAR P, Q R:   POINTER
```

(a) Declaration of a node in a singly linked list T

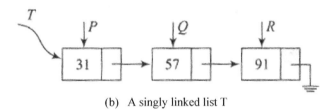

(b)   A singly linked list T

**Figure P6.7.** *(a and b) Declaration of a node in a programming language and the logical representation of a singly linked list T*

i)    P↑.DATA:= Q↑.DATA + R↑.DATA

ii)   Q: = P

iii)  R↑.LINK: = Q

iv)   R↑.DATA:=  Q↑.LINK↑.DATA + 10

## Solution:

The logical representation of list T after every command is shown in Figures P6.7(c–f).

i) P↑.DATA:=    Q↑.DATA + R↑.DATA

   P↑.DATA:=    57 + 91 = 148

ii) Q:=P

Here, Q is reset to point to the node pointed to by P.

iii) R↑.LINK:= Q

The link field of node R is reset to point to Q. In other words, the list T turns into a circularly linked list!

iv) $R\uparrow.\text{DATA}:=\ Q\uparrow.\text{LINK}.\text{DATA}\ +\ 10$

$:=57+10$

$:=67$

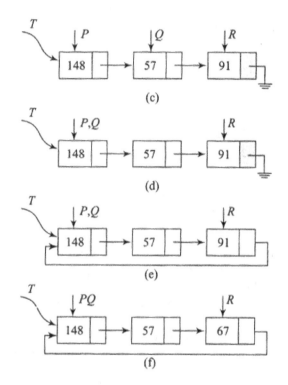

**Figure P6.7.** *(c–f) Logical representation of list T after execution of commands (i)–(iv) of illustrative problem 6.7*

## PROBLEM 6.8.–

Given the logical representations of a list T and the update in its links as shown in Figures P6.8(i)–(iii), write a one-line instruction that will affect the change indicated. The solid lines in the figures indicate the existing pointers, and the broken lines indicate the updated links.

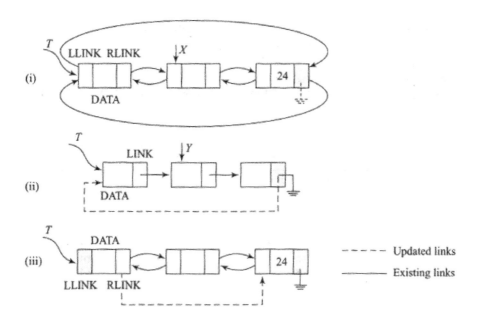

**Figure P6.8.** *Logical representations of a list T and the updated links*

**Solution:**

i) RLINK (RLINK(X)) = NIL

or

RLINK(LLINK(T)) = NIL

ii) LINK(LINK(Y)) = T
iii) RLINK(T) = RLINK(RLINK(T))

**PROBLEM 6.9.–**

Reverse a singly linked list by changing the pointers of the nodes. The data represented by the list should continue to remain in the same nodes of the original list.

For example, given a singly linked list START, as shown in Figure P6.9(a), the list needs to be reversed, as shown in Figure P6.9(b), by manipulating the links alone.

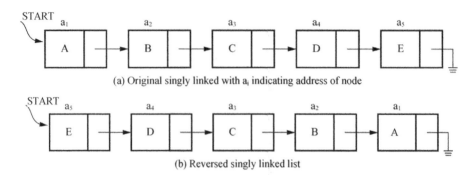

(a) Original singly linked with $a_i$ indicating address of node

(b) Reversed singly linked list

**Figure P6.9.** *Reversing a singly linked list by manipulating links*

### Solution:

We make use of three link variables, namely, PREVIOUS, CURRENT and NEXT, to manipulate the links. The following pseudo-code undertakes the reversal of the list by working on the links of the nodes with the help of the three variables that traverse down the list while chasing one another and remembering/manipulating links in the process.

```
PREVIOUS = NIL
CURRENT = START
NEXT = LINK(CURRENT)
LINK(CURRENT) = NIL
while (NEXT ≠ NIL)
     PREVIOUS = CURRENT
     CURRENT = NEXT
     NEXT = LINK (NEXT)
     LINK(CURRENT) = PREVIOUS
end while
START = CURRENT
```

**PROBLEM 6.10.–**

Given a singly linked list L, where x and y are two data elements that occupy the nodes NODEX and NODEY with PREVIOUSX as the node, which is the previous node of NODEX, write a pseudo-code to swap the date x and y in list L by manipulating the links only (data swapping is not allowed). Assume that x and y are available in the list and are neither neighbors nor the end nodes of list L.

For example, given the list L shown in Figure P6.10(a), with L, NODEX, NODEY and PREVIOUSX marked on it, the swapping should yield the list shown in Figure P6.10(b). NODEX and NODEY are neither immediate neighbors nor the end nodes of list L.

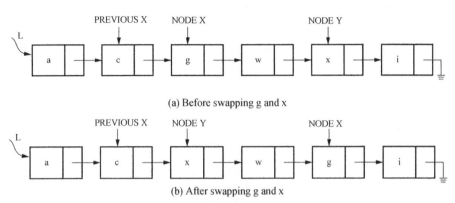

(a) Before swapping g and x

(b) After swapping g and x

**Figure P6.10**. *Swapping of elements in a singly linked list by manipulating links*

### Solution:

The following pseudo-code effects the swapping of x and y without undertaking data swapping and only manipulating the links.

```
TEMP = NODEX
NEXTX = LINK(NODEX)
while (TEMP ≠ NODEY)
     PREVIOUSY = TEMP
     TEMP=LINK(TEMP)
end while
NEXTY = LINK(NODEY)
LINK(PREVIOUSX) = NODEY
LINK(NODEY) = NEXTX
LINK(PREVIOUSY) = NODEX
LINK(NODEX) = NEXTY
```

### PROBLEM 6.11.–

Given a singly linked list L, devise a method to signal true if list L has a cycle and false otherwise. A cycle is spotted when the link of a node points to a node that was already visited while traversing down the list from its start node. Figure P6.11 shows an example list L with a cycle.

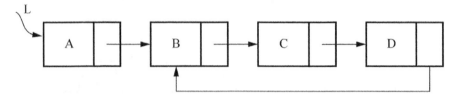

**Figure P6.11.** *A singly linked list with a cycle*

### Solution:

One method to spot a cycle in a list is to maintain an array VISITED, initialized to 0 for the nodes in the list. Every time a new node is encountered during the traversal, whose VISITED flag is 0, the VISITED flag for the node is set to 1. If at any point, the LINK of a node leads to a node whose VISITED flag is already set to 1, then it means the list L has a cycle. In such a case, the check terminates with a true signal. On the other hand, if the VISITED flag checking/resetting to 1 proceeds smoothly until the end of the list is reached, then there is no cycle, and hence, the signal is set to false.

### PROBLEM 6.12.–

Create an unrolled linked list with the minimum level of storage utilization fixed to 2 and the size of the array in the node to be 4, using the data elements 56, 65, 76, 79, 84. Demonstrate the following operations: Insert 95, 98. Delete 79.

### Solution:

Figure P6.12 illustrates the creation of the unrolled linked list and the execution of the insert and delete operations listed.

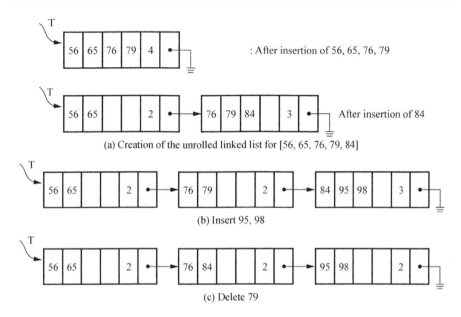

**Figure P6.12.** *Creation of an unrolled linked list and demonstration of insert/delete operations*

## Review questions

The following is a snap shot of a memory that stores a circular doubly linked list TENNIS_STARS that is head node free. Answer questions 1–3 with regard to the list.

| TENNIS_STARS 2 | LLINK | DATA | RLINK |
|---|---|---|---|
| 1 | 9 | Sabatini | 4 |
| 2 | 6 | Graf | 5 |
| 3 | 2 | Navaratilova | 8 |
| 4 | 1 | Mirza | 7 |
| 5 | 2 | Nirupama | 6 |
| 6 | 5 | Chris | 2 |
| 7 | 9 | Myskina | 3 |
| 8 | 8 | Hingis | 1 |
| 9 | 1 | Mandlikova | 9 |

1) The number of data elements in the list TENNIS_STARS is

      a) 3             b) 2             c) 5             d) 9

2) The successor of "Graf" in the list TENNIS_STARS is

      a) Navaratilova    b) Sabatini        c) Nirupama        d) Chris

3) In the list TENNIS_STARS, DATA( RLINK(LLINK(5))) = --------

      a) Mirza       b) Graf    c) Nirupama    d) Chris

4) Given the singly linked list T shown in the illustration below, the following code inserts the node containing the data "where_am_i"

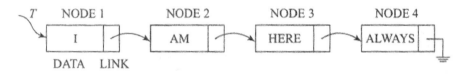

```
T = LINK(T)
P = LINK(LINK(T))
GETNODE(X)
DATA(X)  = "where_am_i"
LINK(X)  = P
LINK(LINK(T)) = X
```

a) Between NODE 1 and NODE 2        b) Between NODE 2 and NODE 3

c) Between NODE 3 and NODE 4        d) After NODE 4

5) For the singly linked list T shown above, after deletion of NODE 3, DATA(LINK(LINK(T))) = -----------

      a) I           b) AM          c) HERE         d) ALWAYS

6) What is the need for linked representations of lists?

7) What are the advantages of circular lists over singly linked lists?

8) What are the advantages and disadvantages of doubly linked lists over singly linked lists?

9) What is the use of a head node in a linked list?

10) What are the conditions for testing whether a linked list T is empty, if T is a (i) simple singly linked list, (ii) headed singly linked list, (iii) simple circularly linked list or (iv) headed circularly linked list?

11) Sketch a multiply linked list representation for the following sparse matrix:

$$\begin{bmatrix} -9 & 0 & 0 & 0 \\ 0 & 0 & 0 & 0 \\ 0 & 5 & 0 & 2 \\ 0 & 7 & 0 & 5 \end{bmatrix}$$

12) Demonstrate the application of singly linked lists for the addition of the polynomials $P_1$ and $P_2$ given below:

$P_1: 19x^6 + 78x^4 + 6x^3 - 23x^2 - 34$

$P_2: 67x^6 + 89x^5 - 23x^3 - 75x^2 - 89x - 21$

13) Modify the pseudo-code shown in illustrative problem 6.10, wherever needed, to handle the cases (i) NODEX and NODEY are immediate neighbors, and (ii) NODEX and NODEY are not immediate neighbors, but are end nodes of list L.

14) Write a pseudo-code that will perform insert/deletion operations on an unrolled linked list, as explained in sections 6.6.2 and 6.6.3.

15) Demonstrate a self-organizing list on the following keywords of a programming language stored as a doubly linked list, when the given list of retrievals is undertaken over the list.

Show how the list reorganizes itself when (i) count, (ii) move to front and (iii) transpose methods are employed. Tabulate the comparisons undertaken for the three methods, while retrieving the keyword **if,** every time it is called in the order given.

List:        **exit and for while if repeat else**

Retrievals:  **if if if if else repeat while if if if**

## Programming assignments

1) Let $X = (x_1, x_2, \dots x_n)$, $Y = (y_1, y_2, \dots y_n)$ be two lists with a sorted sequence of elements. Execute a program to merge the two lists together as a list Z with $m + n$ elements. Implement the lists using singly linked list representations.

2) Execute a program that will split a circularly linked list P with $n$ nodes into two circularly linked lists $P_1$, $P_2$ with the first $\lfloor n/2 \rfloor$ and the last $n - \lfloor n/2 \rfloor$ nodes of the list P in them.

3) Write a menu driven program which will maintain a list of car models, their price, name of the manufacturer, engine capacity, etc., as a doubly linked list. The menu should make provisions for inserting information pertaining to new car models, delete obsolete models, update data such as price, in addition to answering queries such as listing all car models within a price range specified by the client and listing all details, given a car model.

4) Students enrolled for a diploma course in computer science opt for two theory courses, an elective course and two laboratory courses, from a list of courses offered for the programme. Design a multiply linked list with the following node structure:

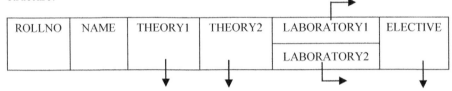

| ROLLNO | NAME | THEORY1 | THEORY2 | LABORATORY1 | ELECTIVE |
|--------|------|---------|---------|-------------|----------|
|        |      |         |         | LABORATORY2 |          |

A student may change their elective course within a week of enrollment. At the end of the period, the department takes into account the number of students who have enrolled for a specific course in the theory, laboratory and elective options.

Execute a program to implement the multiply linked list with provisions to insert nodes, update information, and generate reports as needed by the department.

5) [**Topological Sorting**] The problem of *topological sorting* is to arrange a set of objects $\{O_1, O_2, \ldots O_n\}$ obeying rules of precedence into a linear sequence such that whenever $O_i$ precedes $O_j$, we have $i < j$. The sorting procedure has wide applications in PERT, linguistics, network theory, etc. Thus, when a project comprises a group of activities observing precedence relations among themselves, it is convenient to arrange the activities in a linear sequence to effectively execute the project.

Again, as another example, while designing a glossary for a book, it is essential that the terms $W_i$ are listed in a linear sequence such that no term is used before it has been defined. The illustration below shows the topological sorting of a network.

Network of activities

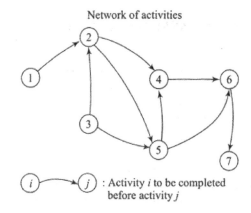

$i$ ─────▶ $j$ : Activity $i$ to be completed
before activity $j$

Topological sorting of activities in the network

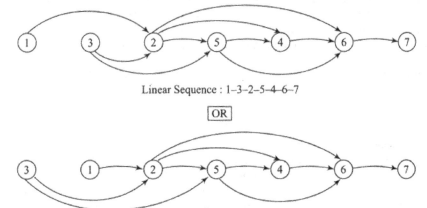

Linear Sequence : 1–3–2–5–4–6–7

OR

Linear Sequence : 3–1–2–5–4–6–7

A simple way to perform topological sorting is to look for objects that are not preceded by any other objects and release them into the output linear sequence. Remove these objects and continue the same with other objects of the network until the entire set of objects have been released into the linear sequence. However, topological sorting fails when the network has a cycle. In other words, if $O_i$ precedes $O_j$ and $O_j$ precedes $O_i$, the procedure is stalled.

Design and implement an algorithm to perform topological sorting of a sequence of objects using a linked list data structure.

6) Write a program FRONTBACK that splits a doubly linked list START with $n$ nodes into two sublists FRONT and BACK, where FRONT points to the $\left\lceil \frac{n}{2} \right\rceil$ nodes

occupying the front of the original list and BACK points to the remaining nodes at the back end of START, but points to the node that is the last in the list.

7) Write a program REMOVE_DUPLICATES that will remove duplicate elements in a list L that occur consecutively. The program should return the list with its elements in the same order of their appearance in the original list, but with the consecutive duplicate elements removed.

For example, for a list with elements {A, B, C, C, C, C, D, D, E, F, F}, the output list produced by REMOVE_DUPLICATES should be {A, B, C, D, E, F}.

8) Write a menu-driven program to create an unrolled linked list and retrieve, insert and delete an element from it. You may take liberties with the operations while implementing them.

9) Implement a self-organizing list by creating a singly linked list of nodes and undertaking frequent retrievals of data in the list repeatedly and at random. Show how the list restructures itself when (i) count, (ii) move to front and (iii) transpose methods are used for the same set of frequent retrievals.

# 7

# Linked Stacks and Linked Queues

In Chapters 4 and 5, we discussed a sequential representation of the stack and queue data structures. Stacks and queues were implemented using arrays and hence inherited all the drawbacks of the sequential data structure.

In this chapter, we discuss the representation of stacks and queues using a linked representation, namely, singly linked lists. The inherent merits of the linked representation render an efficient implementation of the linked stack and linked queue.

We first define a linked representation of the two data structures and discuss the insert/delete operations performed on them. The role played by the linked stack in the management of the free storage pool is detailed. The applications of linked stacks and linked queues in the problems of balancing symbols and polynomial representation, respectively, are discussed later.

## 7.1. Introduction

To review, a stack is an ordered list with the restriction that elements are added or deleted from only one end of the stack termed the *top of stack* with the "inactive" end known as the *bottom of stack*. A stack observes the **Last-In-First-Out (LIFO)** principle and has its insert and delete operations referred to as *Push* and *Pop*, respectively.

The drawbacks of a sequential representation of a stack data structure are as follows:

i) finite capacity of the stack;

ii) check for the **STACK_FULL** condition every time a Push operation is effected.

A queue, on the other hand, is a linear list in which all insertions are made at one end of the list known as the *rear end* and all deletions are made at the opposite end known as the *front end*. The queue observes a **First-In-First-Out (FIFO)** principle, and the insert and delete operations are known as *enqueuing* and *dequeuing*, respectively.

The drawbacks of a sequential representation of a queue are as follows:

i) finite capacity of the queue; and

ii) checking for the **QUEUE_FULL** condition before every insert operation is executed, both in the case of a liner queue and a circular queue.

We now discuss linked representations of a stack and a queue.

### 7.1.1. *Linked stack*

A *linked stack* is a linear list of elements commonly implemented as a singly linked list whose *start pointer performs the role of the top pointer of a stack*. Let *a, b, c* be a list of elements. Figures 7.1(a–c) show the conventional, sequential and linked representations of the stack.

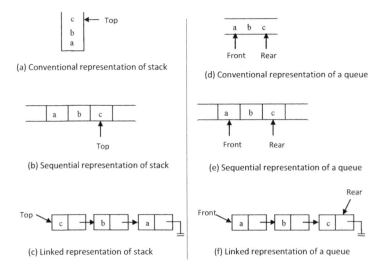

(a) Conventional representation of stack

(d) Conventional representation of a queue

(b) Sequential representation of stack

(e) Sequential representation of a queue

(c) Linked representation of stack

(f) Linked representation of a queue

**Figure 7.1.** *Stack and queue representations (conventional, sequential and linked)*

Here, the start pointer of the linked list is appropriately renamed Top to suit the context.

### 7.1.2. *Linked queues*

A *linked queue* is also a linear list of elements commonly implemented as a singly linked list but with two pointers, namely, front and rear. The *start pointer of the singly linked list plays the role of front*, while the *pointer to the last node is set to play the role of rear*.

Let *a, b* and *c* be a list of three elements to be represented as a linked queue. Figures 7.1(d–f) show the conventional, sequential and linked representations of the queue.

## 7.2. Operations on linked stacks and linked queues

In this section, we discuss the insert and delete operations performed on the linked stack and linked queue data structures and present algorithms for the same.

### 7.2.1. *Linked stack operations*

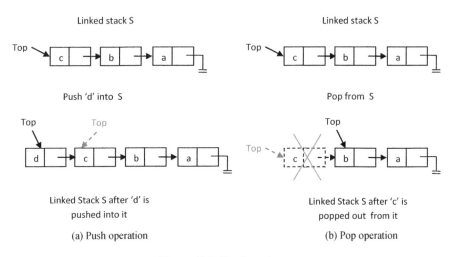

(a) Push operation                    (b) Pop operation

**Figure 7.2.** *Push and pop operations on a linked stack S*

To push an element into the linked stack, we insert the node representing the element as the first node in the singly linked list. The Top pointer, which points to the first element in the singly linked list, is automatically updated to point to the new top element. In the case of a pop operation, the node pointed to by the Top pointer is deleted, and Top is updated to point to the next node as the top element. Figures 7.2(a) and (b) illustrate the push and pop operation on a linked stack S, respectively.

Observe how during the push operation, unlike sequential stack structures, there is no need to check for the STACK-FULL condition due to the unlimited capacity of the data structure.

### 7.2.2. *Linked queue operations*

To insert an element into the queue, we insert the node representing the element as the last node in the singly linked list for which the REAR pointer is reset to point to the new node as the rear element of the queue. To delete an element from the queue, we remove the first node of the list for which the FRONT pointer is reset to point to the next node as the front element of the queue. Figures 7.3(a) and (b) illustrate the insert and delete operations on a linked queue, respectively.

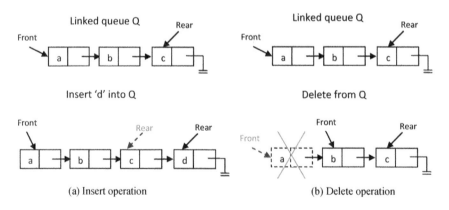

**Figure 7.3.** *Insert and delete operations on the linked queue Q*

The insert operation, unlike insertion in sequential queues, does not exhibit the need to check for the QUEUE_FULL condition due to the unlimited capacity of the data structure. The introduction of circular queues to annul the drawbacks of the linear queues now appears superfluous in light of the linked representation of queues.

Both linked stacks and queues could be represented using a singly linked list with a head node. Additionally, they could be represented as a circularly linked list provided that the fundamental principles of LIFO and FIFO are strictly maintained.

We now present the algorithms for the operations discussed in linked stacks and linked queues.

### 7.2.3. Algorithms for Push/Pop operations on a linked stack

Let S be a linked stack. Algorithms 7.1 and 7.2 illustrate the push and pop operations to be carried out on stack S.

```
procedure PUSH_LINKSTACK (TOP, ITEM)
/* Insert ITEM into stack */

    Call GETNODE(X)
    DATA(X) = ITEM    /*frame node for ITEM */
    LINK(X) = TOP    /* insert node X into stack */
    TOP = X          /* reset TOP pointer */

end PUSH_LINKSTACK.
```

**Algorithm 7.1.** *Push item ITEM into a linked stack S with top pointer TOP*

Note the absence of the STACK_FULL condition. The time complexity of a push operation is $O(1)$.

```
procedure POP_LINKSTACK(TOP, ITEM)
/* pop element from stack and set ITEM to the element */

  if (TOP = 0) then call LINKSTACK_EMPTY
            /* check if linked stack is empty */
  else   { TEMP = TOP
           ITEM = DATA(TOP)
           TOP  = LINK(TOP)
         }
  call   RETURN(TEMP) ;

end POP_LINKSTACK.
```

**Algorithm 7.2.** *Pop from a linked stack S and output the element through ITEM*

The time complexity of a pop operation is $O(1)$. Example 7.1 illustrates the push and pop operation on a linked stack.

### EXAMPLE 7.1.–

Consider the stack DEVICE of peripheral devices illustrated in example 4.1. We implement the same as a linked stack. The insertion of PEN, PLOTTER, JOYSTICK and PRINTER and a deletion operation are illustrated in Table 7.1. We assume the list to be initially empty and Top to be the top pointer of the stack.

### 7.2.4. Algorithms for insert and delete operations in a linked queue

Let Q be a linked queue. Algorithms 7.3 and 7.4 illustrate the insert and delete operations on the queue Q.

```
procedure INSERT_LINKQUEUE(FRONT,REAR,ITEM)
      Call GETNODE (X);
      DATA(X) = ITEM;
      LINK(X) = NIL;    /* Node with ITEM is ready to
                            be inserted into Q */
      if (FRONT = 0)  then FRONT = REAR = X;
             /* If Q is empty then ITEM is the first
                            element in the queue Q */
      else {LINK(REAR) = X;
           REAR = X
           }
end INSERT_LINKQUEUE.
```

**Algorithm 7.3.** *Insert item ITEM into a linear queue Q with FRONT and REAR as the front and rear pointers to the queue*

Observe the absence of the QUEUE_ FULL condition in the insert procedure. The time complexity of an insert operation is $O(1)$.

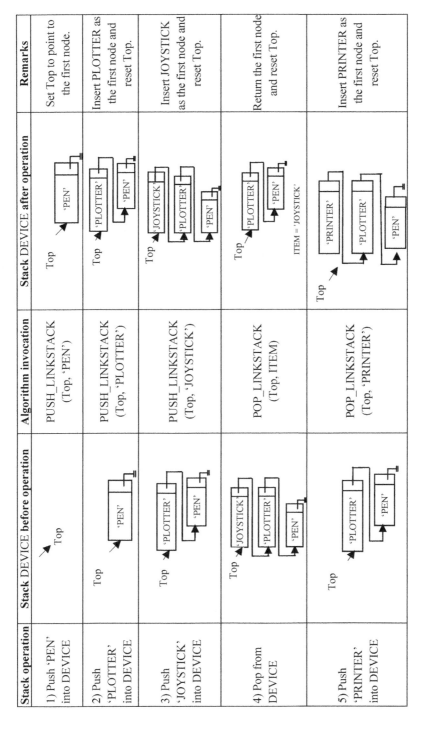

| Stack operation | Stack DEVICE before operation | Algorithm invocation | Stack DEVICE after operation | Remarks |
|---|---|---|---|---|
| 1) Push 'PEN' into DEVICE | Top | PUSH_LINKSTACK (Top, 'PEN') | Top → 'PEN' | Set Top to point to the first node. |
| 2) Push 'PLOTTER' into DEVICE | Top → 'PEN' | PUSH_LINKSTACK (Top, 'PLOTTER') | Top → 'PLOTTER' → 'PEN' | Insert PLOTTER as the first node and reset Top. |
| 3) Push 'JOYSTICK' into DEVICE | Top → 'PLOTTER' → 'PEN' | PUSH_LINKSTACK (Top, 'JOYSTICK') | Top → 'JOYSTICK' → 'PLOTTER' → 'PEN' | Insert JOYSTICK as the first node and reset Top. |
| 4) Pop from DEVICE | Top → 'JOYSTICK' → 'PLOTTER' → 'PEN' | POP_LINKSTACK (Top, ITEM) | Top → 'PLOTTER' → 'PEN'    ITEM = 'JOYSTICK' | Return the first node and reset Top. |
| 5) Push 'PRINTER' into DEVICE | Top → 'PLOTTER' → 'PEN' | POP_LINKSTACK (Top, 'PRINTER') | Top → 'PRINTER' → 'PLOTTER' → 'PEN' | Insert PRINTER as the first node and reset Top. |

**Table 7.1.** *Insert and delete operations on linked stack DEVICE*

```
procedure DELETE_LINKQUEUE (FRONT,ITEM)

   if (FRONT = 0) then call LINKQUEUE_EMPTY;
   /* Test condition to avoid deletion in an empty
      queue */
   else    {TEMP = FRONT;
            ITEM = DATA (TEMP);
            FRONT = LINK (TEMP);
           }
   call RETURN (TEMP);   /* return the node TEMP to
                             the free pool */
end DELETE_LINKQUEUE.
```

**Algorithm 7.4.** *Delete element from the linked queue Q through ITEM with FRONT and REAR as the front and rear pointers*

The time complexity of a delete operation is $O(1)$. Example 7.2 illustrates the insert and delete operations on a linked queue.

### EXAMPLE 7.2.–

Consider the queue BIRDS illustrated in example 5.1. The insertion of DOVE, PEACOCK, PIGEON and SWAN, and two deletions are shown in Table 7.2.

Owing to the linked representation, there is no limitation on the capacity of the stack or queue. In fact, the stack or queue can hold as many elements as the storage memory can accommodate! This dispenses with the need to check for STACK_FULL or QUEUE_FULL conditions during push or insert operations, respectively.

The merits of linked stacks and linked queues are therefore:

i) the conceptual and computational simplicity of the operations;

ii) nonfinite capacity.

The only demerit, if at all, is the requirement of additional space that is needed to accommodate the link fields.

## 7.3. Dynamic memory management and linked stacks

*Dynamic memory management* addresses methods of allocating storage and recycling unused space for future use. The automatic recycling of dynamically allocated memory is also known as *garbage collection*.

If the memory storage pool is thought of as a repository of nodes, then dynamic memory management primarily revolves around the two actions of *allocating nodes* (for use by the application) and *liberating nodes* (after their release by the application). Several intelligent strategies for the efficient allocation and liberation of nodes have been discussed in the literature. However, we have chosen to discuss this topic from the perspective of a linked stack application.

Every linked representation, which makes use of nodes to accommodate data elements, executes procedure GETNODE() to obtain the desired node from the free storage pool and procedure RETURN() to dispose of the node into the storage pool. The free storage pool is also referred to as *Available Space* (AVAIL_SPACE).

When the application invokes GETNODE(), a node from the available space data structure is deleted to be handed over for use by the program, and when RETURN() is invoked, the node disposed of by the application is inserted into the available space for future use.

The most commonly used data structure for the management of AVAIL_SPACE and its insert/delete operation is the *linked stack*. The list of free nodes in AVAIL_SPACE are all linked together and maintained as a linked stack with a top pointer (AV_SP). When GETNODE() is invoked, a pop operation of the linked stack is performed, releasing a node for use by the application, and when RETURN() is invoked, a push operation of the linked stack is performed. Figure 7.4 illustrates the association between the GETNODE() and RETURN() procedures and AVAIL_SPACE maintained as a linked stack.

We now implement the GETNODE() and RETURN() procedures, which in fact are nothing but the POP and PUSH operations on the linked stack AVAIL_SPACE. Algorithms 7.5 and 7.6 illustrate the implementation of the procedures.

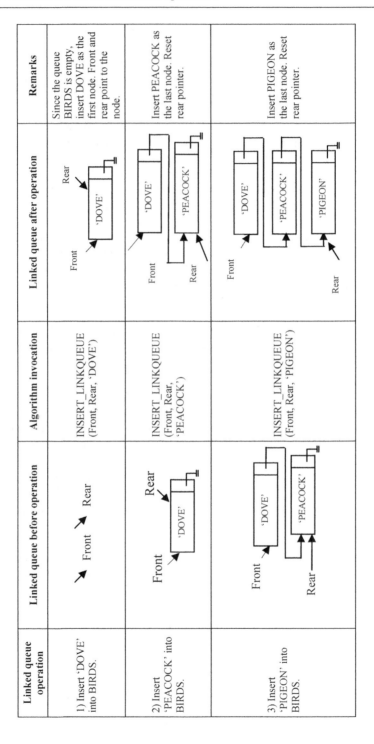

| Linked queue operation | Linked queue before operation | Algorithm invocation | Linked queue after operation | Remarks |
|---|---|---|---|---|
| 1) Insert 'DOVE' into BIRDS. | Front    Rear | INSERT_LINKQUEUE (Front, Rear, 'DOVE') | Rear  Front  'DOVE' | Since the queue BIRDS is empty, insert DOVE as the first node. Front and rear point to the node. |
| 2) Insert 'PEACOCK' into BIRDS. | Rear  Front  'DOVE' | INSERT_LINKQUEUE (Front, Rear, 'PEACOCK') | Front  'DOVE'  Rear  'PEACOCK' | Insert PEACOCK as the last node. Reset rear pointer. |
| 3) Insert 'PIGEON' into BIRDS. | Front  'DOVE'  Rear  'PEACOCK' | INSERT_LINKQUEUE (Front, Rear, 'PIGEON') | Front  'DOVE'  'PEACOCK'  'PIGEON'  Rear | Insert PIGEON as the last node. Reset rear pointer. |

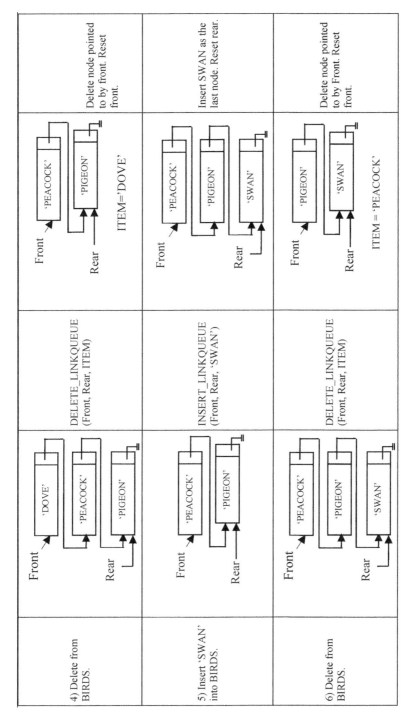

**Table 7.2.** *Insert and delete operations on a linked queue BIRDS*

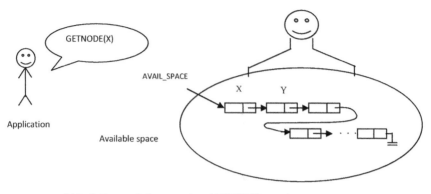

(a) Available space before execution of GETNODE () procedure

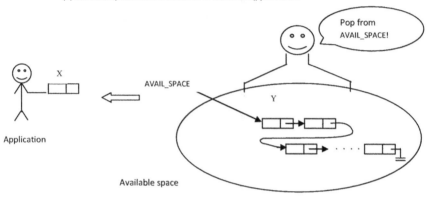

(b) Available space after execution of GETNODE () procedure

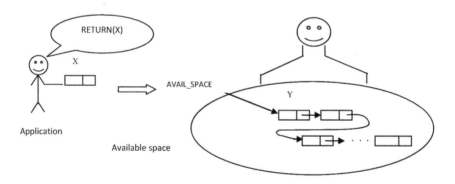

(c) Available space before execution of RETURN () procedure.

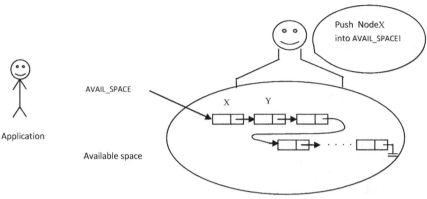

(d) Available space after execution of RETURN () procedure.

**Figure 7.4.** *Association between GETNODE () and*
*RETURN () procedures and AVAIL _SPACE*

```
procedure GETNODE(X)

    if (AV = 0) then call NO_FREE_NODES;
    /* AVAIL_SPACE has no free nodes to allocate * /
    else
        { X  = AV;
          AV = LINK (AV); /* Return the address X of the
        }                    top  node in AVAIL_SPACE */
end GETNODE.
```

**Algorithm 7.5.** *Implementation of procedure GETNODE (X), where*
*AV is the pointer to the linked stack implementation of AVAIL_SPACE*

```
procedure RETURN(X)

    LINK (X)= AV;        /*Push node X into AVAIL_SPACE
                           and reset AV */

    AV = X;
end RETURN.
```

**Algorithm 7.6.** *Implementation of procedure RETURN (X), where*
*AV is the pointer to the linked stack implementation of AVAIL_SPACE*

It is obvious that at a given instance, the adjacent or other nodes in AVAIL_SPACE are neighbors that are physically contiguous in the memory but lie scattered in the list. This may eventually lead to holes in the memory, leading to inefficient use of memory. When variable size nodes are in use, it is desirable to compact memory so that all free nodes form a contiguous block of memory. Such a thing is termed *memory compaction*.

It now becomes essential that the storage manager, for the efficient management of memory, every time a node is returned to the free pool, ensures that the neighboring blocks of memory that are free are coalesced into a simple block of memory to satisfy large requests for memory. This is, however, easier said than done. To look for neighboring nodes that are free, a "brute force approach" calls for a complete search through the AVAIL_SPACE list before collapsing the adjacent free nodes into a single block.

Allocation strategies, such as *the boundary tag method* and *buddy system method* (Knuth 1973), with efficient reservation and liberation of nodes have been proposed in the literature.

## 7.4. Implementation of linked representations

It is emphasized here that nodes belonging to the reserved pool, that is, nodes that are currently in use, coexist with the nodes of the free pool in the same storage area. It is therefore not uncommon to have a reserved node having a free node as its physically contiguous neighbor. While the link fields of the free nodes, which in its simplest form is a linked stack, keep track of the free nodes in the list, the link fields of the reserved pool similarly keep track of the reserved nodes in the list. Figure 7.5 illustrates a naïve scheme of the reserved pool intertwined with the free pool in memory storage.

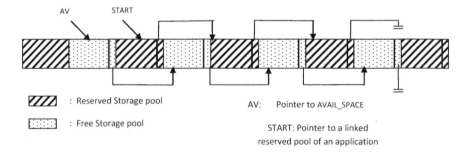

**Figure 7.5.** *The scheme of reserved storage pool and free storage pool in the memory storage*

Example 7.3 illustrates the implementation of a linked representation. For simplicity, we consider a singly linked list occupying the reserved pool.

## EXAMPLE 7.3.–

A snapshot of the memory storage is shown in Figure 7.6. The reserved pool accommodates a singly linked list (START). The free storage pool of used and disposed nodes is maintained as a linked stack with top pointer AV.

DATA    LINK

| | DATA | LINK |
|---|---|---|
| 1 | 22 | 9 |
| 2 | 29 | 8 |
| 3 | -14 | 7 |
| 4 | 36 | 1 |
| 5 | 144 | 10 |
| 6 | -3 | 2 |
| 7 | 116 | 0 |
| 8 | 43 | 3 |
| 9 | 56 | 5 |
| 10 | 34 | 0 |

AV: 6

START: 4

**Figure 7.6.** *A snapshot of the memory accommodating a singly linked list in its reserved pool and the free storage pool*

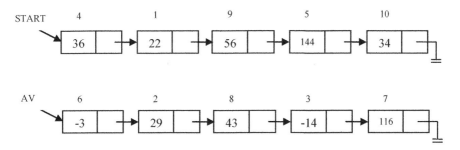

**Figure 7.7.** *Logical representation of the singly linked list and available space shown in Figure 7.6*

Note the memory locations AV and START. AV records the address of the first node in the free storage pool, and START records the address of the singly linked list in the reserved pool. The logical representation of the singly linked list and the available space are illustrated in Figure 7.7.

## 7.5. Applications

All applications of linear queues and linear stacks can be implemented as linked stacks and linked queues. In this section, we discuss the following problems:

i) balancing symbols,

ii) polynomial representation,

as application of linked stacks and linked queues, respectively.

### 7.5.1. *Balancing symbols*

An important activity performed by compilers is to check for syntax errors in the program code. One such error checking mechanism is the balancing of symbols or, specifically, the balancing of parentheses in the context of expressions, which is exclusive to this discussion.

For the balancing of parentheses, every left parenthesis or brace or bracket as allowed by the language syntax must have a closing or matching right parenthesis, brace or bracket, respectively. Thus, the usage of (), or { } or [ ] are correct, whereas (, [, } are incorrect, the former indicative of a balanced occurrence and the latter of an imbalanced occurrence in an expression.

The arithmetic expressions shown in example 7.4 are balanced in parentheses, while those listed in example 7.5 are imbalanced forcing the compiler to report errors.

EXAMPLE 7.4.–

Balanced arithmetic expressions are given as

i) $((A+B)\uparrow C - D) + E - F$

ii) $(- (A+B) * (C - D)) \uparrow F$

EXAMPLE 7.5.–

Imbalanced arithmetic expressions are given as

i) (A+B) * – (C+D+F

ii) – ((A+B+C) * – (E+F)))

The solution to the problem is an easy but elegant use of a stack to check for mismatched parentheses. The general pseudo-code procedure for the problem is illustrated in Algorithm 7.7.

```
procedure BALANCE_ EXPR(E)
/*E is the expression padded with a $ to indicate end of
input*/

 clear stack;
 while not end_of_string(E) do
   read character;/* read a character from string E*/
   if the character is an open symbol
   then push character in to stack;
   if the character is a close symbol
   then
        if stack is empty then ERROR ()
        else {pop the stack;
              if the character popped is not the
                matching symbol
              then ERROR();
              }
 endwhile
 if stack not empty then ERROR();

end BALANCE_EXPR.
```

**Algorithm 7.7.** *To check for the balance of parentheses in a string*

Appropriate to the discussion, we choose a linked representation for the stack in the algorithm. Examples 7.6 and 7.7 illustrate the working of the algorithm on two expressions with balanced and unbalanced symbols, respectively.

### EXAMPLE 7.6.–

Consider the arithmetic expression ((A+B)* C) – D, which has balanced parentheses. Table 7.3 illustrates the working of the algorithm on the expression.

### EXAMPLE 7.7.–

Consider the expression ((A + B) C + G), which has imbalanced parentheses. Table 7.4 illustrates the working of the algorithm on the expression.

### 7.5.2. Polynomial representation

In Chapter 6, section 6.8.1, we discussed the problem of the addition of polynomials as an application of linked lists. In this section, we highlight the representation of polynomials as an application of linear queues.

Consider a polynomial $9x^6 - 2x^4 + 3x^2 + 4$. Adopting the node structure shown in Figure 7.8(a) (reproduction of Figure 6.26(a)), the linked list for the polynomial is as shown in Figure 7.8(b).

| Input string (E) | Stack (S) | Remarks |
|---|---|---|
| ((A+B)* C) – D $ | | Initialization. Note E is padded with $ as end of input symbol |
| (A+B)* C) – D $ | | Push '(' into S |
| A+B)* C) – D $ | | Push '(' into S |
| +B)* C) – D $ | | Ignore character 'A' |
| B)* C) – D $ | | Ignore character '+' |
| )* C) – D $ | | Ignore character 'B' |

| Input string (E) | Stack (S) | Remarks |
|---|---|---|
| * C) – D $<br>↑ | S → [ ( \| ] ⏚ | Pop symbol from S.<br>Matching symbol to<br>")" found. Proceed. |
| C) – D $<br>↑ | S → [ ( \| ] ⏚ | Ignore character '*' |
| ) – D $<br>↑ | S → [ ( \| ] ⏚ | Ignore character 'C' |
| – D $<br>↑ | S ↘ | Pop symbol from S.<br>Matching symbol to<br>')' found. Proceed. |
| D $<br>↑ | S ↘ | Ignore character '–' |
| $<br>↑ | S ↘ | Ignore character 'D' |
| $ | S ↘ | End of input<br>encountered.<br>Stack is empty.<br>Success! |

**Table 7.3.** *Working of algorithm BALANCE_EXPR ()*
*on the expression (A+B)\* C*

| Input string (E) | Stack (S) | Remarks |
|---|---|---|
| ((A+B)*C ↑ G $<br>↑ | S ↘ | Initialization.<br>E is padded with a $<br>as end of input<br>character. |
| (A+B)*C ↑ G $<br>↑ | S → [ ( \| ] ⏚ | Push '(' into S |
| A+B)*C ↑ G $<br>↑ | S → [ ( \| → ] [ ( \| ] ⏚ | Push '(' into S |
| +B)*C ↑ G $<br>↑ | S → [ ( \| → ] [ ( \| ] ⏚ | Ignore character 'A' |

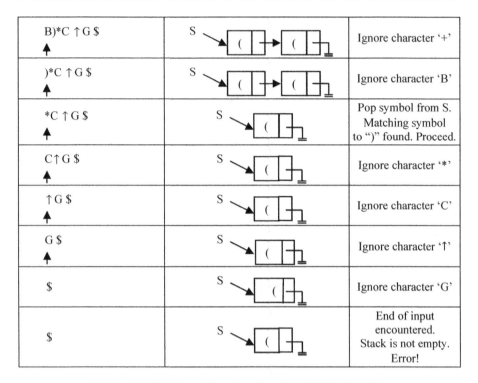

| B)*C ↑G $<br>▲ | S  ( → ( | Ignore character '+' |
| )*C ↑G $<br>▲ | S  ( → ( | Ignore character 'B' |
| *C ↑G $<br>▲ | S  ( | Pop symbol from S.<br>Matching symbol<br>to ")" found. Proceed. |
| C↑G $<br>▲ | S  ( | Ignore character '*' |
| ↑G $<br>▲ | S  ( | Ignore character 'C' |
| G $<br>▲ | S  ( | Ignore character '↑' |
| $ | S  ( | Ignore character 'G' |
| $ | S  ( | End of input<br>encountered.<br>Stack is not empty.<br>Error! |

**Table 7.4.** *Working of the algorithm BALANCE_EXPR ()*
*on the expression ((A+B) \*C↑G)*

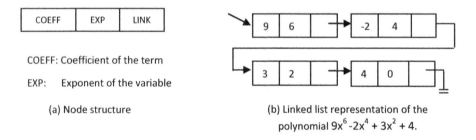

| COEFF | EXP | LINK |

COEFF: Coefficient of the term

EXP:    Exponent of the variable

(a) Node structure

(b) Linked list representation of the
polynomial $9x^6 - 2x^4 + 3x^2 + 4$.

**Figure 7.8.** *Linked list representation of a polynomial*

For easy manipulation of the linked list, we represent the polynomial in its decreasing order of exponents of the variable (in the case of univariable polynomials). It would therefore be easy for the function handling the reading of the polynomial to implement the linked list as a linear queue, since this would entail an elegant construction of the list from the symbolic representation of the polynomial by enqueuing the linear queue with the next highest exponent term. The linear queue representation for the polynomial $9x^6 - 2x^4 + 3x^2 + 4$ is shown in Figure 7.9.

Additionally, after the manipulation of the polynomials (addition, subtraction, etc.) the resulting polynomial can also be elegantly represented as a linear queue. This merely calls for enqueueing the linear queue with the just manipulated term. Recall the problem of the addition of polynomials discussed in section 6.8.1. Maintaining the added polynomial as a linear queue would only call for "appending" the added terms (coefficients of terms with like exponents) to the rear of the list. However, during the manipulation, the linear queue representations of the polynomials are treated as traversable queues. A ***traversable queue*** while retaining the operations of enqueuing and dequeuing permits traversal of the list in which nodes may be examined.

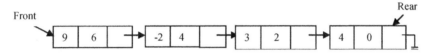

**Figure 7.9.** *Linear queue representation of the polynomial $9x^6 - 2x^4 + 3x^2 + 4$*

## Summary

– Sequential representations of stacks and queues suffer from the limitation of finite capacity besides checking for the STACK_FULL and QUEUE_FULL conditions, each time a push or insert operation is executed, respectively.

– Linked stacks and linked queues are singly linked list implementations of stacks and queues, though a circularly linked list representation can also be attempted without hampering the LIFO or FIFO principle of the respective data structures.

– Linked stacks and linked queues display the merits of conceptual and computational simplicity of insert and delete operations besides the absence of limited capacity. However, the requirement of additional space to accommodate the link fields can be viewed as a demerit.

– The maintenance of available space list calls for the application of linked stacks.

– The problems of balancing of symbols and polynomial representation demonstrate the application of linked stack and linked queue, respectively.

## 7.6. Illustrative problems

### PROBLEM 7.1.–

Given the following memory snapshot where START and AV_ SP store the start pointers of the linked list and the available space, respectively:

i) identify the linked list;

ii) show how the linked list and the available space list are affected when the following operations are carried out:

a) insert 116 at the end of the list,

b) delete 243,

c) obtain the memory snapshot after the execution of operations listed in (a) and (b).

DATA    LINK

| | DATA | LINK |
|---|---|---|
| 1 | 114 | 0 |
| 2 | 176 | 6 |
| 3 | 243 | 9 |
| 4 | 94 | 5 |
| 5 | 346 | 7 |
| 6 | 879 | 8 |
| 7 | 344 | 1 |
| 8 | 465 | 3 |
| 9 | 191 | 10 |
| 10 | 564 | 0 |

START:   2       AV_SP:   4

## Solution:

i) Since the linked list starts at a node whose address is 2, the logical representation of the list is as given below:

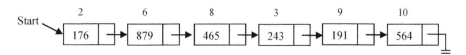

The available space list, which functions as a linked stack and starts from a node whose address is 4, is given by:

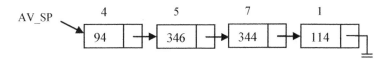

ii) (a) To insert 116 at the end of the list START, we obtain a node from the available space list (invoke GETNODE ()). The node released has address 4. The resultant list and the available space list are as follows:

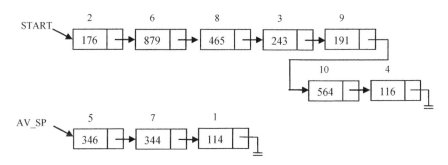

ii) (b) To delete 243, the node holding the element has to be returned to the available space list (invoke (RETURN ()). The resultant list and the available space list are as follows:

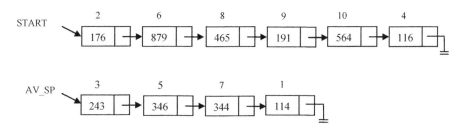

ii) (c) The memory snapshot after the execution of (a) and (b) is as given below:

DATA    LINK

| | DATA | LINK |
|---|---|---|
| 1 | 114 | 0 |
| 2 | 176 | 6 |
| 3 | 243 | 5 |
| 4 | 116 | 0 |
| 5 | 346 | 7 |
| 6 | 879 | 8 |
| 7 | 344 | 1 |
| 8 | 465 | 9 |
| 9 | 191 | 10 |
| 10 | 564 | 4 |

START: 2    AV_SP: 3

## PROBLEM 7.2.–

DATA    LINK

| | DATA | LINK |
|---|---|---|
| 1 | AMTRACK | 7 |
| 2 | FALCON | 5 |
| 3 | BOMBAY_MAIL | 6 |
| 4 | EUROSTAR | 9 |
| 5 | DUTCHFLYER | 4 |
| 6 | RAJDHANI | 0 |
| 7 | FAST_WIND | 8 |
| 8 | DEVILS_EYE | 0 |
| 9 | ORIENT EXPRESS | 0 |
| 10 | BLUE MOUNT | 3 |

L_Q: 1    L_S: 10    AV_SP: 2
(FRONT)

L_Q: 8
(REAR)

Given the above memory snapshot, which stores a linked stack L_S and a linked queue L_Q beginning at the respective addresses, obtain the resulting memory snapshot after the following operations are carried out sequentially.

i) Enqueue CONCORDE into L_Q.

ii) Pop from L_S.

iii) Dequeue from L_Q.

iv) Push "PALACE _ON _WHEELS" into L-S.

## Solution:

It is easier to perform the operations on the logical representations of the lists and available space extracted from the memory before obtaining the final memory snapshot.

The lists are as follows:

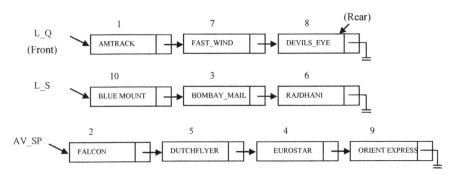

i) Enqueue CONCORDE into L_Q yields:

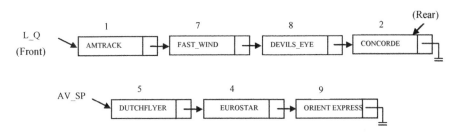

Here, node 2 is popped from AVAIL-SPACE to accommodate CONCORDE, which is inserted at the rear of L_Q.

ii) Pop from L_S yields:

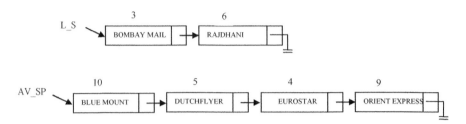

Here, node 10 from L-S is deleted and pushed into AVAIL_SPACE.

iii) Dequeue from L_Q yields:

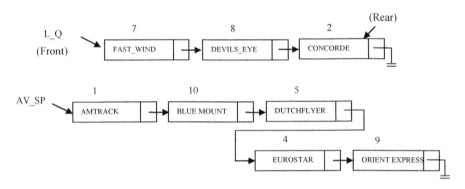

Here, node 1 from L_Q is deleted and pushed into AVAIL_SPACE.

iv) Push "PALACE_ON_WHEELS" into L_S yields:

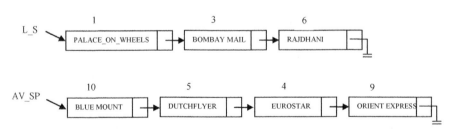

Here, node 1 from AVAIL_SPACE is popped to accommodate "PALACE_ON_WHEELS" before pushing the node into L_S.

The final lists are as follows:

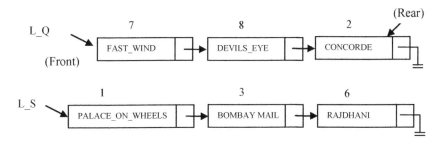

The memory snapshot is given by:

| | DATA | LINK |
|---|---|---|
| 1 | PALACE ON WHEELS | 3 |
| 2 | CONCORDE | 0 |
| 3 | BOMBAY MAIL | 6 |
| 4 | EUROSTAR | 9 |
| 5 | DUTCHFLYER | 4 |
| 6 | RAJDHANI | 0 |
| 7 | FAST_WIND | 8 |
| 8 | DEVILS_EYE | 2 |
| 9 | ORIENT EXPRESS | 0 |
| 10 | BLUE MOUNT | 5 |

L_Q:  7    L_S:  1    AV_SP:  10
(Front)

L_Q:  2
(Rear)

## PROBLEM 7.3.–

Implement an abstract data type STAQUE, which is a combination of a linked stack and a linked queue. Develop procedures to perform an insert and delete operation, termed PUSHINS and POPDEL, respectively, on a non-empty STAQUE. PUSHINS inserts an element at the top or rear of the STAQUE based on an indication given to the procedure, and POPDEL deletes elements from the top/front of the list.

## Solution:

The procedure PUSHINS performs the insertion of an element in the top or rear of the list based on whether the STAQUE is viewed as a stack or queue, respectively. On the other hand, the procedure POPDEL, which performs a pop or deletion of element, is common to a STAQUE, since in both cases, the first element in the list alone is deleted.

```
procedure  PUSHINS(WHERE,     TOP,
REAR, ITEM)
/* WHERE indicates whether the
insertion of ITEM is to be done
as on a stack or as on a queue*/
    Call GETNODE(X);
    DATA(X) = ITEM;
    if (WHERE = 'Stack')
    then {LINK(X)= TOP;
          TOP = X;
         }
    else
         {LINK(REAR) = X;
          LINK(X)=Nil;
          REAR=X;
         }
end PUSHINS
```

```
procedure POPDEL(TOP, ITEM)

    TEMP = TOP;
    ITEM = DATA(TEMP);
    /* delete top element
       of the list through
       ITEM*/
    TOP = LINK(TEMP);
    RETURN(TEMP);
end POPDEL
```

## PROBLEM 7.4.–

Write a procedure to convert a linked stack into a linked queue.

## Solution:

An elegant and easy solution to the problem is to undertake the conversion by returning the addresses of the first and last nodes of the linked stack as FRONT and REAR, thereby turning the linked stack into a linked queue.

```
procedure CONVERT_LINKSTACK(TOP, FRONT, REAR)
/* FRONT and REAR are the variables which return the
addresses of the first and last node of the list
converting the linked stack into a linked queue*/
```

```
if (TOP= Nil)then print("Conversion not possible");
else {FRONT = TOP;
TEMP = TOP;
while (LINK(TEMP) ≠ Nil)do
  TEMP = LINK(TEMP);
  REAR = TEMP;
endwhile
  }
end CONVERT_LINKSTACK.
```

## PROBLEM 7.5.–

An Abstract Data Type STACKLIST is a list of linked stacks stored according to a priority factor, namely, A, B, C, and so on, where A means highest priority, B the next and so on. Elements having the same priority are stored as a linked stack. The following is a structure of the STACKLIST S.

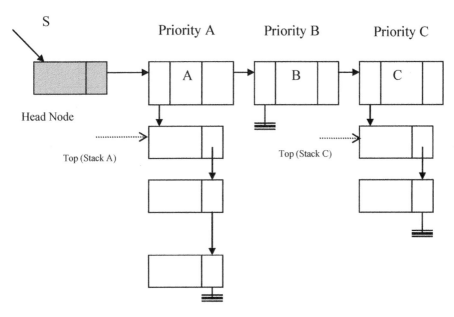

Create a STACKLIST for the following application of process scheduling with the processes having two priorities, namely, R (Real time) and O (On line) listed within brackets.

| 1.  Initiate process P1 (R) | 5.  Initiate process P5(O) |
| 2.  Initiate process P2 (O) | 6.  Initiate process P6 (R) |
| 3.  Initiate process P3 (O) | 7.  Terminate process in linked stack O |
| 4. Terminate process in linked stack R | 8.  Initiate process P7 (R) |

## Solution:

The STACKLIST at the end of Schedules 1–3 is shown below:

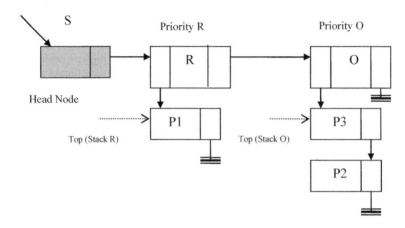

The STACKLIST at the end of Schedule 4 is given as follows:

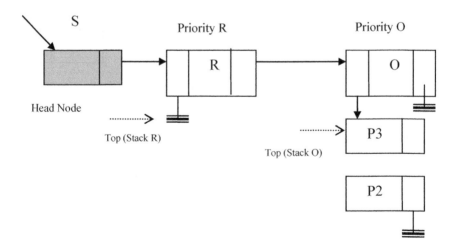

The STACKLIST at the end of Schedules 5–8 is as follows:

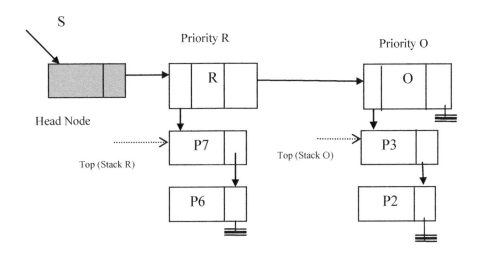

## PROBLEM 7.6.–

Write a procedure to reverse a linked stack implemented as a doubly linked list, with the original top and bottom positions of the stack reversed as bottom and top, respectively.

For example, a linked stack S and its reversed version S$^{rev}$ are shown as follows:

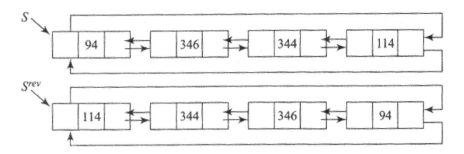

## Solution:

An elegant solution would be to merely swap the LLINK and RLINK pointers of each of the doubly linked lists to reverse the list and remember the address of the last node in the original stack S as the TOP pointer. The procedure is given as follows:

```
procedure REVERSE_STACK(TOP)
/* TEMP and HOLD are temporary variables to hold the
addresses of nodes*/
    TEMP = TOP;
    repeat
        HOLD = LLINK(TEMP);
        LLINK(TEMP)= RLINK(TEMP);
        RLINK(TEMP)= HOLD;/*Swap left and right links for
                            each node*/
        TEMP = LLINK(TEMP);/* Move to the next node*/
    until (TEMP = TOP)
    TOP = RLINK(TEMP);

end REVERSE_STACK.
```

### PROBLEM 7.7.–

What does the following pseudo-code do to the linked queue Q with the addresses of nodes, as shown below:

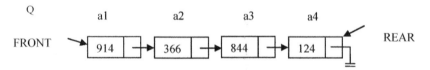

```
procedure WHAT_DO_I_DO(FRONT, REAR)
/* HAVE, HOLD and HUG are temporary variables to hold
the link or data fields of the nodes as the case may
be*/
    HAVE = FRONT;
    HOLD = DATA(HAVE);

    while LINK(HAVE) ≠ Nil do
        HUG = DATA(LINK(HAVE));
        DATA(LINK(HAVE))= HOLD;
        HOLD = HUG;
        HAVE = LINK(HAVE);
    endwhile
    DATA(FRONT)= HOLD;

end WHAT_DO_I_DO
```

## Solution:

The procedure WHAT_DO_I_DO rotates the data items of the linked queue Q to obtain the resultant list given below:

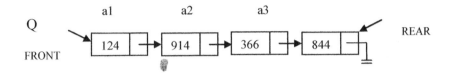

## PROBLEM 7.8.–

Write a procedure to remove the *n*th element (from the top) of a linked stack with the rest of the elements unchanged. Contrast this with a sequential stack implementation for the same problem (illustrative problem 4.2(iii) of Chapter 4).

## Solution:

To remove the *n*th element leaving the other elements unchanged, a linked implementation of the stack merely calls for sliding down the list, which is easily done, and for a reset of a link to remove the node concerned. The procedure is given below. In contrast, a sequential implementation as described in illustrative problem 4.2(iii) calls for the use of another temporary stack to hold the elements popped out from the original stack before pushing them back into it.

```
procedure REMOVE(TOP, ITEM, n)
/*  The nth element is removed through
ITEM*/
    TEMP = TOP;
    COUNT = 1;
    while (COUNT≠ n) do
        PREVIOUS = TEMP;
        TEMP = LINK(TEMP);
        COUNT = COUNT+1;
    endwhile
    LINK(PREVIOUS)= LINK(TEMP);
    ITEM = DATA(TEMP);
    RETURN(TEMP);

end REMOVE
```

## PROBLEM 7.9.–

Given a linked stack L_S and a linked queue L_Q with equal length, what do the following procedures to do the lists? Here, TOP is the top pointer of L_S, and FRONT and REAR are the front and rear of L_Q. What are your observations regarding the functionality of the two procedures?

| | |
|---|---|
| `procedure`<br>`WHAT_IS_COOKING1(TOP,  FRONT,`<br>`REAR)`<br>`/*   TEMP,  TEMP1,  TEMP2 and`<br>`TEMP3         are        temporary`<br>`variables*/`<br>`  TEMP1 = FRONT;`<br>`  TEMP2 = TOP;`<br>`  while (TEMP1≠ Nil AND`<br>`          TEMP2≠ Nil) do`<br>`    TEMP3 = DATA(FRONT);`<br>`    DATA(FRONT)= DATA(TOP);`<br>`    DATA(TOP)= TEMP3;`<br>`    TEMP1 = LINK(TEMP1);`<br>`    PREVIOUS = TEMP2;`<br>`    TEMP2 = LINK(TEMP2);`<br>`  endwhile`<br>`  TEMP = TOP;`<br>`  TOP = FRONT;`<br>`  FRONT = TEMP;`<br>`  REAR = PREVIOUS;`<br>`end WHAT_IS_COOKING 1` | `procedure`<br>`WHAT_IS_COOKING2(TOP,`<br>`FRONT, REAR)`<br>`/*   TEMP,  TEMP1,  TEMP2 and`<br>`TEMP3        are        temporary`<br>`variables*/`<br>`  TEMP = TOP;`<br>`  while (LINK(TEMP)≠ Nil)`<br>`  do`<br>`     TEMP = LINK(TEMP);`<br>`  endwhile`<br>`  TEMP1 = TOP;`<br>`  REAR = TEMP;`<br>`  TOP = FRONT;`<br>`  FRONT = TEMP1;`<br>`end WHAT_IS_COOKING2` |

### Solution:

Both procedures swap the contents of the linked stack L_S and linked queue L_Q. While WHAT_IS_COOKING1 does it by exchanging the data items of the lists, WHAT_IS_COOKING2 does it by merely manipulating the pointers and hence looks elegant.

## PROBLEM 7.10.–

A *queue list* Q is a list of linked queues stored according to orders of priority, namely, A, B, C and so on, with A accorded the highest priority, B the next highest priority and so on. The LEAD nodes serve as head nodes for each of the priority-based queues. Elements with the same priority are stored as a normal linked queue. Figures P7.10(a) and (b) illustrate the node structure and an example queue list, respectively.

The FOLLOW link links together the head nodes of the queues, and the DOWN link connects it to the first node in the respective queue. The LEAD DATA field may be used to store the priority factor of the queue.

Here is a QUEUE LIST Q stored in the memory, a snapshot of which is shown as follows:

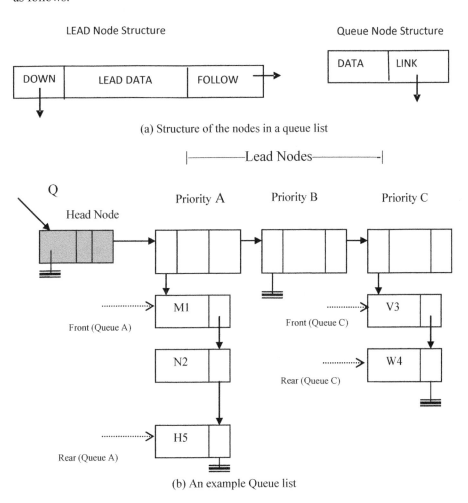

(a) Structure of the nodes in a queue list

(b) An example Queue list

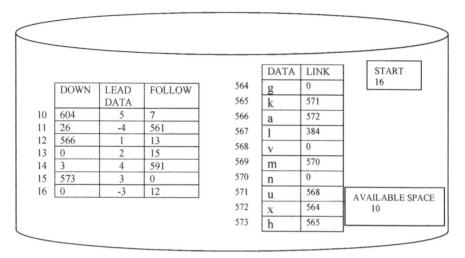

(c) A snapshot of the queue list

**Figure P7.10.** *Queue list: node structure,*
*example and memory snapshot*

There are three queues Q1, Q2 and Q3 with priorities of 1, 2 and 3. The head node of QUEUELIST stores the number of queues in the list as a negative number. The LEAD DATA field stores the priority factor of each of the three queues. START points to the head node of the QUEUELIST and AVAILABLE SPACE the pointer to the free storage pool.

Obtain the QUEUELIST by tracing the lead nodes and nodes of the linked queues.

**Solution:**

The structure of the QUEUELIST is shown as follows:

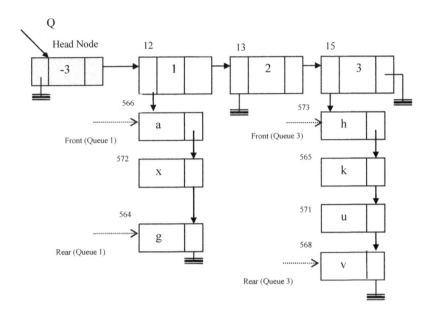

## Review questions

The following is a snapshot of a memory that stores a linked stack VEGETABLES and a linked queue FRUITS beginning at the respective addresses. Answer the following questions with regard to operations on the linked stack and queue, each of which is assumed to be independently performed on the original linked stack and queue.

|  | DATA | LINK |
|---|---|---|
| 1 | CABBAGE | 7 |
| 2 | CUCUMBER | 5 |
| 3 | PEAR | 6 |
| 4 | ONION | 9 |
| 5 | ORANGE | 4 |
| 6 | PEACH | 0 |
| 7 | CELERY | 8 |
| 8 | CARROTS | 0 |
| 9 | LEMON | 0 |
| 10 | PLUM | 3 |

FRUITS

FRONT: 10

REAR: 6

VEGETABLES

TOP: 1

AV_SP

2

1) Inserting PAPAYA into the linked queue FRUITS results in the following changes to the FRONT, REAR and AV_SP pointers, respectively, as given in:

a) 10 2 2              b) 2 6 2              c) 2 6 5              d) 10 2 5

2) Undertaking pop operation on VEGETABLES results in the following changes to the TOP and AV_SP pointers, respectively, as given in:

a) 7 1        b) 7 2              c) 8 2              d) 8 1

3) Undertaking the delete operation on FRUITS results in the following changes to the FRONT, REAR and AV_SP pointers, respectively, as given in:

a) 3 6 2      b) 10 3 6        c) 3 6 10        d) 10 3 2

4) Pushing TURNIPS into VEGETABLES results in the following changes to the TOP and AV_SP pointers, respectively, as given in:

a) 2 5        b) 2 9              c) 1 5              d) 1 9

5) After the push operation of TURNIPS into VEGETABLES (undertaken in review question 4 above),

DATA(2) = ------------- and DATA(LINK(2)) = -------------

a) TURNIPS and CABBAGE    b) CUCUMBER and CABBAGE

c) TURNIPS and CUCUMBER d) CUCUMBER and ORANGE

6) What are the merits of linked stacks and queues over their sequential counterparts?

7) How is the memory storage pool associated with a linked stack data structure for its operations?

8) How are push and pop operations implemented on a linked stack?

9) What are traversable queues?

10) Outline the node structure and a linked queue to represent the polynomial: $17x^5 + 18 x^2 + 9x + 89$.

11) Trace **procedure** BALANCE_EXPR (E)    (Algorithm    7.7) on the following expression to check whether parentheses are balanced:

$$((X + Y + Z) * H) + (D * T)) - 2$$

12) Design a stack MAXSTACK, which functions like an ordinary linked stack supporting the ADT operations of PUSH, POP and EMPTYSTACK, besides

GETMAX. GETMAX is an operation that records the maximum element in the stack. Can you design the stack in such a way that GETMAX merely consumes O(1) time complexity.

13) The evaluation of postfix expressions using stacks is discussed in Algorithm 4.3 of Chapter 4. Can a similar procedure be evolved to evaluate prefix expressions using a linked stack?

Hint: Read the prefix expression from right to left, unlike a postfix expression that was read left to right.

## Programming assignments

1) Execute a program to implement a linked stack to check for the balancing of the following pairs of symbols in a Pascal program. The name of the source Pascal program is the sole input to the program.

Symbols: *begin end, ( ), [ ], { }.*

(i) Output errors encountered during mismatch of symbols.

(ii) Modify the program to set right the errors.

2) Evaluate a postfix expression using a linked stack implementation.

3) Implement the simulation of a time sharing system discussed in Chapter 5, section 5.5, using linked queues.

4) Develop a program to implement a queue list (illustrative problem 7.10), which is a list of linked queues stored according to an order of priority.

Test for the insertion and deletion of the following jobs with their priorities listed within brackets on a queue list JOB_MANAGER with three queues A, B and C listed according to their order of priorities:

| 1. | Insert Job $J_1$ (A) | 6. | Insert Job $J_5$ (C) |
|----|----------------------|-----|----------------------|
| 2. | Insert Job $J_2$ (B) | 7. | Insert Job $J_6$ (C) |
| 3. | Insert Job $J_3$ (A) | 8. | Insert Job $J_7$ (A) |
| 4. | Insert Job $J_4$ (B) | 9. | Delete Queue C |
| 5. | Delete Queue B | 10. | Insert Job $J_8$ (A) |

5) Develop a program to simulate a calculator that performs the addition, subtraction, multiplication and division of polynomials.

# References

Aragon, C.R. and Seidel, R. (1989). Randomized search trees. In *Proc. 30th Symp. Foundations of Computer Science (FOCS 1989)*. IEEE Computer Society Press, Washington, DC.

Donald, K. (1998). *Art of Computer Programming, Vol. III*. 2nd edition. Addison-Wesley Professional, Reading, MA.

Garey, M.R. and David, S.J. (1979). *Computers and Intractability: A Guide to the Theory of NP-Completeness*. W.H. Freeman, New York.

Hoare, C.A.R. (1962). Quick sort. *The Computer Journal*, 5(1), 10–16.

Knuth, D.E. (1973). *The Art of Computer Programming, Volume 1: Fundamental Algorithms*. 2nd edition. Addison-Wesley, Reading, MA.

Malik, S. and Lintao, Z. (2009). Boolean satisfiability, from theoretical hardness to practical success. *Communications of the ACM*, 52(8), 76–82.

Perlis, A.J. and Thornton, C. (1960). Symbol manipulation by threaded lists. *Communications of the ACM*, 3(4), 195–204.

Pugh, W. (1990). Skip lists: A probabilistic alternative to balanced trees. *Communications of the ACM*, 33(6), 668–676.

Shell, D.L. (1959). A high-speed sorting procedure. *Communications of the ACM*, 2(7), 30–32.

References

# Index

## A

Abstract Data Types (ADT), 8, 12, 45, 227, 229
algorithm
  analysis of, 11, 13
  design techniques, 9, 10
  development of an, 5
apriori analysis, 14, 15, 17, 27, 30, 31
array
  bit, 54, 58, 59, 64, 65, 67, 69
  number of elements, 46–48, 61, 63, 66, 100, 102, 114, 131, 171, 172, 175
  one-dimensional, 45, 46, 48–51, 55–58, 60, 99, 102, 140
  operations, 46, 59
  three-dimensional, 48, 52, 53, 67
  two-dimensional, 45–48, 50–52, 57, 114, 130, 131, 140
asymptotic notations, 17, 30, 31
available space, 209, 215, 216, 221–223, 225

## B, C

balancing symbols, 201, 216
base address, 49–51, 53, 60, 62, 63, 66
big oh, 17
circular queue, 101, 105, 106, 108–112, 124, 127, 138–140, 202, 204
circularly linked lists
  advantages of, 155
  disadvantages of, 156
complexity
  space, 13, 17, 30
  time, 13, 17, 19–22, 27, 30–32, 35–37, 40, 42–44, 74, 105, 110, 113, 174, 175, 205, 206, 208, 239
  average case, 22
  best case, 22
  exponential, 20, 43
  polynomial, 19, 43
  worst case, 22

# D

data abstraction, 8
data structures
  classification, 9
  linear, 9, 11, 12, 143, 147, 161
  nonlinear, 9, 11, 12
deque, 101, 117–119, 124, 132, 133, 137, 140, 202, 221
doubly linked lists, 143, 146, 160–165, 182, 186–188, 195–199, 231
  operations on, 163
dynamic memory management, 209

# E, F

expression
  infix, 79, 80, 89, 98
  postfix, 79–83, 89, 90, 98, 99, 239
  prefix, 79–81, 89, 90, 239
First Come First Served (FCFS), 101
First In First Out (FIFO), 101
frequency count, 15–17, 27, 30, 32–37, 42, 44

# J, L, M, O

job scheduling, 101, 119, 120, 122, 124
Last In First Out (LIFO), 72, 97
linear queue, 105, 106, 108, 109, 119, 124, 125, 137–139, 204, 206, 216, 218, 221
little oh, 19
multiply linked list, 143, 146, 166–170, 176, 178–180, 182, 197, 198
omega, 18
ordered list, 54–56, 60, 68, 71, 73, 83, 201

# P, Q

polynomials
  addition of, 175, 176, 182, 218, 221
  representation, 178, 201, 216, 218, 221
posteriori testing, 14, 30
priority queue, 101, 112–114, 119–224, 129, 130, 139, 140
queues
  implementation of, 102, 105

# R, S

recurrence relation, 24, 26–30, 35, 38, 40, 44
recursion, 23, 24, 76, 78, 79, 89, 99
recursive
  functions, 24, 26, 27, 39, 40
  programming, 23, 24, 39, 40, 43, 44, 71, 76, 83, 88, 99
self-organizing lists, 175, 182, 197, 200
singly linked list
  insertion and deletion in a, 149
sparse matrix, 54, 55, 67, 143, 175, 176, 178–180, 182, 197
stack implementation, 73, 79, 213, 231, 233, 239
string, 7, 54, 56–58, 65–67, 69, 141, 217–219

# T, U

theta, 18
Tower of Hanoi puzzle, 25, 26, 28, 29
unrolled linked list, 143, 171–175, 194, 195, 197, 200

# Summary of Volume 2

**Preface**

**Acknowledgments**

**Chapter 8. Trees and Binary Trees**

8.1. Introduction
8.2. Trees: definition and basic terminologies
    8.2.1. Definition of trees
    8.2.2. Basic terminologies of trees
8.3. Representation of trees
8.4. Binary trees: basic terminologies and types
    8.4.1. Basic terminologies
    8.4.2. Types of binary trees
8.5. Representation of binary trees
    8.5.1. Array representation of binary trees
    8.5.2. Linked representation of binary trees
8.6. Binary tree traversals
    8.6.1. Inorder traversal
    8.6.2. Postorder traversal
    8.6.3. Preorder traversal
8.7. Threaded binary trees
    8.7.1. Linked representation of a threaded binary tree
    8.7.2. Growing threaded binary trees

8.8. Applications
    8.8.1. Expression trees
    8.8.2. Traversals of an expression tree
    8.8.3. Conversion of infix expression to postfix expression
    8.8.4. Segment trees
8.9. Illustrative problems

**Chapter 9. Graphs**

9.1. Introduction
9.2. Definitions and basic terminologies
9.3. Representations of graphs
    9.3.1. Sequential representation of graphs
    9.3.2. Linked representation of graphs
9.4. Graph traversals
    9.4.1. Breadth first traversal
    9.4.2. Depth first traversal
9.5. Applications
    9.5.1. Single source shortest path problem
    9.5.2. Minimum cost spanning trees
9.6. Illustrative problems

**Chapter 10. Binary Search Trees and AVL Trees**

10.1. Introduction
10.2. Binary search trees: definition and operations
    10.2.1. Definition
    10.2.2. Representation of a binary search tree
    10.2.3. Retrieval from a binary search tree
    10.2.4. Why are binary search tree retrievals more efficient than sequential list retrievals?
    10.2.5. Insertion into a binary search tree
    10.2.6. Deletion from a binary search tree
    10.2.7. Drawbacks of a binary search tree
    10.2.8. Counting binary search trees
10.3. AVL trees: definition and operations
    10.3.1. Definition
    10.3.2. Retrieval from an AVL search tree
    10.3.3. Insertion into an AVL search tree
    10.3.4. Deletion from an AVL search tree
    10.3.5. R category rotations associated with the delete operation
    10.3.6. L category rotations associated with the delete operation

10.4. Applications
    10.4.1. Representation of symbol tables in compiler design
10.5. Illustrative problems


## Chapter 11. B Trees and Tries

11.1. Introduction
11.2. *m*-way search trees: definition and operations
    11.2.1. Definition
    11.2.2. Node structure and representation
    11.2.3. Searching an *m*-way search tree
    11.2.4. Inserting into an *m*-way search tree
    11.2.5. Deleting from an *m*-way search tree
    11.2.6. Drawbacks of *m*-way search trees
11.3. B trees: definition and operations
    11.3.1. Definition
    11.3.2. Searching a B tree of order *m*
    11.3.3. Inserting into a B tree of order *m*
    11.3.4. Deletion from a B tree of order *m*
    11.3.5. Height of a B tree of order *m*
11.4. Tries: definition and operations
    11.4.1. Definition and representation
    11.4.2. Searching a trie
    11.4.3. Insertion into a trie
    11.4.4. Deletion from a trie
    11.4.5. Some remarks on tries
11.5. Applications
    11.5.1. File indexing
    11.5.2. Spell checker
11.6. Illustrative problems


## Chapter 12. Red-Black Trees and Splay Trees

12.1. Red-black trees
    12.1.1. Introduction to red-black trees
    12.1.2. Definition
    12.1.3. Representation of a red-black tree
    12.1.4. Searching a red-black tree
    12.1.5. Inserting into a red-black tree
    12.1.6. Deleting from a red-black tree
    12.1.7. Time complexity of search, insert and delete operations
on a red-black tree

12.2. Splay trees
12.2.1. Introduction to splay trees
12.2.2. Splay rotations
12.2.3. Some remarks on amortized analysis of splay trees
12.3. Applications
12.4. Illustrative problems

**References**

**Index**

# Summary of Volume 3

**Preface**

**Acknowledgments**

**Chapter 13. Hash Tables**

13.1. Introduction
    13.1.1. Dictionaries
13.2. Hash table structure
13.3. Hash functions
    13.3.1. Building hash functions
13.4. Linear open addressing
    13.4.1. Operations on linear open addressed hash tables
    13.4.2. Performance analysis
    13.4.3. Other collision resolution techniques with open addressing
13.5. Chaining
    13.5.1. Operations on chained hash tables
    13.5.2. Performance analysis
13.6. Applications
    13.6.1. Representation of a keyword table in a compiler
    13.6.2. Hash tables in the evaluation of a join operation on relational databases
    13.6.3. Hash tables in a direct file organization
13.7. Illustrative problems

## Chapter 14. File Organizations

14.1. Introduction
14.2. Files
14.3. Keys
14.4. Basic file operations
14.5. Heap or pile organization
   14.5.1. Insert, delete and update operations
14.6. Sequential file organization
   14.6.1. Insert, delete and update operations
   14.6.2. Making use of overflow blocks
14.7. Indexed sequential file organization
   14.7.1. Structure of the ISAM files
   14.7.2. Insert, delete and update operations for a naïve ISAM file
   14.7.3. Types of indexing
14.8. Direct file organization
14.9. Illustrative problems

## Chapter 15. *k*-d Trees and Treaps

15.1. Introduction
15.2. $k$-d trees: structure and operations
   15.2.1. Construction of a $k$-d tree
   15.2.2. Insert operation on $k$-d trees
   15.2.3. Find minimum operation on $k$-d trees
   15.2.4. Delete operation on $k$-d trees
   15.2.5. Complexity analysis and applications of $k$-d trees
15.3. Treaps: structure and operations
   15.3.1. Treap structure
   15.3.2. Operations on treaps
   15.3.3. Complexity analysis and applications of treaps
15.4. Illustrative problems

## Chapter 16. Searching

16.1. Introduction
16.2. Linear search
   16.2.1. Ordered linear search
   16.2.2. Unordered linear search
16.3. Transpose sequential search
16.4. Interpolation search
16.5. Binary search
   16.5.1. Decision tree for binary search

16.6. Fibonacci search
  16.6.1. Decision tree for Fibonacci search
16.7. Skip list search
  16.7.1. Implementing skip lists
  16.7.2. Insert operation in a skip list
  16.7.3. Delete operation in a skip list
16.8. Other search techniques
  16.8.1. Tree search
  16.8.2. Graph search
  16.8.3. Indexed sequential search
16.9. Illustrative problems

## Chapter 17. Internal Sorting

17.1. Introduction
17.2. Bubble sort
  17.2.1. Stability and performance analysis
17.3. Insertion sort
  17.3.1. Stability and performance analysis
17.4. Selection sort
  17.4.1. Stability and performance analysis
17.5. Merge sort
  17.5.1. Two-way merging
  17.5.2. $k$-way merging
  17.5.3. Non-recursive merge sort procedure
  17.5.4. Recursive merge sort procedure
17.6. Shell sort
  17.6.1. Analysis of shell sort
17.7. Quick sort
  17.7.1. Partitioning
  17.7.2. Quick sort procedure
  17.7.3. Stability and performance analysis
17.8. Heap sort
  17.8.1. Heap
  17.8.2. Construction of heap
  17.8.3. Heap sort procedure
  17.8.4. Stability and performance analysis
17.9. Radix sort
  17.9.1. Radix sort method
  17.9.2. Most significant digit first sort
  17.9.3. Performance analysis
17.10. Counting sort

17.10.1. Performance analysis
17.11. Bucket sort
17.11.1. Performance analysis
17.12. Illustrative problems


## Chapter 18. External Sorting

18.1. Introduction
18.1.1. The principle behind external sorting
18.2. External storage devices
18.2.1. Magnetic tapes
18.2.2. Magnetic disks
18.3. Sorting with tapes: balanced merge
18.3.1. Buffer handling
18.3.2. Balanced P-way merging on tapes
18.4. Sorting with disks: balanced merge
18.4.1. Balanced k-way merging on disks
18.4.2. Selection tree
18.5. Polyphase merge sort
18.6. Cascade merge sort
18.7. Illustrative problems


## Chapter 19. Divide and Conquer

19.1. Introduction
19.2. Principle and abstraction
19.3. Finding maximum and minimum
19.3.1. Time complexity analysis
19.4. Merge sort
19.4.1. Time complexity analysis
19.5. Matrix multiplication
19.5.1. Divide and Conquer-based approach to "high school"
method of matrix multiplication
19.5.2. Strassen's matrix multiplication algorithm
19.6. Illustrative problems


## Chapter 20. Greedy Method

20.1. Introduction
20.2. Abstraction
20.3. Knapsack problem
20.3.1. Greedy solution to the knapsack problem

20.4. Minimum cost spanning tree algorithms
   20.4.1. Prim's algorithm as a greedy method
   20.4.2. Kruskal's algorithm as a greedy method
20.5. Dijkstra's algorithm
20.6. Illustrative problems


## Chapter 21. Dynamic Programming

21.1. Introduction
21.2. 0/1 knapsack problem
   21.2.1. Dynamic programming-based solution
21.3. Traveling salesperson problem
   21.3.1. Dynamic programming-based solution
   21.3.2. Time complexity analysis and applications of traveling salesperson problem
21.4. All-pairs shortest path problem
   21.4.1. Dynamic programming-based solution
   21.4.2. Time complexity analysis
21.5. Optimal binary search trees
   21.5.1. Dynamic programming-based solution
   21.5.2. Construction of the optimal binary search tree
   21.5.3. Time complexity analysis
21.6. Illustrative problems


## Chapter 22. P and NP Class of Problems

22.1. Introduction
22.2. Deterministic and nondeterministic algorithms
22.3. Satisfiability problem
   22.3.1. Conjunctive normal form and Disjunctive normal form
   22.3.2. Definition of the satisfiability problem
   22.3.3. Construction of CNF and DNF from a logical formula
   22.3.4. Transformation of a CNF into a 3-CNF
   22.3.5. Deterministic algorithm for the satisfiability problem
   22.3.6. Nondeterministic algorithm for the satisfiability problem
22.4. NP-complete and NP-hard problems
   22.4.1. Definitions
22.5. Examples of NP-hard and NP-complete problems
22.6. Cook's theorem
22.7. The unsolved problem $P \stackrel{?}{=} NP$
22.8. Illustrative problems

**References**

**Index**

Other titles from

in

Computer Engineering

## 2022

MEHTA Shikha, TIWARI Sanju, SIARRY Patrick, JABBAR M.A.
*Tools, Languages, Methodologies for Representing Semantics on the Web of Things*

SIDHOM Sahbi, KADDOUR Amira
*Systems and Uses of Digital Sciences for Knowledge Organization (Digital Tools and Uses Set – Volume 9)*

ZAIDOUN Ameur Salem
*Computer Science Security: Concepts and Tools*

## 2021

DELHAYE Jean-Loic
*Inside the World of Computing: Technologies, Uses, Challenges*

DUVAUT Patrick, DALLOZ Xavier, MENGA David, KOEHL François, CHRIQUI Vidal, BRILL Joerg
*Internet of Augmented Me, I.AM: Empowering Innovation for a New Sustainable Future*

HARDIN Thérèse, JAUME Mathieu, PESSAUX François,
VIGUIÉ DONZEAU-GOUGE Véronique
*Concepts and Semantics of Programming Languages 1: A Semantical
Approach with OCaml and Python*
*Concepts and Semantics of Programming Languages 2: Modular and
Object-oriented Constructs with OCaml, Python, C++, Ada and Java*

MKADMI Abderrazak
*Archives in The Digital Age: Preservation and the Right to be Forgotten
(Digital Tools and Uses Set – Volume 8)*

TOKLU Yusuf Cengiz, BEKDAS Gebrail, NIGDELI Sinan Melih
*Metaheuristics for Structural Design and Analysis (Optimization Heuristics
Set – Volume 3)*

## 2020

DARCHE Philippe
*Microprocessor 1: Prolegomena – Calculation and Storage Functions –
Models of Computation and Computer Architecture*
*Microprocessor 2: Core Concepts – Communication in a Digital System*
*Microprocessor 3: Core Concepts – Hardware Aspects*
*Microprocessor 4: Core Concepts – Software Aspects*
*Microprocessor 5: Software and Hardware Aspects of Development,
Debugging and Testing – The Microcomputer*

LAFFLY Dominique
*TORUS 1 – Toward an Open Resource Using Services: Cloud Computing
for Environmental Data*
*TORUS 2 – Toward an Open Resource Using Services: Cloud Computing
for Environmental Data*
*TORUS 3 – Toward an Open Resource Using Services: Cloud Computing
for Environmental Data*

LAURENT Anne, LAURENT Dominique, MADERA Cédrine
*Data Lakes*
*(Databases and Big Data Set – Volume 2)*

OULHADJ Hamouche, DAACHI Boubaker, MENASRI Riad
*Metaheuristics for Robotics*
*(Optimization Heuristics Set – Volume 2)*

SADIQUI Ali
*Computer Network Security*

VENTRE Daniel
*Artificial Intelligence, Cybersecurity and Cyber Defense*

## 2019

BESBES Walid, DHOUIB Diala, WASSAN Niaz, MARREKCHI Emna
*Solving Transport Problems: Towards Green Logistics*

CLERC Maurice
*Iterative Optimizers: Difficulty Measures and Benchmarks*

GHLALA Riadh
*Analytic SQL in SQL Server 2014/2016*

TOUNSI Wiem
*Cyber-Vigilance and Digital Trust: Cyber Security in the Era of Cloud Computing and IoT*

## 2018

ANDRO Mathieu
*Digital Libraries and Crowdsourcing*
*(Digital Tools and Uses Set – Volume 5)*

ARNALDI Bruno, GUITTON Pascal, MOREAU Guillaume
*Virtual Reality and Augmented Reality: Myths and Realities*

BERTHIER Thierry, TEBOUL Bruno
*From Digital Traces to Algorithmic Projections*

CARDON Alain
*Beyond Artificial Intelligence: From Human Consciousness to Artificial Consciousness*

HOMAYOUNI S. Mahdi, FONTES Dalila B.M.M.
*Metaheuristics for Maritime Operations*
*(Optimization Heuristics Set – Volume 1)*

JEANSOULIN Robert
*JavaScript and Open Data*


PIVERT Olivier
*NoSQL Data Models: Trends and Challenges*
*(Databases and Big Data Set – Volume 1)*

SEDKAOUI Soraya
*Data Analytics and Big Data*

SALEH Imad, AMMI Mehdi, SZONIECKY Samuel
*Challenges of the Internet of Things: Technology, Use, Ethics*
*(Digital Tools and Uses Set – Volume 7)*

SZONIECKY Samuel
*Ecosystems Knowledge: Modeling and Analysis Method for Information and Communication*
*(Digital Tools and Uses Set – Volume 6)*

# 2017

BENMAMMAR Badr
*Concurrent, Real-Time and Distributed Programming in Java*

HÉLIODORE Frédéric, NAKIB Amir, ISMAIL Boussaad, OUCHRAA Salma, SCHMITT Laurent
*Metaheuristics for Intelligent Electrical Networks*
*(Metaheuristics Set – Volume 10)*

MA Haiping, SIMON Dan
*Evolutionary Computation with Biogeography-based Optimization*
*(Metaheuristics Set – Volume 8)*

PÉTROWSKI Alain, BEN-HAMIDA Sana
*Evolutionary Algorithms*
*(Metaheuristics Set – Volume 9)*

PAI G A Vijayalakshmi
*Metaheuristics for Portfolio Optimization*
*(Metaheuristics Set – Volume 11)*

## 2016

BLUM Christian, FESTA Paola
*Metaheuristics for String Problems in Bio-informatics*
*(Metaheuristics Set – Volume 6)*

DEROUSSI Laurent
*Metaheuristics for Logistics*
*(Metaheuristics Set – Volume 4)*

DHAENENS Clarisse and JOURDAN Laetitia
*Metaheuristics for Big Data*
*(Metaheuristics Set – Volume 5)*

LABADIE Nacima, PRINS Christian, PRODHON Caroline
*Metaheuristics for Vehicle Routing Problems*
*(Metaheuristics Set – Volume 3)*

LEROY Laure
*Eyestrain Reduction in Stereoscopy*

LUTTON Evelyne, PERROT Nathalie, TONDA Albert
*Evolutionary Algorithms for Food Science and Technology*
*(Metaheuristics Set – Volume 7)*

MAGOULÈS Frédéric, ZHAO Hai-Xiang
*Data Mining and Machine Learning in Building Energy Analysis*

RIGO Michel
*Advanced Graph Theory and Combinatorics*

## 2015

BARBIER Franck, RECOUSSINE Jean-Luc
*COBOL Software Modernization: From Principles to Implementation with the BLU AGE® Method*

CHEN Ken
*Performance Evaluation by Simulation and Analysis with Applications to Computer Networks*

CLERC Maurice
*Guided Randomness in Optimization*
*(Metaheuristics Set – Volume 1)*

DURAND Nicolas, GIANAZZA David, GOTTELAND Jean-Baptiste, ALLIOT Jean-Marc
*Metaheuristics for Air Traffic Management*
*(Metaheuristics Set – Volume 2)*

MAGOULÈS Frédéric, ROUX François-Xavier, HOUZEAUX Guillaume
*Parallel Scientific Computing*

MUNEESAWANG Paisarn, YAMMEN Suchart
*Visual Inspection Technology in the Hard Disk Drive Industry*

## 2014

BOULANGER Jean-Louis
*Formal Methods Applied to Industrial Complex Systems*

BOULANGER Jean-Louis
*Formal Methods Applied to Complex Systems:Implementation of the B Method*

GARDI Frédéric, BENOIST Thierry, DARLAY Julien, ESTELLON Bertrand, MEGEL Romain
*Mathematical Programming Solver based on Local Search*

KRICHEN Saoussen, CHAOUACHI Jouhaina
*Graph-related Optimization and Decision Support Systems*

LARRIEU Nicolas, VARET Antoine
*Rapid Prototyping of Software for Avionics Systems: Model-oriented Approaches for Complex Systems Certification*

OUSSALAH Mourad Chabane
*Software Architecture 1*
*Software Architecture 2*

PASCHOS Vangelis Th
*Combinatorial Optimization – 3-volume series, 2ⁿᵈ Edition*
*Concepts of Combinatorial Optimization – Volume 1, 2ⁿᵈ Edition*
*Problems and New Approaches – Volume 2, 2ⁿᵈ Edition*
*Applications of Combinatorial Optimization – Volume 3, 2ⁿᵈ Edition*

QUESNEL Flavien
*Scheduling of Large-scale Virtualized Infrastructures: Toward Cooperative Management*

RIGO Michel
*Formal Languages, Automata and Numeration Systems 1: Introduction to Combinatorics on Words*
*Formal Languages, Automata and Numeration Systems 2: Applications to Recognizability and Decidability*

SAINT-DIZIER Patrick
*Musical Rhetoric: Foundations and Annotation Schemes*

TOUATI Sid, DE DINECHIN Benoit
*Advanced Backend Optimization*

## 2013

ANDRÉ Etienne, SOULAT Romain
*The Inverse Method: Parametric Verification of Real-time Embedded Systems*

BOULANGER Jean-Louis
*Safety Management for Software-based Equipment*

DELAHAYE Daniel, PUECHMOREL Stéphane
*Modeling and Optimization of Air Traffic*

FRANCOPOULO Gil
*LMF — Lexical Markup Framework*

GHÉDIRA Khaled
*Constraint Satisfaction Problems*

ROCHANGE Christine, UHRIG Sascha, SAINRAT Pascal
*Time-Predictable Architectures*

WAHBI Mohamed
*Algorithms and Ordering Heuristics for Distributed Constraint Satisfaction Problems*

ZELM Martin *et al.*
*Enterprise Interoperability*

## 2012

ARBOLEDA Hugo, ROYER Jean-Claude
*Model-Driven and Software Product Line Engineering*

BLANCHET Gérard, DUPOUY Bertrand
*Computer Architecture*

BOULANGER Jean-Louis
*Industrial Use of Formal Methods: Formal Verification*

BOULANGER Jean-Louis
*Formal Method: Industrial Use from Model to the Code*

CALVARY Gaëlle, DELOT Thierry, SÈDES Florence, TIGLI Jean-Yves
*Computer Science and Ambient Intelligence*

MAHOUT Vincent
*Assembly Language Programming: ARM Cortex-M3 2.0: Organization, Innovation and Territory*

MARLET Renaud
*Program Specialization*

SOTO Maria, SEVAUX Marc, ROSSI André, LAURENT Johann
*Memory Allocation Problems in Embedded Systems: Optimization Methods*

## 2011

BICHOT Charles-Edmond, SIARRY Patrick
*Graph Partitioning*

BOULANGER Jean-Louis
*Static Analysis of Software: The Abstract Interpretation*

CAFERRA Ricardo
*Logic for Computer Science and Artificial Intelligence*

HOMÈS Bernard
*Fundamentals of Software Testing*

KORDON Fabrice, HADDAD Serge, PAUTET Laurent, PETRUCCI Laure
*Distributed Systems: Design and Algorithms*

KORDON Fabrice, HADDAD Serge, PAUTET Laurent, PETRUCCI Laure
*Models and Analysis in Distributed Systems*

LORCA Xavier
*Tree-based Graph Partitioning Constraint*

TRUCHET Charlotte, ASSAYAG Gerard
*Constraint Programming in Music*

VICAT-BLANC PRIMET Pascale *et al.*
*Computing Networks: From Cluster to Cloud Computing*

## 2010

AUDIBERT Pierre
*Mathematics for Informatics and Computer Science*

BABAU Jean-Philippe *et al.*
*Model Driven Engineering for Distributed Real-Time Embedded Systems*

BOULANGER Jean-Louis
*Safety of Computer Architectures*

MONMARCHÉ Nicolas *et al.*
*Artificial Ants*

PANETTO Hervé, BOUDJLIDA Nacer
*Interoperability for Enterprise Software and Applications 2010*

SIGAUD Olivier *et al.*
*Markov Decision Processes in Artificial Intelligence*

SOLNON Christine
*Ant Colony Optimization and Constraint Programming*

AUBRUN Christophe, SIMON Daniel, SONG Ye-Qiong *et al.*
*Co-design Approaches for Dependable Networked Control Systems*

## 2009

FOURNIER Jean-Claude
*Graph Theory and Applications*

GUÉDON Jeanpierre
*The Mojette Transform / Theory and Applications*

JARD Claude, ROUX Olivier
*Communicating Embedded Systems / Software and Design*

LECOUTRE Christophe
*Constraint Networks / Targeting Simplicity for Techniques and Algorithms*

## 2008

BANÂTRE Michel, MARRÓN Pedro José, OLLERO Hannibal, WOLITZ Adam
*Cooperating Embedded Systems and Wireless Sensor Networks*

MERZ Stephan, NAVET Nicolas
*Modeling and Verification of Real-time Systems*

PASCHOS Vangelis Th
*Combinatorial Optimization and Theoretical Computer Science: Interfaces and Perspectives*

WALDNER Jean-Baptiste
*Nanocomputers and Swarm Intelligence*

## 2007

BENHAMOU Frédéric, JUSSIEN Narendra, O'SULLIVAN Barry
*Trends in Constraint Programming*

JUSSIEN Narendra
*A TO Z OF SUDOKU*

## 2006

BABAU Jean-Philippe *et al.*
*From MDD Concepts to Experiments and Illustrations – DRES 2006*

HABRIAS Henri, FRAPPIER Marc
*Software Specification Methods*

MURAT Cecile, PASCHOS Vangelis Th
*Probabilistic Combinatorial Optimization on Graphs*

PANETTO Hervé, BOUDJLIDA Nacer
*Interoperability for Enterprise Software and Applications 2006 / IFAC-IFIP I-ESA'2006*

## 2005

GÉRARD Sébastien *et al.*
*Model Driven Engineering for Distributed Real Time Embedded Systems*

PANETTO Hervé
*Interoperability of Enterprise Software and Applications 2005*